Texts and Monographs in Computer Science

W0042663

Texts and Monographs in Computer Science

Thomas W. Reps
Tim Teitelbaum

The
Synthesizer
Generator

A System for Constructing
Language-Based Editors

With 75 Illustrations

Springer-Verlag New York Berlin Heidelberg
London Paris Tokyo

Thomas W. Reps
Computer Sciences Department
University of Wisconsin, Madison
Madison, WI 53706, U.S.A.

Tim Teitelbaum
Department of Computer Science
Cornell University
Ithaca, NY 14853, U.S.A.

Series Editor

David Gries
Department of Computer Science
Cornell University
Ithaca, NY 14853, U.S.A.

Library of Congress Cataloging-in-Publication Data
Reps, Thomas W.
    The synthesizer generator : a system for constructing language
-based editors / Thomas W. Reps, Tim Teitelbaum.
        p.   cm. — (Texts and monographs in computer science)
    Bibliography: p.
    Includes index.
    1. Generators (Computer programs) 2. Linking loaders (Computer
programs) 3. Computer software — Development. I. Teitelbaum,
Tim.
II. Title. III. Series.
QA76.76.G46R46   1988
005.1 — dc19   88-24767

Printed on acid-free paper

Camera-ready copy produced by Impressions, Inc., Madison, Wisconsin.

9 8 7 6 5 4 3 2 1

ISBN-13: 978-1-4613-9625-3   e-ISBN-13: 978-1-4613-9623-9
DOI:10.1007/ 978-1-4613-9623-9

Preface

This book is a detailed account of the Synthesizer Generator, a system for creating specialized editors that are customized for editing particular languages. The book is intended for those with an interest in software tools and in methods for building interactive systems. It is a must for people who are using the Synthesizer Generator to build editors because it provides extensive discussions of how to write editor specifications. The book should also be valuable for people who are building specialized editors "by hand," without using an editor-generating tool.

The need to manage the development of large software systems is one of the most pressing problems faced by computer programmers. An important aspect of this problem is the design of new tools to aid interactive program development. The Synthesizer Generator permits one to create specialized editors that are tailored for editing a particular language. In program editors built with the Synthesizer Generator, knowledge about the language is used to continuously assess whether a program contains errors and to determine where such errors occur. The information is then displayed on the terminal screen to provide feedback to the programmer as the program is developed and modified.

The knowledge incorporated in editors generated with the Synthesizer Generator takes several forms. One form is knowledge of the language's syntax, which is used to detect and prevent syntax errors. Other forms of language knowledge encompass translation, transformation, and analysis of an object being edited. Knowledge of such aspects can be harnessed to check objects for inconsistencies, to prompt the user of the editor with legal alternatives, or to impose constraints on how the user can proceed.

The feature that makes the Synthesizer Generator unique is its use of an *immediate-computation* paradigm to perform analysis, translation, and error reporting while an object is being edited. In the immediate mode of computation, each modification to data has instantaneous effect, as in an electronic spreadsheet. For example, with program editors generated using the Synthesizer Generator, each modification to a program causes all affected analysis, error messages, and generated code to be immediately updated. Errors are detected as soon as they occur, and the delay for compilation that is necessary with traditional program-development tools is eliminated.

The Synthesizer Generator creates a language-specific editor from a specification of a language's abstract syntax, context-sensitive relationships, display format, concrete input syntax, and transformation rules for restructuring objects. The treatment of language syntax by the Synthesizer Generator is of particular importance. The editor-designer's specification of the language's syntax addresses not only context-free syntax but also such context-sensitive conditions as the absence of type mismatches; as the user creates and modifies objects, the generated editor incrementally checks for violations of context conditions that have been specified.

The Synthesizer Generator is of utility in a wide range of applications, including program editors, document-preparation systems, and verification tools. It has been used to create program editors for several different programming languages, including ones with such varying features as context-sensitive "pretty-printing," incremental code generation, detection of program anomalies, and detection of type violations. It has been used to create editors for text and mathematical formulas; in these editors, formatting is performed interactively on a character-by-character basis so that at all times the screen resembles the final page layout. It has also been used to create editors that verify the correctness of mathematical proofs (for several different varieties of logic).

The Synthesizer Generator's specification language (called SSL, for Synthesizer Specification Language) is based on the notion of an *attribute grammar*, which is a very general notation for expressing syntax-directed translations. A number of innovations in SSL make SSL specifications different from specifications written for other systems based on attribute grammars. The primary innovations are the way SSL merges the concepts of abstract-syntax definitions and user-defined attribute types, the introduction of notation that permits specifications to be factored into separate modules, and the manner in which the parser is incorporated into the system.

The Synthesizer Generator has been under development since 1981. It is implemented in C and runs under the UNIX operating system. The system has been licensed to hundreds of sites; further information about the availability of the Synthesizer Generator appears at the end of this volume.

One goal of the book is to present the Synthesizer Generator's specification language. The aim is to describe exactly what is necessary to specify a language-based editor using SSL. However, the book is more than just a user guide for the system; we also discuss issues that motivated the decisions we made when designing the system.

A second goal of the book is to demonstrate the Synthesizer Generator's versatility. We have brought together a collection of examples that demonstrate the widespread applicability of attribute grammars in language-based editors.

A third goal is to describe how to make effective use of the system. In Chapter 8, devoted to practical advice for editor-designers, we provide recommendations about how to start developing a new editor, as well as how to organize an editor specification so as to make it easier to re-use parts of editor specifications in subsequent editors. We also present case studies of how to specify commonly arising editor features.

A fourth goal is to provide an introduction to the implementation of the Synthesizer Generator. In the final two chapters of the book, we describe a number of the algorithms that are used in the system's implementation.

The book is organized as follows: Chapters 2, 3, and 4 provide a tutorial introduction to the Synthesizer Generator; in them, we briefly examine each of the system's major features. In Chapter 2, we use a sample editing session to illustrate the capabilities of editors generated using the Synthesizer Generator. In Chapter 3, we discuss the model of editing upon which the Synthesizer Generator is based. In Chapter 4, we begin discussing the Synthesizer Specification Language, the Synthesizer Generator's specification language; we present the SSL specification used to generate the editor examined in Chapter 2 and describe how each of that editor's major components is specified.

Chapters 5, 6, 7, and 8 provide a more detailed treatment of "programming" in SSL. Chapter 5 is concerned with lists and optional elements, and discusses the issues that arise when writing the parts of editor specifications that concern them. Chapter 6 is devoted to the problem of how to create a harmonious integration of structural and textual perspectives in editors. Chapter 7 discusses how to specify static inferences via attribution. Chapter 8 is devoted to practical advice on a range of topics.

In Chapters 9 and 10 we discuss additional examples that illustrate the power and versatility of the Synthesizer Generator. Chapter 9 is concerned with ways to extend language-based editors with execution facilities. Chapter 10 discusses the use of the Synthesizer Generator to build editors for creating and manipulating proofs in a formal system of logic.

Chapters 11 and 12 discuss technical matters about the system. Chapter 11 provides an introduction to the implementation of the Synthesizer Generator, including a discussion of some of the algorithms that are used in the system. Chapter 12 concerns one of the algorithms used in the system for incremental attribute evaluation.

The four appendices contain miscellaneous documentation of SSL and the Synthesizer Generator.[1] Appendix A contains a context-free grammar for SSL. Appendix B, presented in the standard format for UNIX-manual entries, documents how to build an editor with the Synthesizer Generator by invoking the sgen command. Appendix C, excerpted from *The Synthesizer Generator Reference Manual*, documents some of the commands available in editors generated with the Synthesizer Generator. Appendix D describes workstation-specific information required for running an editor.

Although this book is not specifically intended to be a textbook, there are several roles for it in the computer-science curriculum. One role would be as an adjunct text for a compiler course; a second role would be as a text in an advanced-topics seminar.

One trend of the last few years is that the notion of an attribute grammar has become one of the chief tools used in teaching about compiling. For example, recent compiler texts, such as [Waite83] and [Aho86], make extensive use of attribute grammars for specifying static-semantic analysis (such as name resolution and type checking) and for defining many kinds of translations. Attribute-grammar theory is also a part of many compiler courses; there is an extensive section in [Waite83] about how to create the attribute-evaluation component of a compiler. Because it is based on attribute grammars, the Synthesizer Generator is ideal for use in course projects.

The subject of tools to support software engineering is a topic of great current interest, although it is not currently dealt with in any standard place in the curriculum. A compiler course, especially an advanced course at the graduate level, is a natural place to incorporate more about the subject. This book (as well as the Synthesizer Generator system itself) fits in particularly well because the attribute-grammar concept is one that already plays a major role in the way compiler construction is taught today.

The interested reader may wish to consult an earlier book, titled *Generating Language-Based Environments*, which describes the foundations on which the Synthesizer Generator is based [Reps84]. This is a slightly modified version of

---

[1]For more complete documentation of SSL and the Synthesizer Generator, the reader should consult *The Synthesizer Generator Reference Manual* [Reps88].

Thomas Reps's Ph.D. dissertation; it was published by The M.I.T. Press after it was selected as the winner of the 1983 ACM Doctoral Dissertation Award. The two books are complementary: *Generating Language-Based Environments* describes the algorithmic foundations that underlie the Synthesizer Generator and presents a number of technical results about attribute grammars; the current book provides a thorough discussion of the actual system that we developed for generating language-based environments. In the current book, we have aimed for a mix of theory and practice in an attempt to make the ideas embodied in the system accessible to as wide an audience as possible.

We are indebted to a great number of individuals for their part in the development of the Synthesizer Generator system. Very considerable contributions have been made by the following individuals:

T. Burr	J. Field	D. George	M. Fingerhut
S. Ghemawat	R. Hoover	C. Lagoze	C. Marceau
S. Peckham	W. Pugh	S. Sinofsky	A. Zaring

Countless discussions with our user community have guided us in refining the design and implementation of the system. The assistance of this group is appreciatively acknowledged. The Synthesizer Generator is distributed with many of the demonstration editors that these users have prepared:

S. Ahmad	B. Alpern	R. Ashcroft	T. Ball
C. Beekhuis	M. Belmonte	T. Griffin	S. Horwitz
S. Liu	K. Mughal	A. Palchoudhuri	G. Snelting
B. Vander Zanden			

As always, discussions with Alan Demers have been invaluable. We are indebted to David Gries for his careful reading of the manuscript.

Financial support for our work has been provided by the National Science Foundation, the Office of Naval Research, IBM, DEC, Xerox, and Siemens. We also wish to thank our home institutions, the University of Wisconsin–Madison and Cornell University, as well as the Institut National de Recherche en Informatique et en Automatique (INRIA) in Rocquencourt, France, where we were visiting researchers in 1982-83.

July 1988   Thomas W. Reps
                                                                      Tim Teitelbaum

Contents

CHAPTER 1
Introduction

One of the most pressing practical problems faced by computer programmers is that of managing the development and maintenance of large software systems. This poses a challenge for computer scientists: how can computers best be applied to the software-development process?

An important aspect of meeting this challenge is to design and implement new interactive tools to aid programmers. Recently, research on *language-based programming environments* has developed promising ways to enhance the power of the tools used by programmers. The goal of this work has been to make effective use of knowledge that is specific to a particular language in tools used for programming in that language. Such knowledge can serve several purposes:

- Knowledge of the language's syntax can be used to assess whether a program contains syntax errors and to determine where such errors occur. Syntactic analysis can be either local (to detect context-free errors) or global (to detect context-sensitive errors). Analysis results displayed on the screen provide immediate feedback to the programmer developing or modifying the program. By performing syntactic analysis and type checking during editing rather than compilation, errors may be diagnosed at the time they are introduced.

- Knowledge of a language's semantics can be used to generate and update code incrementally during editing. By incorporating code generation in a language-based editing environment, one can provide programmers with the ability to interleave program development with testing and debugging, without the overhead of lengthy recompilation delays.

- A language's syntax and semantics provide a basis for deriving additional meaningful relationships among program entities. Such knowledge, extracted and maintained automatically during program modification, can serve to guide programmers or even to constrain them. Having such information fosters comprehension; applying it to define meaningful, high-level operations for restructuring programs promotes confidence and security.

- Programs exist not in isolation, but in relation to supporting documents. Whether interleaved with the program or separated from it, designs and specifications become large and unwieldy; these auxiliary languages themselves need language-based tools. By combining knowledge of both the programming language and the design or specification language in a single programming tool, it is possible to furnish programmers with support for creating programs according to particular methodologies.

Although most of this chapter is devoted to issues as they relate to programming environments, many of the ideas discussed have a wider range of application. For example, many of the issues that arise in designing word processors, electronic spreadsheets, and systems for computer-aided design are similar to the ones that arise when building interactive language-based programming environments. In particular, the fundamental problem that confronts the builder of any interactive system is the problem of *incremental change*: the system must be designed to provide its services efficiently as the user makes a sequence of small changes. We need a general theory of incremental computing that addresses users' needs for rapid response; the language-independent techniques that have been developed for incremental analysis in language-based environments are a step in the evolution of such a theory.

Recent work on language-based environments has been influenced both by Lisp environments, which have long exploited the ability to process programs as data objects, and by some work in the 1970s in which program analysis, transformation, and translation facilities were incorporated in language-specific editors for statically-scoped, strongly-typed languages of the Algol family. For example, the MENTOR project [Donzeau-Gouge84], initiated in 1974, created a collection of special-purpose tools for processing Pascal abstract-syntax trees using a general-purpose tree-manipulation language. Around 1979, three systems – GANDALF [Notkin85], LISPEDIT [Alberga81], and the Cornell Program Synthesizer [Teitelbaum81] – explored ways of integrating language-specific program editors with execution and debugging facilities.

In subsequent years, research on interactive, language-based program development environments has flourished; by now, there is a considerable body of published work on the subject, and it is an important topic at major conferences (see, for example, [Henderson84] and [Henderson87]).

Our own work on programming environments has centered around two systems. The first, the Cornell Program Synthesizer, was an interactive programming environment in which we combined a language-based editor for a small subset of PL/I with an incremental compiler and an interpreter.

Our second system, the Synthesizer Generator [Reps84], is a generator of language-based editors. Just as a parser generator creates a parser from a grammar that specifies a language's concrete syntax, the Synthesizer Generator creates a language-based editor from a specification of a language's abstract syntax, context-sensitive relationships, display format, concrete input syntax, and transformation rules for restructuring programs. In developing the Synthesizer Generator, our goal was to facilitate the creation of programming environments similar in spirit to the Cornell Program Synthesizer, but with greatly enhanced capabilities (and for languages other than PL/I).[1]

1.1. Using Structure Editing to Ensure that Programs Are Syntactically Correct

A language-based program editor can apply knowledge of a language's context-free syntax to ensure that programs are always syntactically well formed. In such an editor, a program is represented by its derivation tree with respect to the underlying context-free grammar. In this section, we review the benefits provided by structural editing operations that modify a program's derivation tree.

A *structure editor* reinforces the view that a program is a hierarchical composition of computational structures. Programs are composed of *templates*, which provide predefined, formatted patterns for each of the constructs in the language, such as procedures and loops. Programs are created top-down by inserting new templates at *placeholders* in the skeleton of previously entered templates. For example, in the template

---

[1]The names "Cornell Program Synthesizer" and "Synthesizer Generator" often cause some misunderstanding about the relationship between the two systems. The Synthesizer Generator is a successor system to the Cornell Program Synthesizer, but it is actually a completely separate system. Despite its name, the Synthesizer Generator was not used to create the Cornell Program Synthesizer, although the Synthesizer Generator could now be used to create a system that is functionally equivalent to it.

```
while <exp> do
   <statement>
```

<exp> and <statement> are placeholders that identify where additional inser-
tions may be made.

During editing, the current *selection* (*i.e.* insertion point), can only be moved
from one template to another, or from one template to its constituents, not from
character to character nor from one line of text to another. (In editors generated
with the Synthesizer Generator, the selection is indicated on the display screen
by highlighting the selected region; in our examples, the highlighted characters
on a line of the display are enclosed in a box.)

Templates are inserted into the program by special commands, and the system
checks whether the insertion is legal. For example, if the currently selected element is <statement>, a menu command can be invoked to insert an if-
statement into the program, automatically indented in the body of the loop, as
follows:[2]

```
while <exp> do
   if <exp> then
      <statement>
   else <statement>
```

The menu of insertion commands need not provide the same choices in all
contexts; restricting the choices offered to the insertions that are legal in the
context of the current selection forbids the user from making inappropriate
insertions. For example, because an if-statement is not an appropriate derivation
of an <exp>, the if-statement choice would not be offered in the menu when the
loop-condition is selected.

With a structure editor, changes to a program are accomplished by removal
and insertion of entire, well-formed, program fragments. This highly disci-
plined mode of modification guarantees the syntactic integrity of the program at
every step.

Transformation operations in a structure editor provide a mechanism for making controlled changes in a single step. Construct-to-construct transformation
operations emphasize the abstract computational meaning of program units.
Consider, for example, the following Pascal function that multiplies two integers
by repeated addition:

---

[2]Note that the three boxes shown in the example constitute *one* selection, not three separate selections.

```
function multiply (a, b: integer): integer;
var
    y, z: integer;
begin
    y := b;
    z := 0;
    while y > 0 do
        begin
            y := y – 1;
            z := z + a
        end ;
    multiply := z
end;
```

In one operation, this fragment can be transformed into the equivalent implementation:

```
function multiply (a, b: integer): integer;
var
    y, z: integer;
begin
    y := b;
    z := 0;
    if y > 0 then
        repeat
            y := y – 1;
            z := z + a
        until y <= 0 ;
    multiply := z
end;
```

A structure editor's capabilities for *elision* allow a program's display to be controlled according to its hierarchical structure. Users may be allowed manual control of the display, which permits them to hide unnecessary detail; alternatively, the system may automatically furnish a derived view of the program by selectively choosing to suppress certain parts of it. For example, one of the ways that might be chosen for displaying the first version of function multiply is

```
function multiply (a, b: integer): integer;
var . . . ;
begin
    y := b;
    z := 0;
    while y > 0 do . . . ;
    multiply := z
end;
```

Here the ellipses (. . .) indicate portions of the program whose display representation has been suppressed.

Structure editing has a number of attractive properties. The integrated behavior of templates and the editor's selection enforces the view that a program is a hierarchy of nested components. Placeholders in templates serve both as prompts and as syntactic constraints, by identifying places that can or must be refined, as well as by restricting the range of choices to legitimate insertions.

Templates eliminate mundane tasks of program development and let the programmer focus on the intellectually challenging aspects of programming. Each template insertion is syntactically correct because template commands are valid only in appropriate contexts. Indentation is automatic, both when a template is introduced and when it is moved. Typographical errors in structural units are impossible; the templates are predefined and immutable, so after a template has been inserted, errors cannot be introduced by subsequently modifying it. Thus, a program developed with a structure editor is always well formed, regardless of whether it is complete.

Templates correspond to abstract computational units. Because they are inserted and manipulated as units, the process of programming begins and continues at a high level of abstraction.

Do not get the idea that text editing and structure editing are incompatible. Structure editors can be augmented with text-editing facilities to create hybrid tree-and-text editors that have the advantages of both. While permitting both text editing and structure editing, a hybrid design can still preclude the creation of syntactically incorrect programs; all components that are inserted or modified textually (*e.g.* character-by-character) must be validated by the editor. A good strategy is to parse the text of the current selection (and *only* the text of the current selection) as soon as the programmer selects some other element of the program to work on; if the phrase contains an error, a message can be printed and an indicator positioned at (or close to) the site of the error.

1.2. Using Immediate Computation to Locate Errors in Programs

Recently, language-based editors have been developed that use an *immediate-computation* paradigm for program analysis, error reporting, and code generation. For example, to provide a user with feedback about errors that exist in a program, the editor performs static-semantic analysis of the program in between the user's editing modifications. The exploitation of spare machine cycles for such purposes is just one example of a general trend to immediate computation, as we describe below.

The path between the keypunch and the computer center was a very familiar route to early computer users. Data prepared in advance were submitted as batches of input to be processed by the central machine. Although timesharing improved matters considerably – the interval between successive runs was reduced from hours to seconds and the trip to the computer center was eliminated – the essence of the batch mode, an alternation between data preparation and program execution, remained dominant.

Recently, a new way of computing has begun to take hold; the dedicated processors of inexpensive personal computers are bringing about a shift to *immediate computation*. In the immediate mode of computation, the editing function is embedded within the application program itself. Each modification to a datum is processed by the application and has essentially instantaneous effect. An important result is that a computation is always consistent with the current state of the data, thereby providing useful, immediate feedback to the user as the data are manipulated. Extra computation is required, of course, because the data pass through many intermediate states that do not arise in the batch mode. These extra steps are often acceptable, however, because immediate processing can use surplus processing capacity. (While the unused cycles of timeshared computers are at the disposal of others, the spare cycles of single-user computers go to waste.) Where applicable, the immediate-computation paradigm appears certain to take hold, especially as more powerful workstations appear.

The trend towards immediate computation is illustrated by developments in three areas: word processing, electronic spreadsheets, and language-based program editors.

Many recent word-processing systems use the immediate-computation paradigm. In the traditional batch-processing mode, an input file, consisting of interleaved formatting commands and textual data, is prepared using a conventional text editor. The page layout is created only when this file is submitted to a document compiler. With the newer systems, formatting is performed interactively on a character-by-character basis, and at all times the screen resembles the final page layout. Such editors are called WYSIWYG editors, because What You See Is What You Get.

In Figure 1.1, the information displayed in (a) is used by the batch-oriented word-processing software of the UNIX operating system. This typical input file consists of the interleaved text and commands to produce the formatted document (b). With a WYSIWYG editor, the formatted page, such as the one in (b), is displayed on the screen at all times while the document is being modified.

```
.pp
This is a right justified paragraph containing
\f(HOitalicized\fP and \f(HBboldface\fP words.
In batch mode, it is difficult to tell from
the input file what the final page will look like.
.ip "1)"
This is an indented paragraph containing
the formula $x sup 2 - y sup 2$.
```

(a)

> This is a right justified paragraph containing *itali-cized* and **boldface** words. In batch mode, it is difficult to tell from the input file what the final page will look like.
>
> 1) This is an indented paragraph containing the formula x^2-y^2.

(b)

Figure 1.1. A comparison of word processing by a batch method (a) and by an immediate-processing method (b).

Electronic spreadsheets also follow the immediate-computation paradigm. In such a system, a collection of related arithmetic calculations is displayed on the screen, and a modification to the definition of any cell, either a single datum or a formula that expresses how the cell gets its value as a function of other cells, causes all affected computations to be updated immediately.

In the example in Figure 1.2, the Item, UnitPrice, and Quantity columns are user data: the Amount column and the Total are results of computations. A

Item	UnitPrice	Quantity	Amount	
pen	$0.50	2	$1.00	
pad	$0.75	3	$2.25	
			$3.25	Total

Figure 1.2. An electronic spreadsheet is an example of a system that follows the immediate-computation paradigm. Each time a cell definition is revised, the screen is updated to reflect the consequences of the change.

change in data would immediately be reflected in the computations. For example, if the Quantity of pens were changed, the Amount and Total would be immediately recomputed and displayed. Entering an improper value, such as a nonarithmetic Quantity, would result in an error message.

Language-based program editors have been developed that use immediate computation to perform program analysis, to report errors, and to generate code while the program is being edited. With these systems, errors are detected early, and the delay for compilation necessary with traditional program-development tools is eliminated. As in a WYSIWYG text editor, formatting according to program structure is immediate; as in an electronic spreadsheet, each modification to the program causes all affected analysis, error messages, and generated code to be immediately updated.

In the Pascal program shown in Figure 1.3(a), the names size, index, list, and A are defined in terms of each other. In Figure 1.3(b), after redefinition of size from 10 to x, an error message appears because the name x has not been defined in the program. Changing x to −1 removes this error, but introduces another error at a different location, as illustrated in Figure 1.3(c). This editor is, in effect, a spreadsheet for Pascal programs; the computations, updated after each editing transaction and displayed on the screen, concern correctness conditions for Pascal programs that can be determined by means of static inference.

One of the earliest programming systems that incorporated an editor with this kind of immediate error-analysis capability was the Cornell Program Synthesizer [Teitelbaum81]. In the Synthesizer Generator, this capability has been expanded by incorporating a very general mechanism for implementing immediate computations on abstract-syntax trees. Although our own systems have promoted the immediate-computation paradigm only for static program analysis, others have explored its application for program execution as well [Henderson85].

1.3. Using Incremental Code Generation to Support Program Testing

To provide programmers with the ability to combine program development with testing and debugging, program editors can support incremental translation as programs are created. A program can be translated into executable form during editing, and the code can be maintained as the program is modified. Having the program executable at all times allows the programmer to interleave editing with preliminary tests of the program.

```
program p;
const
    size = 10;
type
    index = 1 . . size;
    list = array [index] of integer;
var
    A: list;
begin
    A[10] := 0
end.
```

(a)

```
program p;
const
    size = x { CONSTANT IDENTIFIER NOT DECLARED } ;
type
    index = 1 . . size;
    list = array [index] of integer;
var
    A: list;
begin
    A[10] := 0
end.
```

(b)

```
program p;
const
    size = -1;
type
    index = 1 . . size { EMPTY RANGE NOT ALLOWED } ;
    list = array [index] of integer;
var
    A: list;
begin
    A[10] := 0
end.
```

(c)

Figure 1.3. The three screen images shown above, taken from a Pascal program editor generated with the Synthesizer Generator, illustrate the editor's immediate error-analysis capability. In (b), after size is redefined from 10 to x, an error message appears because the name x is not defined in the program. Changing x to −1 removes this error, but introduces a different one, as shown in (c).

For example, when programs were developed using the Cornell Program Synthesizer, execution could be initiated at any time and began immediately,

without any delay for compilation. The programmer could interrupt an executing program, modify it, and, as long as the program still contained the structure
associated with the point of interruption, execution could be resumed. It was
even possible to run incomplete programs: execution was suspended when a
missing program element was encountered, but could be resumed after the
required code was inserted.

Incremental translation is advantageous both for generating intermediate code
for interpretive systems like the Cornell Program Synthesizer and for generating
machine code, as in GANDALF's Incremental Programming Environment
[Medina-Mora81]. Another situation where it can be of great benefit is in a
cross-development environment. Incremental translation can be used as the
basis for a cross-debugger where programs are developed on a host machine and
executed on a slave machine; the editor on the host machine ships code to the
slave machine in small increments, thereby avoiding long delays for download-
ing a program that has been modified only slightly [Fritzson84, Fritzson84a].

1.4. Supporting Program-Development Methodologies

One of the responses to the "software crisis" has been to identify methodologies
for program development. Immediate computation has the potential to play an
important role in tools to support these methodologies.

One school holds that a program should be developed in stages. During the
first stage, the programmer should not be concerned with the efficiency with
which a program solves the given problem; rather, the programmer's initial
creation should provide an executable statement of a solution for which it is
easy to prove that the problem's requirements are satisfied. In later stages, the
program is rewritten through a sequence of correctness-preserving transformations until an efficient implementation is achieved. Support for this methodology can be provided by building in knowledge of language semantics and using
it to determine if editing operations preserve correctness.

A second school holds that a program should be developed hand-in-hand with
a proof that the program satisfies its specification. Support for this methodology
can be provided in the form of a proof editor that permits a programmer to
create and modify program proofs. The editor provides the programmer with
feedback about errors that exist in a proof as it is developed, using knowledge
embedded within the editor of the programming logic's inference rules.

A program and a proof of correctness can be presented as a *proof outline*. In
a proof outline, the program is annotated with a pre-condition and a post-
condition, and an invariant assertion is provided for each loop; these annotations
provide a formal specification of the program's intended behavior. In a conven-

tional program-verification system, a verification-condition generator reduces the question of consistency between a program and a purported proof of correctness to that of the validity of formulae in the underlying theory. One drawback of conventional verification tools is that the formulae generated are divorced from the program context in which they arise.

In contrast, it is possible to build a specialized proof editor that determines which proof obligations are not satisfied and displays information about the location of unsatisfied obligations [Reps84a]. Such an editor uses the immediate-computation paradigm: the editor keeps the user informed of errors and inconsistencies in a proof by reexamining the proof's obligations after each modification to it. It then annotates the proof with warning messages to indicate locations where proof obligations are not satisfied. (See Chapter 10 for a more lengthy discussion about using immediate computation in an interactive program verifier.)

1.5. The Need for Incremental Algorithms

Widespread adoption of the immediate mode of computation by new application software is making the study of *incremental algorithms* very important.

Suppose a program computes the function f on the user's data x, where x and $f(x)$ can be either scalars or vectors. If the program follows the immediate-computation paradigm, then the moment the user changes the data from x to x' the program must compute $f(x')$ and discard $f(x)$. Of course, $f(x')$ could be calculated from scratch, but this would usually be too slow to provide adequate response. What is needed is an algorithm that re-uses old information to avoid as much recomputation as possible. Because the increment from x to x' is often small, the increment from $f(x)$ to $f(x')$ is often also small. An algorithm that uses information from the old computation of $f(x)$ to compute the new value $f(x')$ is called *incremental*.

The advantage of an incremental algorithm is illustrated by what happens on the screen when a document is corrected on a word processor that has a WYSIWYG editor. In the WYSIWYG editor, x is the internal data structure used to represent the document, $f(x)$ is the initial formatted document and $f(x')$ is the corrected version. Suppose a small change, such as inserting a single character in the middle of a document, is made. It is possible that a major change in the format would result, but this is unlikely for two reasons: *independence* and *quiescence*. The format of the text that precedes the inserted character in no way depends on that character and is thus unaffected by the change. This is independence. In the text that follows the inserted character, the format usually changes only locally. Even if the inserted character causes some words to wrap around to succeeding lines, the propagation of changes will die out if there is enough space on the last line of the paragraph to prevent the addition of an extra line; the remainder of the document will be unaffected. This is quiescence. An incremental formatting algorithm can exploit independence and quiescence to minimize the amount of reanalysis performed.

We can distinguish between two approaches to incremental algorithms: *selective recomputation* and *differential evaluation*. In selective recomputation, values independent of changed data are never recomputed. Such values may be either intermediate results of scalar computations or individual components of vector calculations. Values that are dependent on changed data are recomputed; but after each partial result is obtained, the old and new values of that part are compared, and when changes die out, no further recomputations take place. In differential evaluation, rather than recomputing $f(x')$ in terms of the new data x', the old value $f(x)$ is updated by some difference Δf computed as a function of x, x', and $f(x)$.

The spreadsheet example of Figure 1.2 can be used to illustrate the two approaches.

To illustrate selective recomputation, suppose that $UnitPrice_{pen}$ and $Quantity_{pen}$ are changed to $1.00 and 1 respectively. Dependence information can be used to determine that $Amount_{pad}$ need not be recomputed, since it cannot change. Although $Amount_{pen}$ must be recomputed, it turns out to be unchanged, so $Total$ need not be recomputed.

To illustrate differential evaluation, suppose that $UnitPrice_{pen}$ is changed to $1.00 and $Quantity_{pen}$ is left unchanged. Then the differences

$$\Delta UnitPrice_{pen} = \$0.50$$
$$\Delta Amount_{pen} = \Delta UnitPrice_{pen} \times Quantity_{pen} = \$1.00$$
$$\Delta Total = \Delta Amount_{pen} = \$1.00$$

can be computed and used for updating $Amount_{pen}$ and $Total$. Note that with differential evaluation, even if there are hundreds of lines of data, $Total$ can be updated with a single addition.

Sophisticated incremental algorithms are not always needed because exhaustive recomputation can be fast enough for small problems. But for language-based tools to have a major effect on the productivity of software production, they must apply to large software systems. The larger the application, the more crucial the need for incremental methods.

The Cornell Program Synthesizer's editor did not employ an incremental algorithm because exhaustive recomputation was fast enough for small student programs. The system whetted appetites, but did not incorporate methods that would scale-up to meet professional requirements. Thus, in 1981 we turned our attention to the problem of devising an incremental reanalysis algorithm for language-based editing environments. In an early paper, we proposed the use of a formalism known as *attribute grammars* [Knuth68] and showed how incremental analysis could be done in this framework [Demers81]. Shortly thereafter, we discovered an optimal algorithm for incremental attribute updating [Reps82]. The algorithm follows the selective-recomputation paradigm described above. It is optimal in the sense that the amount of processing required in response to a given editing change is proportional to the amount of computed information that changes in value. (See Chapters 3 and 12 for additional details.)

1.6. Adapting Specifications for Immediate Computation

In traditional batch-mode systems, such as word processors and compilers, data items from the input file are processed sequentially. In contrast, in systems that follow the immediate-computation paradigm, data items are inserted and deleted in arbitrary order, with the system's response reflecting the current state of the user's data.

The absence of any predetermined order for processing data, together with the desire to employ incremental algorithms for this task, creates additional complexity in the design of systems that perform immediate computation. The actions of batch-mode systems are specified *imperatively*; that is, they are implemented with an imperative programming language in which a computation follows an ordered sequence of state transitions. Although imperative specifications have also been employed in immediate-mode systems, several systems have made use of an alternative approach, namely *declarative specifications*, defined as collections of simultaneous equations whose solution is the desired computation.

The salient features of declarative specifications are that

- the order of solution is left unspecified; and
- the dependence of variables on data and on one another is implicit in the equations. Whenever the data change, an incremental algorithm can be used to re-solve the equations, retaining as much of the previous solution as possible.

For example, the "program" executing the spreadsheet of Figure 1.2 is merely the set of equations:

$\text{UnitPrice}_{\text{pen}} = \$0.50$
$\text{Quantity}_{\text{pen}} = 2$
$\text{UnitPrice}_{\text{pad}} = \$0.75$
$\text{Quantity}_{\text{pad}} = 3$
$\text{Amount}_{\text{pen}} = \text{UnitPrice}_{\text{pen}} \times \text{Quantity}_{\text{pen}}$
$\text{Amount}_{\text{pad}} = \text{UnitPrice}_{\text{pad}} \times \text{Quantity}_{\text{pad}}$
$\text{Total} = \text{Amount}_{\text{pen}} + \text{Amount}_{\text{pad}}$

Changing data is, in effect, changing some of the equations, after which those equations and, perhaps, other equations must be re-solved.

The *attribute grammar* formalism adopted by the Synthesizer group for defining immediate error-analysis in language-based editors is such a declarative specification language. For each object that a user may create, the attribute grammar defines a corresponding set of simultaneous equations whose solution expresses the deductions of the editor about errors in the object. Each unknown variable in these equations represents a deduction relevant to a particular point in the object. During editing, each modification to the object causes a related change to the set of equations and their solution. Error messages that appear and disappear on the screen (as in Figure 1.3) are merely the values of textual variables that change from time to time as the equations are re-solved.

For example, suppose the + operator of the language denotes addition of integer operands (and is not overloaded for adding other kinds of operands). Then the expression 1 + 5 would be associated with the following set of equations:

$\text{typeOf}_{+} = \text{integer}$
$\text{typeOf}_{\text{leftOperand}} = \text{integer}$
$\text{typeOf}_{\text{rightOperand}} = \text{integer}$
$\text{error}_{+} = $ **if** $\text{typeOf}_{\text{leftOperand}} = \text{integer}$ **and** $\text{typeOf}_{\text{rightOperand}} = \text{integer}$
$\qquad\qquad\qquad$ **then** ""
$\qquad\qquad\qquad$ **else** "TYPE MISMATCH" **fi**

In the solution of these equations, variable error_{+} has the value "" (the empty string). If, however, the expression were changed to 1 + "a string", then the equations would be:

$\text{typeOf}_+ = \text{integer}$
$\text{typeOf}_{\text{leftOperand}} = \text{integer}$
$\text{typeOf}_{\text{rightOperand}} = \text{string}$
$\text{error}_+ = $ **if** $\text{typeOf}_{\text{leftOperand}} = \text{integer}$ **and** $\text{typeOf}_{\text{rightOperand}} = \text{integer}$
                    then ""
                    else "TYPE MISMATCH" **fi**

In the solution of the latter equations, variable error_+ has the value "TYPE MISMATCH".

Attribute grammars have several desirable qualities as a notation for specifying language-based editors. A language is specified in a modular fashion by an attribute grammar: syntax is defined by a context-free grammar; attribution is defined in an equally modular fashion, because the arguments to each attribute equation are local to one production. Propagation of attribute values through the derivation tree is not specified explicitly in an attribute grammar; rather, it is implicitly defined by the equations of the grammar and the form of the tree.

The benefit of using attribute grammars to handle the problem of incremental change in language-based editors is that the *repropagation* of consistent attribute values after a modification to an object is implicit in the formalism. Thus, there is no need for the notions of "undoing a semantic action" or "reversing the side-effects of a previous analysis," which would otherwise be necessary. When an object is modified, consistent relationships among the attributes can be reestablished automatically by incrementally re-solving the system of attribute equations. Consequently, when an editor is specified with an attribute grammar, the method for achieving a consistent state after an editing modification is not part of the specification.

Apart from its use to specify name analysis and type checking, the attribute-grammar formalism provides a basis for specifying a large variety of other computations on tree-structured data, including type inference (as distinct from type checking), code generation, proof checking, and text formatting (including filling and justification, as well as equation formatting).

1.7. Generating Language-Based Programming Environments

Today's powerful stand-alone computers provide virtually free processing, but to make full use of their potential, the impressive advances in hardware must be accompanied by the development of appropriate, innovative software. Much of the capacity of hardware, which can perform millions of operations between every pair of consecutive keystrokes, is currently going to waste. Language-based editors offer a way to put this capacity to work.

Many language-based environments are currently under development world-wide. With some exceptions, such as MENTOR, GANDALF, and the Synthesizer Generator, most are hand-tailored for the particular application, be it a programming language, design language, specification language, system-modeling language, theorem prover, and so forth.

All language-based environments share many language-independent features. These include maintaining an abstract representation of the object being edited and a collection of derived information as the object changes. For example, a program editor must maintain the correct type assignments for each subexpression as variable declarations change; a proof editor must maintain its verification that a given proof proves a given proposition as both proof and proposition are modified; a WYSIWYG editor must maintain the spacing values that effect right-justification of text, and so forth. While these examples are domain-specific, the notion of incrementally maintaining a collection of derived information, and many of the techniques for doing so efficiently, are language-independent.

In addition to these tasks, every editing environment must provide many mundane, language-independent services, such as commands for navigating through the object and for allowing the user to save and restore the object using the file system. A user interface must be developed, with bindings of key sequences to the environment's generic commands (such as selection of sub-objects) as well as to application-specific commands. Buffers for edited objects need to be created, maintained, and interfaced to the windowing systems under which the environment is to run. Editing operations (deletion, in-place text editing, *etc.*) must not only affect the internal representation of the object, but the display of the object must be incrementally updated. In general, the size of the language-independent code dominates that of the language-specific code.

When people build language-based editors in an *ad hoc* manner, there is a lamentable duplication of effort and misspent expertise as specialists in many different application areas struggle with the same details of windowing systems, parsing of input commands, and the like. The resulting systems also suffer from *ad hoc* solutions to problems for which systematic solutions have been found, for example, incremental change propagation of derived information.

In contrast, editor-generating systems facilitate the creation of editing systems that are individually tailored for different languages. Although each different editor produced with an editor-generating system results in an editor with different characteristics, all share the common user-interface of the generator's editing kernel.

1.8. The Synthesizer Generator

The Synthesizer Generator is one such system for generating language-based editors. It creates a language-specific editor from an input specification that defines a language's abstract syntax, context-sensitive relationships, display format, concrete input syntax, and transformation rules for restructuring objects. From this specification, the Generator creates a display editor for manipulating objects according to these rules.

The treatment of language syntax by the Generator is of particular importance. The editor-designer's specification of the language's syntax addresses not only context-free syntax but also such context-sensitive conditions as type correctness. As the user creates and modifies objects, the generated editor incrementally checks for violations of context conditions that have been specified.

Context conditions are expressed by introducing certain attributes whose attribute equations indicate whether or not a constraint is satisfied. The manner in which objects are annotated with information about violations of context conditions is expressed by the editor's *unparsing* specification, which determines how objects are displayed on the screen. Attributes used in the unparsing specification cause the display to be annotated with values of attribute instances. In particular, the attributes that indicate satisfaction or violation of context-dependent constraints can be used to annotate the display to indicate the presence or absence of errors. If an editing operation modifies an object in such a way that formerly satisfied constraints are now violated (alternatively, formerly violated constraints are now satisfied), the attributes that indicate satisfaction of constraints will receive new values. The changed image of these attributes on the screen provides the user with feedback about new errors introduced and old errors corrected.

Editor specifications are written in the Synthesizer Specification Language (SSL), which is built around the concepts of an attribute grammar and a type-definition facility, although certain features are tailored to the application domain of language-based editors. In SSL, an attribute's type can be either one of the built-in primitive types or a user-defined, composite type. In an editor specification, one uses precisely the same sort of rules to define new attribute types as one uses to define abstract syntax. This design, in which the abstract-syntax tree being edited and the attributes attached to it are all elements of a single domain of values, permits writing attribution schemes whose computations create new syntactic objects.

The Synthesizer Generator has been used to produce prototype editors for a wide variety of applications, including WYSIWYG editors for both text and mathematical formulas, editors that verify the correctness of proofs in several varieties of mathematical logic, and program editors for several different programming languages (including an editor for full Pascal with complete static-semantic checking).

The Synthesizer Generator is written in C and runs under Berkeley UNIX. Editors can be generated for the X Window System and for SunView, as well as for video display terminals. Editors generated for X or SunView support multiple overlapping windows and the use of the mouse to make selections in edited objects, to select commands and transformations from menus, and to scroll, resize, and iconify windows.

CHAPTER 2

Demonstration of a Sample Editor

Chapter 2 demonstrates the nature of editors generated using the Synthesizer Generator. We present a sample editing session using an editor whose facilities are tailored to a simple programming language. The language is a miniature Algol-like language with two kinds of data – integer and boolean – and four kinds of statements – an assignment-statement, a conditional-statement, a while-statement, and a compound-statement. The language is strongly typed; each variable used in a program must be declared as either integer or boolean, and programs can be statically type-checked to ensure that an integer is never used in a context that requires a boolean, and *vice versa*.

The session illustrates structure editing, pretty-printing, list manipulation, and text editing. It also shows how an editor can incrementally check for violations of context-sensitive conditions; in the sample editor, the program is continuously checked for three kinds of errors:

- Uses of identifiers in expressions and on the left-hand side of assignment statements are checked against the declarations in the program to find undeclared identifiers.
- Expressions and statements are checked to verify that their constituents have compatible types.
- Declarations are checked for identifiers that are declared more than once.

For each such error in the program, the editor displays a comment indicating its location.

The editor to be described illustrates only one of the possible ways that features can be tailored to a particular language. We have tried to make the example representative of the Synthesizer Generator's capabilities, but it has been necessary to keep the specification simple so that it may be explained completely in Chapter 4. Throughout the book, we will discuss how other editors with quite different features can be created with the Synthesizer Generator.

We first examine the screen as it appears when an editing session is initiated. In the diagrams that follow, the border of the editor's screen is indicated with a double-ruled box; highlighted characters (ones displayed in reverse-video) are outlined with a single-ruled box.

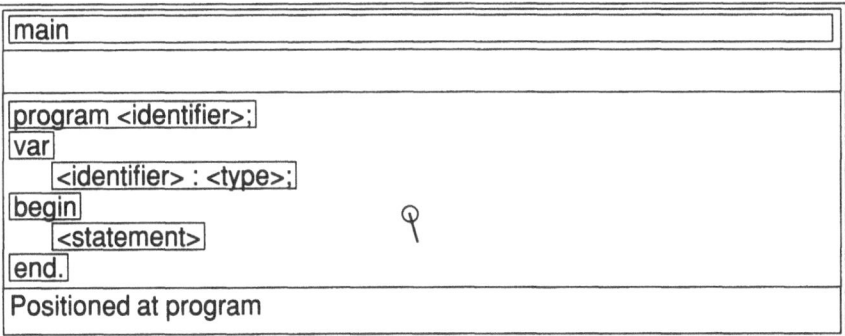

The top line of the screen has a highlighted *title bar* displaying the name of the current buffer. The rest of the screen is divided into three regions: the *command line*, the *help pane*, and the *object pane*. The command line, just below the title bar, is where commands are echoed and also where system messages are displayed. The help pane, which takes up the last few lines at the bottom, provides information about what constituent is currently selected. The object pane, displaying the buffer's program fragment, covers the remaining portion of the screen.

The editor is a screen-oriented structure editor. The object being edited has hierarchical structure; it is not just a sequence of characters and lines. The initial content of the object pane consists of a *template* for a program. A template is a formatted pattern of keywords and *placeholders*, where the placeholders identify locations at which additional components can be inserted. Programs are created top down by inserting new statements and expressions within the skeleton of previously entered templates. Operations on the object pane are defined in terms of this structure and the current *selection* – an individual component of the program that is denoted in the display by highlighting. In the example shown above, the entire program is selected, which is indicated by highlighting the entire program.

However, the editor is not just a structure editor; it also supports character- and line-oriented operations to insert and delete text. During text editing, the selection contains within it a *character selection*, denoted on the screen as an unhighlighted character or I-beam within the highlighted selection. Text editing is not initiated until the user types or erases a character; thus, at the start of an editing session there is no character selection within the selection.

The structural selection and the character selection can both be changed by using the *locator* to point to a new location in the program. On a workstation equipped with a mouse, the locator is an arrow or some other graphic icon; in the screen image shown above, the symbol "♀" represents the locator. The locator's position is changed by moving the mouse, but the selection is not changed until the user executes the **select** command by clicking the mouse's selection button. On a video display terminal, the locator is the terminal's cursor, and it can be moved using one of the commands **pointer-up** <ESC-p>, **pointer-down** <ESC-d>, **pointer-left** <ESC-b>, and **pointer-right** <ESC-f>.[1] The **select** command is normally bound to the sequence <ESC-@>.

The editor incorporates knowledge about a language's syntax, which it uses to prevent syntax errors from being introduced into the program. One way this is done is by requiring that certain templates be immutable; that is, when certain components are selected, the user is not permitted to make textual modifications.

For instance, in our example editor, it is impossible to modify the program template by textual operations. If the user types a character anyway, the character is rejected, a warning signal sounds, and the message text entry not permitted here is displayed on the command line, as shown below:

```
┌─────────────────────────────────────────────────────────────┐
│ │main                                                       │ │
│ ├───────────────────────────────────────────────────────────┤ │
│ text entry not permitted here                                 │
│ ┌─────────────────────────┐                                  │
│ │program <identifier>;│                                       │
│ ┌───┐                                                         │
│ │var│                                                         │
│ └───┘    ┌──────────────────────┐                             │
│          │<identifier> : <type>;│                             │
│ ┌─────┐  └──────────────────────┘                            │
│ │begin│                              ♀                        │
│ └─────┘  ┌───────────┐                                        │
│          │<statement>│                                        │
│ ┌────┐   └───────────┘                                        │
│ │end.│                                                        │
│ └────┘                                                        │
│ Positioned at program                                         │
└─────────────────────────────────────────────────────────────┘
```

---

[1]For the convenience of readers who are experimenting with the editor, the standard key bindings for the commands mentioned in the chapter are indicated in the text between angle brackets (*e.g.* **redraw-display** <^L>).

In this case, we must move the selection elsewhere before we can modify the program. The selection can be changed to a different element of the program by repositioning the locator and invoking the **select** command <ESC-@>. Suppose we have decided to enter the program's statements first; we select the statement placeholder of the program's body by pointing the locator at any of the characters of <statement> and invoking **select**:

```
┌────────────────────────────────────────────────────────────┐
│ ┌──────────────────────────────────────────────────────┐   │
│ │main                                                    │   │
│ └──────────────────────────────────────────────────────┘   │
│                                                              │
│ program <identifier>;                                        │
│ var                                                          │
│     <identifier> : <type>;                                   │
│ begin                                                        │
│     ┌─────────────┐                                          │
│     │<statement>  │                                          │
│     └─────────────┘                                          │
│ end.      \                                                  │
│ Positioned at stmtList   assign    if   while   begin   (begin │
└────────────────────────────────────────────────────────────┘
```

The highlighted region changes to indicate the extent of the new selection and the help pane is updated to provide information about the currently selected component. The new selection is a stmtList, a list of statements that, for the moment, consists of just one <statement> placeholder.

When the selection is positioned at a stmtList, we are permitted to enter statements into the program directly as text; for the moment, however, we choose to modify the program by an alternative method: *template insertion*. The names of all templates available are displayed in the help pane. In this case, they correspond to the different kinds of statements in the language; for example, assign is bound to the template for an assignment-statement.

There are three ways in which a template may be selected. On a workstation equipped with a mouse, it can be chosen from a pop-up menu of choices displayed when the mouse's structure-menu button is depressed, or it can be inserted by just clicking on its name in the help pane. On a standard video display terminal, the user escapes to the command line by invoking the **execute-command** command <^I or ESC-x>[2] and then types some unambiguous prefix of the template name.

The **execute-command** command echoes the prompt COMMAND: on the command line to signify command mode, after which subsequent characters are

---

[2]The control character ^I is TAB.

directed to the command line. After typing the template name assign, the
screen appears as:

```
┌─────────────────────────────────────────────────────────┐
│┌────────────────────────────────────────────────────────┐│
││main                                                      ││
│├────────────────────────────────────────────────────────┤│
││COMMAND: assign                                           ││
│├────────────────────────────────────────────────────────┤│
││program <identifier>;                                     ││
││var                                                       ││
││     <identifier> : <type>;                               ││
││begin                                                     ││
││     ┌───────────┐                                        ││
││     │<statement>│                                        ││
││     └───────────┘                                        ││
││end.                                                      ││
│├────────────────────────────────────────────────────────┤│
││Positioned at stmtList   assign   if  while  begin  (begin││
│└────────────────────────────────────────────────────────┘│
└─────────────────────────────────────────────────────────┘
```

Template commands can be terminated by any of the several commands for
moving the buffer's selection. Below we use the **forward-with-optionals** command <^M>,[3] which moves the cursor to the next resting place in a preorder
traversal of the program's derivation tree.

```
┌─────────────────────────────────────────────────────────┐
│┌────────────────────────────────────────────────────────┐│
││main                                                      ││
│├────────────────────────────────────────────────────────┤│
││                                                          ││
│├────────────────────────────────────────────────────────┤│
││program <identifier>;                                     ││
││var                                                       ││
││     <identifier> : <type>;                               ││
││begin                                                     ││
││     ┌────────────┐                                       ││
││     │<identifier>│ := <exp>                              ││
││     └────────────┘                                       ││
││end.                                                      ││
│├────────────────────────────────────────────────────────┤│
││Positioned at identifier                                  ││
│└────────────────────────────────────────────────────────┘│
└─────────────────────────────────────────────────────────┘
```

An assignment-statement template, such as the one that has just been inserted,
has two placeholders: one for the left-hand-side identifier and one for the right-
hand-side expression. Because the terminating **forward-with-optionals** command is applied after the template is inserted, the selection has been moved to
the identifier placeholder.

Note that when positioned at <identifier>, the help pane does not list any
template commands, indicating that no templates are provided in this context.
As an experiment, however, let us try using the same command again. We
invoke the **execute-command** command <^l or ESC-x> and type assign.

---

[3]The control character ^M is RETURN.

```
┌─────────────────────────────────────────────────────────┐
│ main                                                      │
├───────────────────────────────────────────────────────────┤
│ COMMAND: assign                                           │
├───────────────────────────────────────────────────────────┤
│ program <identifier>;                                     │
│ var                                                       │
│     <identifier> : <type>;                                │
│ begin                                                     │
│     <identifier> := <exp>                                 │
│ end.                                                      │
├───────────────────────────────────────────────────────────┤
│ Positioned at identifier                                  │
└─────────────────────────────────────────────────────────┘
```

We then attempt to initiate the template insertion by **forward-with-optionals**
<^M>. This time, the command has no effect on the program. Instead, the edi-
tor sounds a warning signal, the message assign is unknown command is
displayed in the command line, and a second buffer is provided that lists all the
system commands together with their key bindings:

```
┌─────────────────────────────────────────────────────────┐
│ main                                                      │
├───────────────────────────────────────────────────────────┤
│ assign is unknown command                                 │
├───────────────────────────────────────────────────────────┤
│ program <identifier>;                                     │
│ var                                                       │
│     <identifier> : <type>;                                │
│ begin                                                     │
│     <identifier> := <exp>                                 │
│ end.                                                      │
├───────────────────────────────────────────────────────────┤
│ Positioned at identifier                                  │
└─────────────────────────────────────────────────────────┘
```

```
┌─────────────────────────────────────────────────────────┐
│ help                                                      │
├───────────────────────────────────────────────────────────┤
│                                                           │
├───────────────────────────────────────────────────────────┤
│ advance-after-transform              (none)               │
│ advance-after-parse                  (none)               │
│ apropos                              <ESC ?>              │
│ ascend-to-parent                     <ESC ^>              │
└─────────────────────────────────────────────────────────┘
```

The help buffer can be removed from the screen with the **delete-other-windows**
command <^X1>. For additional information about manipulating buffers and
windows, consult *The Synthesizer Generator Reference Manual*. (*The Synthesizer Generator Reference Manual* also provides complete documentation for
each of the other system commands.)

As the last example illustrated, a particular template command may only apply at certain placeholders. The template commands that are acceptable at the currently selected placeholder are listed in the help pane and in the pop-up template menu. A command that fails to match any of the acceptable template names is interpreted as a system command.

The Synthesizer Generator lets an editor-designer create *hybrid* editors that allow making character- and line-oriented operations on the program text in addition to structural operations, such as template insertion. For structure editing, the editor-designer specifies templates and template-insertion commands; for text editing, the editor-designer specifies the syntactic categories at which it is permissible to enter text, as well as the concrete syntax allowed as input in each category. Text editing does not have to be permitted for all constructs; the input forms allowed (concrete input syntax for textual input and template-insertion commands for structural input) can depend on context. This capacity gives the editor-designer complete freedom to design whatever mix of structural editing and text editing is desired.

Thus, it is possible to edit some selections as text. For this purpose, the textual representation of the selection is captured into a *text buffer*. During such text editing, the selection exists as text, not as structure, and operations within the selection are defined on individual characters, not on program structures. The text buffer is displayed in place within the program, so its presence is almost imperceptible. A text buffer contains a *character selection* denoted on the screen as an unhighlighted character or I-beam within the highlighted selection. Character insertions and deletions occur at the position of the character selection. In the screen image shown below, the symbol I represents the I-beam.

In the example editor, identifiers may be entered by text editing. When the first character is entered, the placeholder disappears. For example, after typing 12345, the screen appears as:

```
┌─────────────────────────────────────────────────────────────┐
│ │main                                                      │  │
│ ├──────────────────────────────────────────────────────────┤ │
│ │                                                           │ │
│ │program <identifier>;                                      │ │
│ │var                                                        │ │
│ │    <identifier> : <type>;                                 │ │
│ │begin                                                      │ │
│ │   │12345│    := <exp>                                     │ │
│ │end.                                                       │ │
│ ├──────────────────────────────────────────────────────────┤ │
│ │Positioned at identifier                                   │ │
│ └──────────────────────────────────────────────────────────┘ │
└─────────────────────────────────────────────────────────────┘
```

Just as the commands that move the buffer's selection initiate a template insertion, they also initiate the processing of a textual entry. Because text is typed by the user, it can be syntactically incorrect in the context of the current selection. To check syntactic correctness, a parser is invoked when text entry is terminated. If an error is detected, a warning signal sounds, the message syntax error is displayed on the command line, and the character selection is located at the last character of the leftmost error. Thus, after execution of **forward-with-optionals** <^M>, the screen appears as:

```
┌─────────────────────────────────────────────────────────────┐
│ │main                                                      │  │
│ ├──────────────────────────────────────────────────────────┤ │
│ │syntax error                                               │ │
│ ├──────────────────────────────────────────────────────────┤ │
│ │program <identifier>;                                      │ │
│ │var                                                        │ │
│ │    <identifier> : <type>;                                 │ │
│ │begin                                                      │ │
│ │   │1234│5│    := <exp>                                    │ │
│ │end.                                                       │ │
│ ├──────────────────────────────────────────────────────────┤ │
│ │Positioned at identifier                                   │ │
│ └──────────────────────────────────────────────────────────┘ │
└─────────────────────────────────────────────────────────────┘
```

because the use of an integer constant on the left-hand side of an assignment-statement is illegal.

After an error is detected, the user may resume text editing to correct the syntax error. In the screen image below, the constant 12345 has been removed by first invoking **delete-selection** <^K> and then typing the identifier i.

```
┌─────────────────────────────────────────────────────────┐
│┌───────────────────────────────────────────────────────┐│
││ main                                                    ││
│└───────────────────────────────────────────────────────┘│
│┌───────────────────────────────────────────────────────┐│
││                                                         ││
│├───────────────────────────────────────────────────────┤│
││ program <identifier>;                                   ││
││ var                                                     ││
││     <identifier> : <type>;                              ││
││ begin                                                   ││
││    [i]            := <exp>                              ││
││ end.                                                    ││
│├───────────────────────────────────────────────────────┤│
││ Positioned at identifier                                ││
│└───────────────────────────────────────────────────────┘│
└─────────────────────────────────────────────────────────┘
```

Invoking **forward-with-optionals** <^M> again causes the text to be parsed; this time it is accepted, the identifier is inserted in the program, and the selection moves to the right-hand side of the assignment-statement:

```
┌─────────────────────────────────────────────────────────┐
│┌───────────────────────────────────────────────────────┐│
││ main                                                    ││
│└───────────────────────────────────────────────────────┘│
│┌───────────────────────────────────────────────────────┐│
││                                                         ││
│├───────────────────────────────────────────────────────┤│
││ program <identifier>;                                   ││
││ var                                                     ││
││     <identifier> : <type>;                              ││
││ begin                                                   ││
││    i { NOT DECLARED } := [<exp>]                        ││
││ end.                                                    ││
│├───────────────────────────────────────────────────────┤│
││ Positioned at exp                                       ││
│└───────────────────────────────────────────────────────┘│
└─────────────────────────────────────────────────────────┘
```

However, although the text is syntactically correct, the program does not contain a declaration for variable i; the editor announces the undeclared-variable error by attaching the comment { NOT DECLARED } to the undeclared identifier.

The existence of such an error does not place any constraints on the user. The error can either be corrected immediately by moving to the declaration place-holder and creating a declaration for i, or it can be ignored for the time being. We choose to do the latter and proceed to enter the expression for the right-hand side of the assignment-statement by typing 1.

```
┌─────────────────────────────────────────────────────────┐
│┌───────────────────────────────────────────────────────┐│
││main                                                     ││
│└───────────────────────────────────────────────────────┘│
│                                                          │
│program <identifier>;                                     │
│var                                                       │
│    <identifier> : <type>;                                │
│begin                                                     │
│    i { NOT DECLARED } := [1]│                            │
│end.                                                      │
│Positioned at exp                                         │
└─────────────────────────────────────────────────────────┘
```

When **forward-with-optionals** <ˆM> is executed, 1 correctly parses as an expression, and the selection is advanced to the next possible placeholder for an insertion:

```
┌─────────────────────────────────────────────────────────┐
│┌───────────────────────────────────────────────────────┐│
││main                                                     ││
│└───────────────────────────────────────────────────────┘│
│                                                          │
│program <identifier>;                                     │
│var                                                       │
│    <identifier> : <type>;                                │
│begin                                                     │
│    i { NOT DECLARED } := 1;                              │
│    <statement>                                           │
│end.                                                      │
│Positioned at stmtList  assign   if  while  begin  (begin │
└─────────────────────────────────────────────────────────┘
```

The next placeholder where an insertion is possible is an optional stmtList placeholder that is materialized following the assignment-statement i := 1. Note that the semicolon joining successive statements has also appeared automatically.

This example illustrates how lists, such as stmtList, are manipulated in the editor. Conceptually, each item in a list is preceded and followed by an additional placeholder, but such placeholders appear only if they are the current selection (or when there are no elements in the list). The command **forward-with-optionals** means: "Advance the selection to the next template, phrase, or placeholder, *including list placeholders*."

Let us continue developing this program for a few more steps. First, a while-loop is inserted. We need only type **execute-command** <ˆl or ESC-x> followed by **w**, a unique prefix of the template name while.

```
┌─────────────────────────────────────────────────────┐
│ main                                                  │
├─────────────────────────────────────────────────────┤
│ COMMAND: w                                            │
├─────────────────────────────────────────────────────┤
│ program <identifier>;                                 │
│ var                                                   │
│     <identifier> : <type>;                            │
│ begin                                                 │
│     i { NOT DECLARED } := 1;                          │
│     <statement>                                       │
│ end.                                                  │
├─────────────────────────────────────────────────────┤
│ Positioned at stmtList  assign   if  while  begin  (begin │
└─────────────────────────────────────────────────────┘
```

The template is inserted and the selection is advanced to the next insertion point as soon as **forward-with-optionals <^M>** is executed:

```
┌─────────────────────────────────────────────────────┐
│ main                                                  │
├─────────────────────────────────────────────────────┤
│                                                       │
├─────────────────────────────────────────────────────┤
│ program <identifier>;                                 │
│ var                                                   │
│     <identifier> : <type>;                            │
│ begin                                                 │
│     i { NOT DECLARED } := 1;                          │
│     while <exp> do                                    │
│         <statement>                                   │
│ end.                                                  │
├─────────────────────────────────────────────────────┤
│ Positioned at exp                                     │
└─────────────────────────────────────────────────────┘
```

The loop's condition is expanded by typing the inequality i<>100 in place, followed by **forward-with-optionals <^M>**:

```
┌──────────────────────────────────────────────────────────────────┐
│ ┌──────────────────────────────────────────────────────────────┐ │
│ │main                                                            │ │
│ └──────────────────────────────────────────────────────────────┘ │
│ ┌──────────────────────────────────────────────────────────────┐ │
│ │                                                                │ │
│ ├──────────────────────────────────────────────────────────────┤ │
│ │program <identifier>;                                           │ │
│ │var                                                             │ │
│ │    <identifier> : <type>;                                      │ │
│ │begin                                                           │ │
│ │    i { NOT DECLARED } := 1;                                    │ │
│ │    while (i { NOT DECLARED } <> 100) do                        │ │
│ │        ┌─────────────┐                                         │ │
│ │        │<statement>  │                                         │ │
│ │        └─────────────┘                                         │ │
│ │end.                                                            │ │
│ ├──────────────────────────────────────────────────────────────┤ │
│ │Positioned at stmt   assign   if   while   begin   (begin       │ │
│ └──────────────────────────────────────────────────────────────┘ │
└──────────────────────────────────────────────────────────────────┘
```

The expression i<>100 parses successfully and the selection advances to the next placeholder where an insertion can be made. As before, the system attaches a comment to identifier i to indicate the absence of a declaration for i. Note that the expression has been enclosed within parentheses. The sample editor uses a straightforward rule for generating parentheses: each subexpression whose outermost operator is binary is enclosed in a single pair of parentheses. However, it is possible to specify more elaborate rules using the Synthesizer Generator. (See Section 6.3, "Defining Computed Display Representations.")

Finally, the loop-body is filled in by typing an assignment-statement i:=i+1. Earlier, when an assignment-statement was entered into the program, it was inserted using an assignment template; to illustrate that the editor supports textual insertion of assignment statements in addition to providing the assignment template, this time we choose to type in the entire statement i:=i+1 directly, as shown below:

```
┌──────────────────────────────────────────────────────────┐
│ main                                                       │
├──────────────────────────────────────────────────────────┤
│                                                            │
│ program <identifier>;                                      │
│ var                                                        │
│     <identifier> : <type>;                                 │
│ begin                                                      │
│     i { NOT DECLARED } := 1;                               │
│     while (i { NOT DECLARED } <> 100) do                   │
│         i:=i+1                                             │
│ end.                                                       │
├──────────────────────────────────────────────────────────┤
│ Positioned at stmt  assign   if  while  begin  (begin     │
└──────────────────────────────────────────────────────────┘
```

Then, upon **forward-with-optionals** <^M>, the text i:=i+1 is parsed, its display
is annotated with error messages, and the selection is advanced to the next
placeholder where an insertion can made. No further insertions are possible
within the body of the while-statement, because in our example editor the body
of a while-statement is defined to be just a single statement. Thus, the new
selection is automatically advanced to a newly displayed <statement> placeholder beyond the entire while-statement. The indentation level of the placeholder reveals that the location is after, rather than within, the while-statement:

```
┌──────────────────────────────────────────────────────────┐
│ main                                                       │
├──────────────────────────────────────────────────────────┤
│                                                            │
│ program <identifier>;                                      │
│ var                                                        │
│     <identifier> : <type>;                                 │
│ begin                                                      │
│     i { NOT DECLARED } := 1;                               │
│     while (i { NOT DECLARED } <> 100) do                   │
│         i { NOT DECLARED } := (i { NOT DECLARED } + 1);    │
│     <statement>                                            │
│ end.                                                       │
├──────────────────────────────────────────────────────────┤
│ Positioned at stmtList  assign   if  while  begin  (begin │
└──────────────────────────────────────────────────────────┘
```

At this point, we finally add a declaration for variable i. First, we select the
declaration placeholder by pointing the locator at the : within the declaration
and invoking the **select** command <ESC-@>:

```
┌─────────────────────────────────────────────────────────────────┐
│ ┌─────────────────────────────────────────────────────────────┐ │
│ │ main                                                        │ │
│ └─────────────────────────────────────────────────────────────┘ │
│ ┌─────────────────────────────────────────────────────────────┐ │
│ │                                                             │ │
│ └─────────────────────────────────────────────────────────────┘ │
│  program <identifier>;                                           │
│  var                                                             │
│      ┌────────────────────────┐                                 │
│      │<identifier> ◌ <type>│ ;                                 │
│      └────────────────────────┘                                 │
│  begin                          \                                │
│     i { NOT DECLARED } := 1;                                     │
│     while (i { NOT DECLARED } <> 100) do                         │
│         i { NOT DECLARED } := (i { NOT DECLARED } + 1)           │
│  end.                                                            │
│ ─────────────────────────────────────────────────────────────── │
│  Positioned at declList                                          │
└─────────────────────────────────────────────────────────────────┘
```

The optional <statement> placeholder disappears as soon as the selection moves to the declaration. The phrase <identifier> : <type> is an example of a *compound placeholder* – a placeholder that contains other placeholders. As soon as we type i, the first character of the declaration, the entire compound placeholder is replaced by i. Continuing to type, we intentionally make the mistake of declaring i to be a boolean variable by entering i:boolean.

```
┌─────────────────────────────────────────────────────────────────┐
│ ┌─────────────────────────────────────────────────────────────┐ │
│ │ main                                                        │ │
│ └─────────────────────────────────────────────────────────────┘ │
│ ┌─────────────────────────────────────────────────────────────┐ │
│ │                                                             │ │
│ └─────────────────────────────────────────────────────────────┘ │
│  program <identifier>;                                           │
│  var                                                             │
│      ┌──────────────┐                                           │
│      │ i:boolean ▮ │            ;                               │
│      └──────────────┘                                           │
│  begin                                                           │
│     i { NOT DECLARED } := 1;                                     │
│     while (i { NOT DECLARED } <> 100) do                         │
│         i { NOT DECLARED } := (i { NOT DECLARED } + 1)           │
│  end.                                                            │
│ ─────────────────────────────────────────────────────────────── │
│  Positioned at declList                                          │
└─────────────────────────────────────────────────────────────────┘
```

When we invoke **forward-with-optionals** <^M>, the new text is parsed and the selection is advanced. In addition, as a side effect of the insertion, the error messages throughout the program are revised:

```
┌─────────────────────────────────────────────────────────┐
│┌─────────────────────────────────────────────────────┐ │
││main                                                    │ │
│└─────────────────────────────────────────────────────┘ │
│┌─────────────────────────────────────────────────────┐ │
│└─────────────────────────────────────────────────────┘ │
│program <identifier>;                                     │
│var                                                       │
│    i : boolean;                                          │
│    ┌──────────────────────┐                              │
│    │<identifier> : <type> │;                             │
│    └──────────────────────┘                              │
│begin                                                     │
│    i := 1 { INCOMPATIBLE TYPES IN := };                  │
│    while (i <> { INCOMPATIBLE TYPES } 100) do            │
│        i := (i + { INCOMPATIBLE TYPES } 1) { INCOMPATIBLE TYPES│
│        IN := }                                           │
│end.                                                      │
├─────────────────────────────────────────────────────────┤
│Positioned at declList                                    │
└─────────────────────────────────────────────────────────┘
```

Adding the declaration has corrected the undeclared-variable errors in the program, but because i is declared as **boolean**, it has introduced type errors in a number of other locations. The left-hand and right-hand sides of the two assignment-statements now have incompatible types, which the editor has reported by annotating them with the comment

{ INCOMPATIBLE TYPES IN := }.

In addition, the comparison operation in the loop-condition and the addition operation have type errors. This has been signaled by the comment

{ INCOMPATIBLE TYPES }.

Now consider what happens when we change the type of variable i from **boolean** to **integer**. First, we select the declaration's type expression by pointing the locator at any of the characters in **boolean** and invoking **select** <ESC-@>:

```
┌─────────────────────────────────────────────────────────────────────┐
│┌─────────────────────────────────────────────────────────────────┐  │
││ main                                                              │  │
│└─────────────────────────────────────────────────────────────────┘  │
│                                                                      │
│ program <identifier>;                                                │
│ var                                                                  │
│     i : [boolea̱ṉ];                                                   │
│ begin                     ⟍                                          │
│     i := 1 { INCOMPATIBLE TYPES IN := };                             │
│     while (i <> { INCOMPATIBLE TYPES } 100) do                       │
│         i := (i + { INCOMPATIBLE TYPES } 1) { INCOMPATIBLE TYPES     │
│         IN := }                                                      │
│ end.                                                                 │
│ Positioned at typeExp                                                │
└─────────────────────────────────────────────────────────────────────┘
```

Then, we delete boolean by invoking **delete-selection** <^K>, which causes the <type> placeholder to reappear. As soon as the type component of i's declaration is deleted, the type errors annotating the display disappear because, in this editor, a variable that is declared but whose type has not been specified is considered to be type-compatible in any context:

```
┌─────────────────────────────────────────────────────────────────────┐
│┌─────────────────────────────────────────────────────────────────┐  │
││ main                                                              │  │
│└─────────────────────────────────────────────────────────────────┘  │
│                                                                      │
│ program <identifier>;                                                │
│ var                                                                  │
│     i : [<type>];                                                    │
│ begin                                                                │
│     i := 1;                                                          │
│     while (i <> 100) do                                              │
│         i := (i + 1)                                                 │
│ end.                                                                 │
│ Positioned at typeExp   integer boolean                              │
└─────────────────────────────────────────────────────────────────────┘
```

Entering an integer type expression introduces no new type incompatibilities into the program. We type integer followed by **forward-with-optionals** <^M>:

```
┌─────────────────────────────────────────────────────────────┐
│ main                                                          │
├─────────────────────────────────────────────────────────────┤
│                                                               │
│ program <identifier>;                                         │
│ var                                                           │
│     i : integer;                                              │
│     <identifier> : <type> ;                                   │
│ begin                                                         │
│     i := 1;                                                   │
│     while (i <> 100) do                                       │
│         i := (i + 1)                                          │
│ end.                                                          │
├─────────────────────────────────────────────────────────────┤
│ Positioned at typeExp                                         │
└─────────────────────────────────────────────────────────────┘
```

Now suppose we want to add additional statements to the body of the while-loop. The while body has syntactic type stmt, not stmtList, which means we need to introduce a compound-statement into the loop. Because the body already contains a statement, the most convenient way to perform the insertion is to use a command that encloses the existing statement in a begin-end. First, to select the assignment-statement, we point the locator at the := symbol and invoke **select** <ESC-@>. The declaration placeholder disappears as soon as the selection moves away. Next, we type **execute-command** <ˆl or ESC-x> to escape to the command line, where we type the command (begin:

```
┌─────────────────────────────────────────────────────────────┐
│ main                                                          │
├─────────────────────────────────────────────────────────────┤
│ COMMAND: (begin                                               │
├─────────────────────────────────────────────────────────────┤
│ program <identifier>;                                         │
│ var                                                           │
│     i : integer;                                              │
│ begin                                                         │
│     i := 1;                                                   │
│     while (i <> 100) do                                       │
│         i := (i + 1)                                          │
│ end.                                                          │
├─────────────────────────────────────────────────────────────┤
│ Positioned at stmt   (begin                                   │
└─────────────────────────────────────────────────────────────┘
```

Heretofore, the only structural commands we have illustrated have been template-insertion commands used at placeholders. In addition to template commands, the Synthesizer Generator allows the definition of *transformation commands*, which provide operations for restructuring programs. Each

template-insertion command, such as the assign and while commands used earlier, are really transformation commands of a particularly simple form – they
transform a placeholder into a template. (In the previous screen image, they are
not itemized in the help pane, since the selection is not currently a statement
placeholder.) The Synthesizer Generator's transformation commands allow the
editor-designer to specify more general source-to-source transformations. For
instance, (begin is the name of a transformation that encloses a statement in a
compound-statement. We now invoke this transformation by executing
forward-with-optionals <ˆM>:

```
 main

 program <identifier>;
 var
     i : integer;
 begin
     i := 1;
     while (i <> 100) do
         begin
             i := (i + 1)
         end
 end.
 Positioned at stmt   (begin )begin
```

As expected, the loop-body has been enclosed within a begin-end pair. The
selection now encompasses the inserted compound-statement. In addition to the
(begin transformation, which can be used to introduce an additional enclosing
begin-end, a second transformation is now enabled. This transformation, named
)begin, strips off a compound-statement when the body of the begin-end consists of only a single statement.

    The observant reader may be mystified by the selection that resulted when we
applied the (begin transformation. In particular, why was the selection not
advanced to some placeholder? The following fine point should dispel the con-
fusion. The **forward-with-optionals** command, when executed alone, advances
the selection forward in preorder through the abstract-syntax tree of the object.
Any optional placeholders encountered *en route* are materialized and serve as
stopping places. For example, were **forward-with-optionals <ˆM>** to be executed at this moment, the selection would change as follows:

```
┌────────────────────────────────────────────────────────────────┐
│┌────────────────────────────────────────────────────────────────┐│
││main                                                              ││
│├──────────────────────────────────────────────────────────────────│
││                                                                  ││
│├──────────────────────────────────────────────────────────────────│
││program <identifier>;                                             ││
││var                                                               ││
││     i : integer;                                                 ││
││begin                                                             ││
││     i := 1;                                                      ││
││     while (i <> 100) do                                          ││
││         begin                                                    ││
││            │<statement>│;                                        ││
││             i := (i + 1)                                         ││
││         end                                                      ││
││end.                                                              ││
│├──────────────────────────────────────────────────────────────────│
││Positioned at stmtList   assign   if   while   begin   (begin     ││
│└────────────────────────────────────────────────────────────────┘│
└────────────────────────────────────────────────────────────────┘
```

However, when used in conjunction with either textual input or a transformation command, the **forward-with-optionals** command behaves differently. In particular, after a transformation the selection is advanced to the first placeholder (not counting optionals) within the transformed component, but if no such placeholder exists, the selection remains at the site at which the transformation was invoked.

This brief session has illustrated several of the capabilities of editors generated with the Synthesizer Generator. There are many additional editing features that have not been illustrated, including, for instance, those relating to scrolling, to suppressing the display of portions of the program, and to rearranging the program (*i.e.* moving sections from one place to another). Further information about editing can be found in *The Synthesizer Generator Reference Manual*.

CHAPTER 3

The Attribute-Grammar Model of Editing

As the example session of the previous chapter illustrates, a modification to one part of a program may introduce an error in some other part of the program and simultaneously correct an error in yet a third part. Detecting violations of language constraints may thus require a widespread analysis of the object being edited. This section gives a brief introduction to the analysis method that is employed in the Synthesizer Generator.

The Synthesizer Generator is based on the concept of an *attribute grammar* [Knuth68], which provides a powerful mechanism for specifying how widely separated parts of a tree are constrained in the context provided by the rest of the tree. An attribute grammar is a context-free grammar extended by attaching *attributes* to the nonterminal symbols of the grammar and by supplying *attribute equations* to define attribute values. In every production $p: X_0 \rightarrow X_1 \cdots X_k$, each X_i denotes an *occurrence* of a grammar symbol, and associated with each nonterminal occurrence is a set of *attribute occurrences* corresponding to the nonterminal's attributes.

Each production has a set of attribute equations; each equation defines one of the production's attribute occurrences as the value of an *attribute-definition function* applied to other attribute occurrences in the production. The attributes of a nonterminal are divided into two disjoint classes: *synthesized* attributes and *inherited* attributes. Each attribute equation defines a value for a synthesized attribute occurrence of the left-hand-side nonterminal or an inherited attribute occurrence of a right-hand-side nonterminal.

By convention, we deal only with attribute grammars that are *well formed*: an attribute grammar is well formed when the root symbol of the grammar has no inherited attributes and each production has exactly one attribute equation for each of the left-hand-side nonterminal's synthesized attribute occurrences and the right-hand-side nonterminals' inherited attribute occurrences. Finally, we restrict our attention to the *noncircular* grammars; a grammar is noncircular if it is not possible to build a derivation tree in which attributes are defined circularly.

Example. As a running example to illustrate these concepts, we will use a simple programming language with declaration, assignment, conditional, and iteration statements. The language is essentially the one supported by the editor described in Chapter 2, but without type expressions in variable declarations. The concrete syntax of the language is defined by the context-free grammar given in Figure 3.1. (For brevity, we have not shown the productions that can be derived from the nonterminals identifier and exp.) We define a scheme to compute the set of declared names by attaching the attributes *id* and *env* to certain nonterminals of the grammar. Attribute *id* is a synthesized attribute of the nonterminal identifier; its value is an identifier name. Attribute *env* is a synthesized attribute of declList and an inherited attribute of stmtList and stmt; its value is a set of identifier names.

Attribute equations define how the values of attributes are related to the values of other attributes. A collection of equations that define the propagation of declaration information through a program of the language is presented in Figure 3.2. (In the equations in Figure 3.2, we have used conventionally accepted notation to express operations on sets; we have used "." as the operator for selecting an attribute of a nonterminal; and we have used subscripts to distinguish among multiple occurrences of the same nonterminal.) Rules (2) and (3) of Figure 3.2 describe how a set of declared names is generated from the

---

(1) program → **program** identifier **var** declList **begin** stmtList **end**

(2) declList → **declare** identifier

(3) declList → **declare** identifier ; declList

(4) stmtList → stmt

(5) stmtList → stmt ; stmtList

(6) stmt → identifier := exp

(7) stmt → **if** exp **then** stmt **else** stmt

(8) stmt → **while** exp **do** stmt

(9) stmt → **begin** stmtList **end**

Figure 3.1. A context-free grammar that defines a simple programming language.

(1) program → **program** identifier **var** declList **begin** stmtList **end**
      stmtList.env = declList.env

(2) declList → **declare** identifier
      declList.env = {identifier.id}

(3) declList₁ → **declare** identifier ; declList₂
      declList₁.env = {identifier.id} ∪ declList₂.env

(4) stmtList → stmt
      stmt.env = stmtList.env

(5) stmtList₁ → stmt ; stmtList₂
      stmt.env = stmtList₁.env
      stmtList₂.env = stmtList₁.env

(6) stmt → identifier := exp
      exp.env = stmt.env

(7) stmt₁ → **if** exp **then** stmt₂ **else** stmt₃
      exp.env = stmt₁.env
      stmt₂.env = stmt₁.env
      stmt₃.env = stmt₁.env

(8) stmt₁ → **while** exp **do** stmt₂
      exp.env = stmt₁.env
      stmt₂.env = stmt₁.env

(9) stmt → **begin** stmtList **end**
      stmtList.env = stmt.env

Figure 3.2. Attribute equations that express the propagation of declaration information using the attributes *id* and *env*.

declarations of a program; rule (1) causes the set of declared names to be passed from the declarations to the statements of the program; rules (4)–(9) describe how the set of declared names is propagated to the individual statements of the program.

A derivation-tree node that is an instance of symbol X has an associated set of *attribute instances* corresponding to the attributes of X. An *attributed tree* is a derivation tree together with an assignment of either a value or the special token **null** to each attribute instance of the tree. To analyze a program according to its attribute-grammar specification, first construct its derivation tree with an assignment of **null** to each attribute instance; then evaluate as many attribute instances as possible, using the appropriate attribute equation as an assignment-statement. The latter process is termed *attribute evaluation*.

Functional dependences among attribute occurrences in a production p (or attribute instances in a tree T) can be represented by a directed graph,[1] called a *dependence graph*, denoted by $D(p)$ (respectively, $D(T)$) and defined as follows:

1) For each attribute occurrence (instance) b, the graph contains a vertex b'.
2) If attribute occurrence (instance) b appears on the right-hand side of the attribute equation that defines attribute occurrence (instance) c, the graph contains an edge (b', c'), directed from b' to c'.

A grammar is noncircular when the dependence graphs of all of the grammar's derivation trees are acyclic.

Example. The diagram shown in Figure 3.3 depicts the derivation tree and dependence graph of the following program scheme:

program p
var
        declare q ;
        declare r
begin
        stmt ;
        stmt ;
        stmt
end

The nonterminals of the derivation tree are connected by dashed lines; the dependence graph consists of the instances of the attributes *env* and *id*, linked by their functional dependences, shown as solid arrows. (The solid arrows emanating from the tree's identifier leaves indicate dependences on tree components; strictly speaking, they are not part of the dependence graph.)

Attribute grammars have several desirable qualities as a notation for specifying language-based editors. A language is specified in a modular fashion by an attribute grammar. Syntax is defined by a context-free grammar; attribution is defined in an equally modular fashion, because the arguments to each attribute equation are local to one production. Propagation of attribute values through the derivation tree is not specified explicitly in an attribute grammar; rather, it is implicitly defined by the equations of the grammar and the form of the tree.

When an editor-designer creates an editor with the Synthesizer Generator, part of the editor specification consists of attribute equations that express

---

[1] A *directed graph* $G = (V, E)$ consists of a set of *vertices* V and a set of *edges* E, where $E \subseteq V \times V$. Each edge $(b, c) \in E$ is directed from b to c.

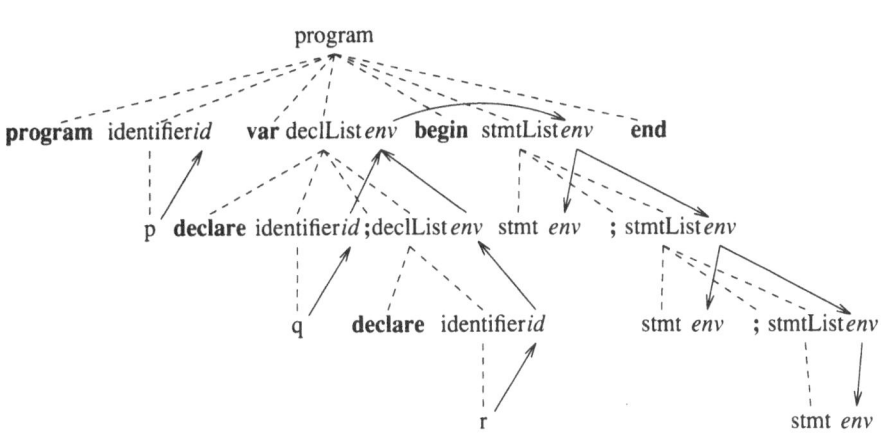

Figure 3.3. A partial derivation tree and its associated dependence graph.

context-sensitive language constraints or computations of derived information. As an object is edited with the generated editor, it is represented as a derivation tree that is *consistently attributed* in accordance with the grammar's equations. A tree is consistently attributed when the value of each attribute instance in the tree is equal to the value of the appropriate attribute-definition function applied to the values of the appropriate (neighboring) attribute instances in the tree. When a tree is modified by editing operations, say by replacing one of its sub-trees, some of the attributes may no longer have consistent values. Incremental analysis is performed by updating attribute values throughout the tree in response to modifications; by following the dependence relationships between attributes as defined in the editor specification, it is possible to reestablish consistent values throughout the tree.

In the Synthesizer Generator, context-sensitive language constraints are expressed by having certain attributes in the specification indicate whether the constraint is satisfied. In addition to the attribute grammar component of an editor specification, the editor-designer also furnishes an *unparsing* specification that determines how objects are displayed on the screen. Attributes used in the unparsing specification cause the screen to be annotated with values of attribute instances. In particular, the attributes that indicate satisfaction or violation of context-dependent constraints can be used to annotate the display to indicate the presence or absence of errors. If an editing operation modifies an object in such a way that formerly satisfied constraints are now violated (alternatively, formerly violated constraints are now satisfied), the attributes that indicate satisfaction of constraints will receive new values; the changed image of these attributes on the screen provides the user with feedback about new errors introduced and old errors corrected.

Fundamental to this approach is the idea of an *incremental attribute evaluator*, an algorithm to produce a consistent, fully attributed tree after each restructuring operation. Of course, any non-incremental attribute evaluator could be applied to reevaluate the tree completely, but the goal is to minimize work by confining the scope of reevaluation.

After each modification to a program tree, only a subset of attributes, denoted by AFFECTED, requires new values. It should be understood that when updating begins, it is not known which attributes are members of AFFECTED; AFFECTED is determined as a result of the updating process itself. In [Demers81, Reps82, Reps83, Reps84], we have described algorithms that identify attributes in AFFECTED and recompute their values. Some of these algorithms have cost proportional to the size of AFFECTED, which means that they are asymptotically *optimal* in time, because, by definition, the work needed to update the tree can be no less than |AFFECTED|.

The chief drawback to the use of attribute grammars for creating program editors that perform immediate computation is the question of whether certain efficiency problems prevent the approach from scaling up. The problem is that attribute grammars have strictly local dependences among attribute values, and, at least conceptually, attributed trees have a large number of intermediate attribute values that must be updated. By contrast, imperative methods for implementing checks on a language's context conditions can, by using auxiliary data structures to record nonlocal dependences in the tree, skip over arbitrarily large sections of the tree that attribute-updating algorithms visit node by node.

For example, suppose we want to enforce the constraint that the declarations and uses of identifiers in a program be consistent. An imperative approach can implement this constraint with a symbol table for each block, in which the entry for an identifier i points to a chain of all uses of i in that block. When a declaration is deleted or inserted, the use chains are employed to immediately access uses of variables that were formerly declared. With the attribute grammar approach, when a declaration is deleted or inserted, the incremental attribute evaluator traverses the entire scope of the declaration.

Some recent work on attribute-grammar extensions, including [Demers85], [Johnson85], [Reps86], and [Hoover87], has been directed towards abandoning the restriction to purely local attribute dependences. This matter remains a topic for additional research; incorporation of such techniques into the Synthesizer Generator is planned for future releases.

CHAPTER 4

Specification of a Sample Editor

Chapter 4 introduces the basic features of editor definitions as written in the Synthesizer Specification Language (SSL). The specification used to generate the sample program editor demonstrated in Chapter 2 is explained completely. This example is sufficient to illustrate how the major components of any editor are specified in SSL.

An editor specification consists of a collection of declarations. The different kinds of declarations are introduced in the sections indicated below: abstract-syntax declarations, discussed in Section 4.1, define the language's underlying structure; attribute declarations and attribute equations, discussed in Section 4.2, express the language's context-sensitive relationships; unparsing declarations, discussed in Section 4.3, express how programs are formatted on the display screen; concrete-input-syntax declarations, discussed in Section 4.4, define the input language that is accepted (for text editing); transformation declarations, discussed in Section 4.5, define commands for restructuring programs.

4.1. Abstract Syntax

The core of an editor specification is the definition of the language's abstract syntax, given as a set of grammar rules. An object being edited is represented by its derivation tree with respect to this grammar. Regardless of whether the editor's user interface allows textual modifications, structural modifications, or some combination of both, the effect of each editing modification is to change the underlying syntax tree.

The abstract syntax of our example programming language is defined by the rules given in Figure 4.1. It consists of a collection of *productions* of the form

$$x_0 : op\ (\ x_1\ x_2\ \cdots\ x_k\ )\ ;$$

where *op* is an *operator* name and each x_i is a nonterminal of the grammar, or, as we call it, the name of a *phylum* (borrowing the word from abstract alge-

---

```
root program;
program :           Prog(identifier declList stmtList);
list declList;
declList  :         DeclListNil( )
          |         DeclListPair(decl declList)
          ;
decl      :         Declaration(identifier typeExp);
typeExp  :          EmptyTypeExp( )
          |         IntTypeExp( )
          |         BoolTypeExp( )
          ;
identifier:         IdentifierNull( )
          |         Identifier(IDENTIFIER)
          ;
list stmtList;
stmtList  :         StmtListNil( )
          |         StmtListPair(stmt stmtList)
          ;
stmt      :         EmptyStmt( )
          |         Assign(identifier exp)
          |         IfThenElse(exp  stmt  stmt)
          |         While(exp stmt)
          |         Compound(stmtList)
          ;
exp       :         EmptyExp( )
          |         IntConst(INTEGER)
          |         True( )
          |         False( )
          |         Id(identifier)
          |         Equal(exp exp)
          |         NotEqual(exp exp)
          |         Add(exp exp)
          ;
IDENTIFIER:         IdentLex< [a-zA-Z][a-zA-Z_0-9]* >;
INTEGER:            IntegerLex< [0-9]+ >;
```

Figure 4.1. Rules defining abstract syntax.

bra).[1] The phylum associated with a given nonterminal is the set of derivation trees that can be derived from it. These derivation trees are known as *terms*. With the exception of the operators, whose purpose is to identify the production instances in a derivation tree, the SSL grammar rule acts exactly as the context-free production

$$x_0 \rightarrow x_1 x_2 \cdots x_k$$

Although several rules may have structurally identical right-hand sides, the unique operator name differentiates among the various alternatives that would otherwise have been indistinguishable. For example, in Figure 4.1, the operator names Equal, NotEqual, and Add distinguish between three kinds of expression pairs.

Because terms are a focal point of our discussion, we introduce the following notation: a term is denoted by an expression in which a k-ary operator is applied to k constants of the appropriate phyla; for terms of nullary operators, the parentheses may be omitted.[2] For example,

Equal(Id(IdentifierNull), Id(IdentifierNull))

denotes a term containing, as subterms, two instances of the term Id(IdentifierNull). Each instance of the term Id(IdentifierNull) itself contains a subterm, the nullary term IdentifierNull. This notation for terms matches the SSL notation for denoting constants. Although this notation is used in the expressions of an editor's specification, it never appears on the screen of a generated editor, where terms are always displayed in the "sugared" form specified by the unparsing rules of the specification. For example, the above term would be displayed as the string

(<identifier> = <identifier>)

as will be explained in Section 4.3, "Unparsing Schemes."

Some expressions that do not denote terms are Equal(IdentifierNull, True), because IdentifierNull denotes a term that is not of an appropriate phylum to be used as the first argument of Equal, and Equal(True), because the binary operator Equal is applied to the wrong number of argument terms.

---

[1]More precisely, definitions of alternative productions can be separated by vertical bars, without repeating the left-hand-side phylum name, as is done in Figure 4.1.

[2]The empty parentheses may *not* be omitted from the declaration of the nullary operator, however.

In defining abstract syntax, one phylum is distinguished as the *root phylum*. The first line of Figure 4.1 declares program to be the root phylum of the sample editor. The editable objects of a generated editor are terms of this root phylum. For example, the first screen image of the editor demonstration given in Chapter 2, showing an empty edit buffer, was

```
 main

 program <identifier>;
 var
      <identifier> : <type>;
 begin
      <statement>
 end.
 Positioned at program
```

which is actually the unparsing of the following ten-node term of phylum program

Prog(IdentifierNull,
      DeclListPair(Declaration(IdentifierNull, EmptyTypeExp), DeclListNil),
      StmtListPair(EmptyStmt, StmtListNil)
)

The first operator declared for each phylum, such as the operator Prog of phylum program and the operator IdentifierNull of phylum identifier, is called the *completing operator* and plays a special role in the editor specification. The completing operator is used to construct a default representative for the phylum, called the *completing term*. The completing term is created by applying the completing operator to the completing terms of its argument phyla.[3] For example, the completing term for phylum decl defined in Figure 4.1 is the term

Declaration(IdentifierNull, EmptyTypeExp)

i.e. the completing operator for decl applied to the completing terms of phylum identifier and phylum typeExp.

An instance of the appropriate completing term is used at each unexpanded occurrence of a phylum in a derivation tree. For instance, the placeholders in

---

[3] Phyla declared to be lists or optional are an exception to this rule, as described below.

the program created in Chapter 2 are examples of completing terms supplied at unexpanded phyla. This means that a tree containing placeholders, which a naive user might consider to be a partial derivation tree, is really a complete derivation tree from the system's point of view.

An additional aspect of defining a language's abstract syntax is the designation of certain phyla as *lists*. Because generated editors provide special built-in actions for manipulating list phyla, the list-property declarations in the specification play an important role in specifying how a user of the editor will be able to manipulate objects. As illustrated in Chapter 2, when the command **forward-with-optionals** is used to move the selection through a list, the editor automatically supplies list-insertion points that precede and follow each list element.

The abstract-syntax rules for a list phylum must have exactly two operators, one being a nullary operator and the other a binary operator that is right recursive. For example, in Figure 4.1, phylum declList is declared to be a list phylum and has operators of the required form; the nullary operator is DeclListNil and the binary operator is DeclListPair.

The declaration of a phylum as a list alters how its completing term is created. According to our earlier explanation, if the nullary operator were declared first, the completing term would be an empty list, *e.g.* DeclListNil, whereas if the binary operator were declared first, the completing term would be an infinite list. Thus, for list phyla, the following definition of the completing term is substituted for the one given earlier:

> The completing term of a list phylum is the (singleton) list constructed by applying the binary operator to the completing term of its left-argument phyla and to the list's nullary operator.

For instance, the completing term of phylum declList is the term

DeclListPair(Declaration(IdentifierNull, EmptyTypeExp), DeclListNil)

i.e. DeclListPair applied to the completing term of phylum decl and to the term DeclListNil.

Let us now be more specific about the list-insertion points that the editor automatically supplies (and removes) before and after each element of a list. For brevity, let us use P to stand for the completing term of phylum decl, *i.e.* the term

Declaration(IdentifierNull, EmptyTypeExp).

For brevity, we abbreviate list expressions with the same notation that is used in SSL: the right associating infix operator :: denotes the *concatenation* operation;

it attaches a single element to the head of a list, where the element and list are of appropriate phyla. For example, if A and B are both terms of phylum decl, the term $A :: B ::$ DeclListNil is the declList term

DeclListPair(A, DeclListPair(B, DeclListNil)).

The command **forward-sibling-with-optionals** <ESC-^M> is similar to **forward-with-optionals** in automatically supplying list-insertion points before and after list elements; however, it bypasses all resting places contained within the current selection and advances to the next sibling in the tree. Thus, **forward-sibling-with-optionals** successively modifies the list

$A :: B ::$ DeclListNil

by inserting and removing instances of P in the following fashion:

$A :: B ::$ DeclListNil	(selection precedes the list)
$P :: A :: B ::$ DeclListNil	(P selected)
$A :: B ::$ DeclListNil	(A selected)
$A :: P :: B ::$ DeclListNil	(P selected)
$A :: B ::$ DeclListNil	(B selected)
$A :: B :: P ::$ DeclListNil	(P selected)
$A :: B ::$ DeclListNil	(selection follows the list)

A succession of **forward-with-optionals** commands behaves similarly, except that A is traversed after the third step and B is traversed after the fifth step.

The definitions of the phyla INTEGER and IDENTIFIER in the last two lines of Figure 4.1 illustrate regular expressions, which permit defining subclasses of the built-in phylum STR of strings. (Other predefined phyla include INT, BOOL, CHAR, and REAL.)

4.2. Attributes and Attribute Equations

In addition to grammar rules that define the language's abstract syntax, an editor specification contains declarations that define how to make static inferences about the objects being edited.

In Chapter 2, the comments that annotate the program arise from static inferences about whether the program violates context-sensitive constraints on the language's syntax. The conditions checked require that

- a declaration must be supplied for all identifiers used in a program,
- an identifier must be declared at most once, and

● the constituents of expressions and statements must have compatible types.

As the user creates and modifies programs, the generated editor incrementally checks for violations of these conditions. The comments indicating such violations are, in fact, STR-valued attributes that are displayed as part of the display representation of the term being edited. When an error is present, the attribute value is the appropriate message; when no error is present, the attribute value is the null string. As the user edits a term, the values of its attributes are updated, if necessary, before the screen is refreshed. Thus, the information displayed is always current.

The declarations presented in Figures 4.2, 4.3, and 4.4 define the appropriate attributes to implement the desired analysis. Figure 4.2 defines, at the root of the program, an environment attribute named env that contains the type binding of each declared identifier. In addition, each expression and subexpression has an associated type attribute. The type of each identifier used in an expression is determined by accessing the environment at the root. The type of each other expression is uniquely determined by what sort of an expression it is. Figure 4.3 makes use of the env and type attributes defined in Figure 4.2 to define STR-valued attributes that contain appropriate messages. Figure 4.4 contains auxiliary functions that are used in defining the attributes.

In SSL, each attribute associated with a phylum is declared in an *attribute declaration* that specifies the name of the phylum, the type of the attribute, and

---

```
exp, identifier    { synthesized typeExp type; };
program :          Prog {
                        local declList env;
                        env = declList;
                        }

    ;
identifier :       IdentifierNull    { identifier.type = EmptyTypeExp; }
    |              Identifier         { identifier.type =
                                         LookupType(identifier, {Prog.env}); }

    ;
exp        :       EmptyExp          { exp.type = EmptyTypeExp; }
    |              IntConst          { exp.type = IntTypeExp; }
    |              True, False       { exp.type = BoolTypeExp; }
    |              Id                { exp.type = identifier.type; }
    |              Equal, NotEqual   { exp$1.type = BoolTypeExp; }
    |              Add               { exp$1.type = IntTypeExp; }
    ;
```

Figure 4.2. Rules defining the attributes env and type.

whether the attribute is synthesized or inherited. An attribute's type can be either one of the predefined phyla or a user-defined phylum. For example, the declaration

exp { synthesized typeExp type; };

associates a synthesized typeExp-valued attribute named type with phylum exp. The first line of Figure 4.2 declares that phylum exp and phylum identifier both have such attributes. (Phylum typeExp is declared in Figure 4.1, since it is also used in the abstract syntax of programs.)

Local attributes are attributes that are associated with a particular production rather than with every production of a phylum. Local attribute declarations differ from the declarations of ordinary attributes in that the keyword local is used in place of synthesized or inherited; they also differ in that local attribute declarations are placed among a production's attribute equations. The third line of Figure 4.2 declares the local attribute env, of type declList, to be associated with production Prog. (As with typeExp, phylum declList is declared in Figure 4.1.)

The values of attributes are defined by the *attribute equations* associated with each production. Each equation defines one of the production's attribute occurrences as the value of an attribute-definition function applied to other attribute occurrences in the production.[4] In an attribute equation, attribute a of occurrence i of phylum n in a given production is referred to as $n\$i.a$, where $\$i$ is optional if there is only one occurrence of n in the production.

The easiest attribute equations to understand are the ones defining exp.type in the second half of Figure 4.2. The equations define exp.type to be Int-TypeExp if exp is an integer constant or an addition, BoolTypeExp if exp is true, false, or a predicate, and EmptyTypeExp if exp is unexpanded. In each case, the attribute definition function is just a constant of phylum typeExp. If exp is an identifier then exp.type is defined to be identifier.type, the type of the identifier.

Next, we consider the equations in Figure 4.2 that define identifier.type. When identifier is unexpanded, *i.e.* when the production is IdentifierNull, its type attribute is defined to be EmptyTypeExp. When identifier is expanded, *i.e.* when the production is Identifier, the defining equation is

---

[4]*Syntactic references* and *upward remote attribute sets*, described later in the section, extend the class of permissible arguments to attribute-definition functions.

identifier.type = LookupType(identifier, {Prog.env});

which determines the value of identifier.type by looking up identifier in the environment attribute Prog.env at the root of the program. LookupType is an auxiliary procedure whose definition, in Figure 4.4, will be examined later. For the moment, assume that LookupType(i, e) is the first type bound to identifier i in environment e. If no type is bound to i in e, then LookupType(i, e) is EmptyTypeExp.

The expression {Prog.env}, by which we refer to the local attribute env at the root of the program, is an example of an *upward remote attribute set*. For a given instance p of the Identifier production, {Prog.env} refers to the value of the env attribute of the first Prog operator that appears on the path from p to the root of the tree. In this case, there is never more that one Prog operator on this path — the one at the root of the tree; however, in general, there may be several instances of the objects referred to in an upward remote attribute set.

Upward remote attribute sets are a convenience that often saves the bother of writing many inherited attribute definitions and equations. In this case, the alternative to using upward remote attribute sets is to attach explicit env attributes to each phylum and to write appropriate attribute equations that pass the value down the term, as is done in Figure 3.2 of Chapter 3.

The upward remote attribute sets illustrated in the sample editor do not make use of the concept in its full generality. In general, one is allowed to list several attributes between the braces; the value is the first instance of a set element encountered on the path to the root.

The final equation of Figure 4.2 to be explained is the one that defines the environment attribute Prog.env itself. We have declared Prog.env to have type declList, *i.e.* a list of zero or more <identifier, typeExp> pairs. Prog.env should contain one <identifier, typeExp> pair for each identifier declaration in the program. But recall from Figure 4.1 that production Prog is defined as follows:

program: Prog(identifier declList stmtList);

The second argument of Prog, the declaration list of the program, is itself a term of type declList. It is, in fact, exactly the value desired and can be used directly in the equation that defines env. Note that the name declList is used in two distinct ways in the rules for operator Prog:

```
program:        Prog {
                        local declList env;
                        env = declList;
                        }

        ;
```

In the declaration of local attribute env, declList specifies the type of the attribute. In the equation defining the value of env, declList is the name of a value, in particular, the second argument of Prog.

The use, in an attribute definition function, of a part of the term being edited is called a *syntactic reference*. This extension to conventional attribute grammars is provided in the Synthesizer Generator in recognition of the fact that often a piece of the abstract-syntax tree is itself a sufficiently convenient representation of a value needed for attribute computations. In a system such as GAG [Kastens82], where a syntax tree is a different sort of object from an attribute value, one must resort to replicating the syntactic tree in the attribute domain. However, in the Synthesizer Generator, an attribute's type is a phylum that is defined with the same kind of rules that are used to define syntactic objects; a program's attribute values and the program itself are all elements of either primitive phyla or phyla defined in the editor specification. Thus, we were able to use phylum declList as both the type of the declaration list of a program and the type of the Prog.env attribute.

In general, any of a production's phylum occurrences can be used as a value in the expression on the right-hand side of an attribute equation. A second example of a syntactic reference occurred, without our remarking on it, in the equation

identifier.type = LookupType(identifier, {Prog.env});

The first argument passed to LookupType actually refers to a phylum occurrence of the production

identifier :   Identifier(IDENTIFIER);

Thus, when the value of IDENTIFIER is "i", for example, LookupType will actually be passed Identifier("i") as its first argument.

This completes our discussion of Figure 4.2. The env and type attributes defined there are used in the next part of the specification, Figure 4.3, to define the STR-valued attributes that describe type incompatibilities and undeclared variables in the program.

First, note the liberal scattering of local attribute declarations in Figure 4.3. Observe that not every operator of decl, stmt, and exp has such attributes. The

```
decl  :  Declaration {
            local STR error;
            error = (identifier != IdentifierNull
                    && NumberOfDecls(identifier, {Prog.env}) > 1)
                        ? " { MULTIPLY DECLARED }" : "";
         }
      ;
stmt  :  Assign {
            local STR assignError;
            local STR error;
            assignError = IncompatibleTypes(identifier.type, exp.type)
                        ? " { INCOMPATIBLE TYPES IN := }" : "";
            error = (identifier == IdentifierNull || IsDeclared(identifier, {Prog.env}))
                        ? "" : "{ NOT DECLARED }";
         }
      |  IfThenElse, While {
            local STR typeError;
            typeError = IncompatibleTypes(exp.type, BoolTypeExp)
                        ? " { BOOLEAN EXPRESSION NEEDED }" : "";
         }
      ;
exp   :  Id {
            local STR error;
            error = (identifier == IdentifierNull || IsDeclared(identifier, {Prog.env}))
                        ? "" : " { NOT DECLARED }";
         }
      |  Equal, NotEqual {
            local STR error;
            error = IncompatibleTypes(exp$2.type, exp$3.type)
                        ? " { INCOMPATIBLE TYPES } " : "";
         }
      |  Add {
            local STR leftError;
            local STR rightError;
            leftError = IncompatibleTypes(exp$2.type, IntTypeExp)
                        ? " { INT EXPRESSION NEEDED }" : "";
            rightError = IncompatibleTypes(exp$3.type, IntTypeExp)
                        ? "{ INT EXPRESSION NEEDED } " : "";
         }
      ;
```

Figure 4.3. Rules defining error attributes.

chief virtue of local attributes is that they permit defining a computation in one production of a phylum without requiring the computation in all, as would be the case, for example, if the attributes were synthesized.

Each local error attribute – error, assignError, typeError, leftError, and rightError – is declared to have type STR, the built-in phylum of strings in

SSL. Each attribute will be either the null string, if there is no error, or the appropriate error message.

Each error attribute is defined by a *conditional expression*. In SSL, conditional expressions have the form:

expression ₁ *?* *expression* ₂ : *expression* ₃

The value of the conditional expression is *expression* ₂ if *expression* ₁ is true and *expression* ₃ otherwise. The infix operations **&&**, **||**, **==**, and **!=** denote the Boolean operations logical-and, logical-or, equality, and inequality, respectively.

Some predicates make use of the auxiliary functions NumberOfDecls, IncompatibleTypes, and IsDeclared, whose definitions in Figure 4.4 will be examined shortly. For the moment, assume that they perform the operations suggested by their names.

The main subtlety in defining the error attributes is the correct treatment of unexpanded program elements. We cannot assume that the program is complete. For example, the predicate testing whether an identifier has been declared must take into account the possibility that the identifier is IdentifierNull (*i.e.* that no identifier has yet been provided). Similarly, when a type should be boolean, we test for compatibility, not equality, with BoolTypeExp. EmptyTypeExp is defined to be compatible with BoolTypeExp in order to take into account the possibility that an identifier is either undeclared or is declared but with an as yet unspecified type.

This completes our discussion of Figure 4.3. At this stage, the reader may benefit from a review of the screen images of Chapter 2. In each case, it should be possible to comprehend how the error attributes have taken on their given values.

We turn now to the definitions of the auxiliary recursive functions, which have already been used in defining type and error attributes. The four functions are declared in Figure 4.4. The form of a *function declaration* is:

phylum function (*formal-parameter-list*) {
    expression
    };

where *function* is the name of the function, *phylum* is the result type, and *expression* is the function body. Each formal parameter name is declared with a type, and the *expression* that is the function body must have type *phylum*. For

---

```
/* Determine the first type bound to i in e, or EmptyTypeExp if there is none. */
typeExp LookupType(identifier i, declList e) {
        with (e) (
                DeclListNil: EmptyTypeExp,
                DeclListPair(Declaration(id, t), dl):
                        (i == id) ? t : LookupType(i, dl)
                )
        };

/* Return true iff there exists a type bound to i in e. */
BOOL IsDeclared(identifier i, declList e) {
        with (e) (
                DeclListNil: false,
                DeclListPair(Declaration(id, t), dl):
                        (i == id) ? true : IsDeclared(i, dl)
                )
    };

/* Determine the number of types bound to i in e. */
INT NumberOfDecls(identifier i, declList e) {
        with (e) (
                DeclListNil: 0,
                DeclListPair(Declaration(id, *), dl):
                        ((i == id) ? 1 : 0) + NumberOfDecls(i, dl)
                )
        };

/* Return true iff neither t1 nor t2 is EmptyTypeExp and t1 is not equal to t2. */
BOOL IncompatibleTypes(typeExp t1, typeExp t2) {
        (t1 != EmptyTypeExp) && (t2 != EmptyTypeExp) && (t1 != t2)
        };
```

Figure 4.4. Function declarations that define the auxiliary functions LookupType, IsDeclared, NumberOfDecls, and IncompatibleTypes.

example, IncompatibleTypes takes two typeExp arguments t1 and t2 and returns a BOOL result.

We have illustrated that the SSL expression language permits infix expressions, function applications, and conditional expressions. Another form of expression, the construction of new terms, is not illustrated in the sample specification until Section 4.4. A term is constructed by applying a k-ary operator to k argument expressions of the appropriate phyla. For example, the 2-ary operator Declaration, when applied to two expressions of type identifier and typeExp respectively, may be used to create a new decl object, such as Declaration(Identifier("j"), IntTypeExp).

The final form of expression to be illustrated is a generalized conditional expression that allows discrimination based on pattern matching. This construct, called a *with-expression* in SSL, follows a style originally proposed in [Burstall69]. The form of a with-expression is

with (*expression*$_0$) (
      pattern$_1$: *expression*$_1$,
      pattern$_2$: *expression*$_2$,
      . . .
      pattern$_n$: *expression*$_n$
)

The value of a with-expression is computed as follows. *Expression*$_0$ is compared with the patterns, in order, until one matches. The value of the with-expression is the value of the *expression*$_i$ that corresponds to the first matching *pattern*$_i$. The patterns are required to be comprehensive, *i.e.* one of the patterns is guaranteed to match.

Patterns have the form of terms, except that some subterms may be replaced by *pattern variables*. If *pattern*$_i$ is the matching pattern, its pattern variables are bound to subterms of the value of *expression*$_0$. *Expression*$_i$ can then be computed in terms of these pattern variables.

Consider, for example, the with-expression in procedure LookupType:

```
typeExp LookupType(identifier i, declList e) {
        with (e) (
                DeclListNil: EmptyTypeExp,
                DeclListPair(Declaration(id, t), dl):
                        (i == id) ? t : LookupType(i, dl)
                )
        };
```

The first pattern is simply the constant DeclListNil. This matches the declList e precisely when e is the term DeclListNil, *i.e.* an empty declList. If it matches, the value of LookupType is EmptyTypeExp. If e is not DeclListNil, it is guaranteed to have the form

DeclListPair(Declaration(*, *), *)

where * stands for any subterm. In the pattern

DeclListPair(Declaration(id, t), dl)

the pattern variables are id, t, and dl. When this pattern matches, id, t, and dl will be bound to the corresponding subterms in e. Thus, the value of Lookup-Type can be computed as (i == id) ? t : LookupType(i, dl)

That is, if id is i, the identifier whose type we are looking for, return t, its type; otherwise, continue looking for i in dl, the rest of the declList e.

The recursive functions IsDeclared and NumberOfDecls behave similarly and need not be discussed further.

Taken together, the definitions given in Figures 4.1 through 4.4 specify the language's underlying abstract syntax and define how a program's abstract-syntax tree is annotated with STR-valued attributes that indicate the presence or absence of type errors and undeclared variables. We next describe how display representations are specified.

4.3. Unparsing Schemes

The unparsing schemes in an editor specification define not only the display format of a term, but also which nodes of the abstract-syntax tree are selectable and which productions of an object are editable as text. Each production's unparsing scheme consists of a sequence of strings, names of attribute occurrences, names of right-hand-side phylum occurrences, and *selection symbols*. The unparsing scheme defines a rule for formatting the production in mix-fix notation, that is, with strings before and after each right-hand-side phylum occurrence.

The unparsing rules for the sample editor are given in Figure 4.5, which defines a display representation for each production of the abstract syntax presented in Figure 4.1. Each of the rules has one of two forms:

phylum : *operator* [*left-side* : *right-side*] ;
phylum : *operator* [*left-side* ::= *right-side*] ;

The unparsing scheme between the square brackets should be seen as an image of the corresponding production. The choice of the symbol : or ::= determines whether or not a production can be edited as text. The symbol ::= indicates that it is permitted to edit the production's text; the symbol : indicates that the production is (customarily) treated only as an indivisible structural unit. Note that not all operators of a given phylum have to use the same symbol. For example, EmptyStmt and Assign use ::=, while IfThenElse, While, and Compound use :.

The display is generated by a left-to-right traversal of the tree that interprets the unparsing schemes. Indentation and line breaks are controlled by control characters that can be included in the strings of an unparsing scheme. In particular, the characters %t, %b, and %n have the following meanings:

program :	Prog	[@ : "program " @	";%n"
		"var"	"%t%n"
		@ ";"	"%b%n"
		"begin"	"%t%n"
		@	"%b%n"
		"end."]	
	;		
declList :	DeclListNil	[@ ::=]	
	DeclListPair	[@ ::= ^ [";%n"] @]	
	;		
decl :	Declaration	[^ : @ error " : " @];	
typeExp :	EmptyTypeExp	[@ : "<type>"]	
	IntTypeExp	[@ : "integer"]	
	BoolTypeExp	[@ : "boolean"]	
	;		
identifier :	IdentifierNull	[@ ::= "<identifier>"]	
	Identifier	[^ ::= ^]	
	;		
stmtList :	StmtListNil	[@ :]	
	StmtListPair	[@ : ^ [";%n"] @]	
	;		
stmt :	EmptyStmt	[^ ::= "<statement>"]	
	Assign	[^ ::= @ error " := " @ assignError]	
	IfThenElse	[^ : "if " @ typeError " then" "%t%n"	
		@ "%b%n"	
		"else%t%n"	
		@ "%b"]	
	While	[^ : "while " @ typeError " do" "%t%n"	
		@ "%b"]	
	Compound	[^ : "begin" "%t%n"	
		@ "%b%n"	
		"end"]	
	;		
exp :	EmptyExp	[^ ::= "<exp>"]	
	IntConst	[^ ::= ^]	
	True	[^ ::= "true"]	
	False	[^ ::= "false"]	
	Id	[^ ::= ^ error]	
	Equal	[^ ::= "(" @ " = " error @ ")"]	
	NotEqual	[^ ::= "(" @ " <> " error @ ")"]	
	Add	[^ ::= "(" @ leftError " + " rightError @ ")"]	
	;		

Figure 4.5. Grammar rules defining display representations.

%t   move the left margin one indentation unit to the right
%b   move the left margin one indentation unit to the left
%n   break the line and move to the left margin of the next line

Each *selection symbol*, either @ or ^, represents the position of one of the phylum occurrences in the production's mix-fix display representation. An additional selection symbol for the left-hand-side occurrence is separated from the rest of the unparsing declaration by the : or ::=; the remaining selection symbols match up with the right-hand-side phylum occurrences in the order in which they occur in the abstract-syntax definition.

A selection symbol defines the *selectability property* for the corresponding node in the tree. Selections may only be made at *resting places*, which are determined by the selection symbols of the unparsing declarations. When the user selects an item on the display, the selection is moved to the nearest resting place that encloses that item. The selection symbol @ specifies that a phylum occurrence is a resting place; the symbol ^ specifies that it is not. Note that a syntax-tree node is an instance of *two* phylum occurrences: a left-hand-side occurrence in one production and a right-hand-side occurrence in another. A node is a resting place if either of its two corresponding occurrences is specified with @.

With the unparsing declarations given above, a selection in an expression will select the smallest subexpression whose display representation includes the selected character. If all of the @ selection symbols in the Equal, NotEqual, and Add productions were changed to ^ symbols, then a selection anywhere in an expression would select the entire expression.

Selections in lists are handled somewhat specially, so care should be made to define the selection symbols as has been done above for DeclListPair and StmtListPair; that is, the two occurrences of the list phylum should be defined with @ and the element-phylum occurrence, in the first argument position, should be defined with ^. This avoids having an extra resting place at the element-phylum occurrence, yet allows selecting a sublist by pointing and dragging. (See Section 5.3, "Sublist Manipulations.")

The unparsing declarations for DeclListPair and for StmtListPair illustrate *conditional unparsing* of list separators. The unparsing declaration of the binary production of a list phylum may have items enclosed in square brackets; these items are suppressed from the display of production instances that occur at the end of a list. Thus, the [";%n"] in the unparsing declarations for DeclListPair and StmtListPair causes the lists to be printed with a semi-colon/line-feed separator.

Attribute occurrences in the unparsing declaration cause the display representation of the attribute's value to be included in the display. In the example above, the unparsing declarations use this facility to indicate the location of type errors, undeclared variables, and multiply-declared variables. The attribute equations of the specification define these attributes to contain a warning message when an error exists at a location, and the null string otherwise. The incremental reevaluation of attributes that is performed after each program modification guarantees that the program's display reflects appropriate error messages.

4.4. Input Interfaces

We have seen that edited objects in the Synthesizer Generator are represented as terms. There are numerous advantages to this representation. First, the terms are guaranteed to be structurally correct with respect to the context-free syntax. Second, static inferences, computed in attributes of the term, can provide users with valuable feedback, for example, messages announcing violations of context-sensitive constraints. Third, the terms provide a hierarchy for structure editing and for pretty-printing.

While structure editing has its advantages, text editing is often more appropriate. For example, although structure editing is convenient for manipulating statements in a Pascal-like programming language, text editing is preferable for entering and modifying expressions. Text editing provides a temporary escape from the rigor of the syntax-directed discipline, for while a subterm is being text edited, it can be any string whatsoever. When editing is complete, the string is parsed and translated to the corresponding term of the abstract syntax.

To specify the translation from text to term, productions are given for a concrete input grammar, along with attribute equations that synthesize the term as an attribute of the parse tree. Figure 4.7 contains the productions of the input grammar of the sample editor; Figure 4.6 presents the declarations of the attributes, which must come first.

The sample editor permits text entry at every phylum except program. Therefore, associated with each phylum of the abstract syntax except program is a corresponding phylum in the input syntax. We have chosen to use the same names for the related phyla, merely capitalizing those of the input grammar.[5] Each phylum P of the input grammar has a synthesized attribute named t of type p, the corresponding phylum in the abstract grammar.

The correspondence between selections in the abstract-syntax tree being edited and entry points within the input syntax is established by the specification's *entry declarations*, which appear in the second half of Figure 4.6. Each entry declaration has the form

---

[5]In the case of identifier, the name Identifier was already used for another purpose, so we have called the input phylum Ident.

DeclList	{synthesized declList t; };	
Decl	{synthesized decl t; };	
TypeExp	{synthesized typeExp t; };	
Ident	{synthesized identifier t;};	
StmtList	{synthesized stmtList t; };	
Stmt	{synthesized stmt t; };	
Exp	{synthesized exp t;};	
declList	~	DeclList.t;
decl	~	Decl.t;
typeExp	~	TypeExp.t;
identifier	~	Ident.t;
stmtList	~	StmtList.t;
stmt	~	Stmt.t;
exp	~	Exp.t;

Figure 4.6. Rules that define the association between the abstract syntax and the input syntax.

$$p \sim P.t \; ;$$

which indicates that when the currently selected component of the program is a member of phylum p, input is to be parsed to see if it is a member of phylum P, and, if so, attribute t is to be inserted in the abstract-syntax tree, replacing the current selection. The parse tree is a transient structure – it is discarded as soon as the attribute t is extracted.

The grammar rules shown in Figure 4.7 begin with definitions of lexical phyla. There is one rule for each keyword and other multi-character token of the language. The token WHITESPACE has special significance: every occurrence of a WHITESPACE token is ignored during a parse.

The remaining rules of Figure 4.7 define the syntax of the concrete input language. The phylum declarations that define the concrete input language, or *parsing declarations*, are distinguished from the other phylum/operator declarations of an SSL specification by the use of the symbol ::= to separate the left-hand-side phylum name from the symbols on the right-hand side. Another difference between parsing declarations and ordinary phylum declarations is that *tokens* – single characters enclosed in quotes – may be interspersed among the phylum symbols on the right-hand side of a parsing declaration. For example, the token '=' appears in the operator declaration for parsing an equality expression:

Exp   ::=   (Exp '=' Exp)   {Exp$1.t = Equal(Exp$2.t, Exp$3.t);};

In this rule's attribute equation, which defines attribute Exp$1.t, the right-

```
WHITESPACE:     Whitespace< [\ \t\n] >;
ASSIGN:         AssignLex< ":=" >;
NOTEQUAL:       NotEqualLex< "<>" >;
INTKW:          IntKeyWordLex< "integer" >;
BOOLKW:         BoolKeyWordLex< "boolean" >;
TRUE:           TrueLex< "true" >;
FALSE:          FalseLex< "false" >;

nonassoc '=', NOTEQUAL;
left '+';

DeclList ::=    ( Decl )                {DeclList.t = (Decl.t :: DeclListNil);}
         |      ( Decl ';' DeclList)    {DeclList$1.t = (Decl.t :: DeclList$2.t);}
         ;
Decl     ::=    (Ident ':' TypeExp)     {Decl.t = Declaration(Ident.t, TypeExp.t);};
TypeExp::=      (INTKW)                 {TypeExp.t = IntTypeExp; }
         |      (BOOLKW)                {TypeExp.t = BoolTypeExp; }
         ;
Ident    ::=    (IDENTIFIER)            {Ident.t = Identifier(IDENTIFIER);};
StmtList ::=    ( Stmt )                {StmtList.t = (Stmt.t :: StmtListNil);}
         |      ( Stmt ';' StmtList)    {StmtList$1.t = (Stmt.t :: StmtList$2.t);}
         ;
Stmt     ::=    (Ident ASSIGN Exp)      {Stmt.t = Assign(Ident.t, Exp.t);};
Exp      ::=    (INTEGER)               {Exp.t = IntConst(INTEGER);}
         |      (TRUE)                  {Exp.t = True;}
         |      (FALSE)                 {Exp.t = False;}
         |      (Ident)                 {Exp.t = Id(Ident.t);}
         |      (Exp '=' Exp)           {Exp$1.t = Equal(Exp$2.t, Exp$3.t);}
         |      (Exp NOTEQUAL Exp prec NOTEQUAL)
                                        {Exp$1.t = NotEqual(Exp$2.t, Exp$3.t);}
         |      (Exp '+' Exp)           {Exp$1.t = Add(Exp$2.t, Exp$3.t);}
         |      ('(' Exp ')')           {Exp$1.t = Exp$2.t;}
         ;
```

Figure 4.7. Rules that define the input syntax and its translation to a term of the abstract syntax.

hand-side expression uses the operator Equal to construct the corresponding term of the abstract syntax. Note that concrete syntax can be specified with ambiguous productions and disambiguating precedence rules, as is done for the tokens '+', '=', and NOTEQUAL.

A phylum defined by a regular expression may also appear on the right-hand side of a parsing declaration; it denotes the corresponding lexical token, as in the rule

```
Exp    ::=    (INTEGER)               {Exp.t = IntConst(INTEGER);};
```

In the accompanying attribute equation, the argument to constructor IntConst is a syntactic reference to the token INTEGER itself.

The sample specification of this chapter has used only synthesized attributes in the translation of concrete syntax to abstract syntax. Chapter 6 illustrates how inherited attributes may also be used to advantage.

The mechanism for translating input text to an abstract-syntax tree provides an editor-designer with the ability to define textual and structural interfaces in whatever balance is desired. This ability is discussed in detail in Chapter 6, along with many examples that illustrate how different combinations of text-editing and structure-editing interfaces can be defined.

4.5. Templates and Transformations

Transformation declarations specify commands for restructuring an object when the current selection matches a given pattern. One use of transformations is to insert templates. In this case, whenever the selection is a placeholder, it can be replaced by the given template. This is a somewhat degenerate form of transformation, since the replacing value does not depend at all on the original selection. More general transformations compute a replacement for the selection in terms of its former value.

The transformation rules that are part of our sample editor specification are shown in Figure 4.8. The first two groupings are template-insertion transformations for the phyla typeExp and stmt, respectively. The final grouping contains two source-to-source transformations, one that encloses a statement in a begin-end pair and a second that removes the begin-end pair.

```
transform typeExp
          on "integer"    <typeExp>: IntTypeExp,
          on "boolean"    <typeExp>: BoolTypeExp
          ;
transform stmt
          on "assign"     <stmt>: Assign(<identifier>, <exp>),
          on "if"         <stmt>: IfThenElse(<exp>, <stmt>, <stmt>),
          on "while"      <stmt>: While(<exp>, <stmt>),
          on "begin"      <stmt>: Compound(<stmtList>)
          ;
transform stmt
          on "(begin"     s: Compound(StmtListPair(s,StmtListNil)),
          on ")begin"     Compound(StmtListPair(s,StmtListNil)): s
          ;
```

Figure 4.8. Rules defining transformations.

In general, the form of a transformation declaration is

transform *phylum* on *transformation-name pattern* : *expression* ;

Suppose the current selection is a term *s* of the given *phylum*; then the transformation is said to be enabled if the *pattern* matches *s*. The *transformation-names* of all enabled transformations are listed in the help pane of the current window and are updated whenever the selection is moved. The effect of invoking the transformation is to replace *s* with the value of the *expression*. As in the case of with-expressions, the *pattern* contains pattern variables that are bound to sub-terms of *s*. By using these pattern variables in the *expression*, it is possible to restructure the selection.

Consider the two source-to-source transformations of Figure 4.8. The pattern of the transformation named (begin is just the pattern variable *s*. A pattern variable, by itself, matches anything. Thus, whenever the selection is a stmt, (begin is enabled. Invoking this transformation will replace *s* by the term

Compound(StmtListPair(s,StmtListNil))

This transformation was illustrated at the end of Chapter 2.

The transformation)begin is the inverse of (begin. Its pattern is

Compound(StmtListPair(s,StmtListNil))

which matches only a stmt that is a Compound containing a singleton stmtList. Whenever this pattern matches, *s* is bound to that single statement. Invoking)begin will replace the selection with *s*.

We turn now to the template-insertion transformations of Figure 4.8. These declarations make use of a notation that has not been previously introduced: each expression in Figure 4.8 of the form *<phylum>* denotes the *placeholder term* of the given *phylum*. The concept of a phylum's placeholder term is similar to that of the phylum's completing term – both are default representatives of the phylum. In general, the two concepts are not identical; however, we will not explain the difference between them at this point. For now, it suffices to say that in our sample specification the placeholder term of each phylum is exactly the same as its completing term. A discussion of the difference between a phylum's placeholder term and its completing term can be found in Section 5.2, "Specifying Lists and Optional Elements in SSL."

In each of the template transformations, the pattern denotes the appropriate placeholder term. Therefore, the template transformations are enabled only when the selection is at a placeholder. It is thus not possible to accidentally replace an existing statement with a template, thereby wiping out a large part of a developed program.

A final subtlety will have escaped the attention of all but the most astute readers. Review of the sample session of Chapter 2 reveals that the transformations listed for stmt are also enabled when the selection is a singleton sublist of a stmtList term. This is true in general: whenever the selection is a singleton sublist, transformations of both the list phylum and the item phylum are candidates. This feature of the Synthesizer Generator supports the goal of minimizing distinctions between the singleton sublist and the list item itself; it is discussed further in Section 5.4, "Selections of Singleton Sublists Versus Selections of List Elements."

This completes the specification of the sample editor demonstrated in Chapter 2. Figures 4.1 through 4.8 constitute a complete definition of that editor and illustrate the most important features of SSL.

CHAPTER 5

Lists, Optional Elements, and Placeholders

Lists and optional elements are such an important aspect of editor specifications that they deserve to be discussed in more detail. Although iterated elements (lists) and optional elements are concepts that are commonly found in many extended BNF notations, the form that they take in the Synthesizer Specification Language is different from the familiar notions. The chief motivation for SSL's notation for lists and optional elements is to provide a uniform notation for specifying the attribution of terms and their unparsing. The attribute equations and, with one small exception, the unparsing declarations that one writes for list phyla and optional phyla are no different in form from those that are used for ordinary phyla. For example, because all lists are terminated by an instance of the list phylum's nullary operator, there is no need for special-case rules covering the cases of an empty list, a singleton list, and a list of length two or more, as would otherwise have been necessary.

This chapter describes the behavior of lists and optional elements in generated editors and discusses the issues that arise when writing the parts of editor specifications that concern them. Sections 5.1 and 5.2 describe how certain editing operations in generated editors automatically supply placeholders before and after list elements and at unexpanded optional elements. Section 5.3 discusses operations for manipulating sublists. Section 5.4 concerns text-entry definitions for lists and transformations of list elements. Section 5.5 describes how to write parsing and translation rules that translate concrete text into the correct list structure of the underlying abstract syntax. Section 5.6 concerns attribute equations for the completing terms of lists and optional elements.

5.1. Transient Placeholders

One of the important concepts of the user interface of generated editors is that of *placeholders*, which represent "unexpanded" nodes in the derivation tree. A new subterm can be inserted when the currently selected component is a placeholder. Deleting the current selection leaves a placeholder behind.

For phyla that are lists or optional elements, generated editors take special actions that insert and delete additional placeholders automatically. Because these placeholders are automatically deleted as well as automatically inserted, we refer to them as *transient placeholders*. The mechanism provided in SSL for enabling this behavior has an important role in specifying how the user will be able to manipulate abstract-syntax trees. In this section, we describe the manner in which transient placeholders are automatically inserted and deleted. Section 5.2 discusses this mechanism from the point of view of an editor-designer specifying editors with the Synthesizer Generator.

Recall that at all times one subterm of the edited abstract-syntax tree is identified as the selection. Two kinds of commands permit the user to change the selection to a different subterm: *traversal* commands and *selection* commands. Each traversal command moves the selection to the next node in a predefined traversal sequence; that is, on each invocation of the command, the position of the new selection is determined from its position relative to the selection's previous position. Examples of traversal commands include

forward-preorder <^N>
>   Change the selection to the next resting place in a preorder traversal of the abstract-syntax tree.

forward-sibling <ESC-^N>
>   Bypass all resting places contained within the current selection, and advance to the next sibling in the abstract-syntax tree. If there is no next sibling, ascend to the enclosing resting place and advance to its next sibling, *etc.*

ascend-to-parent <ESC->
>   Change the selection to the closest enclosing resting place.

Alternatively, the selection can be changed by using the locator (mouse) to point to a new location in the tree's display and invoking a selection command. The new selection is determined from the position of the locator on the screen. Each position in the display is associated with a particular selection in the abstract-syntax tree; the new selection is the one that corresponds to the locator's position when the selection command is issued.

We will refer to the commands that insert and delete placeholders automatically as *placeholder-inserting commands*. The placeholder-inserting commands consist of the selection commands and some of the traversal commands. All selection commands and traversal commands, even ones that are not placeholder-inserting commands, are *placeholder-deleting* commands; that is, all commands that move the selection will eliminate a transient placeholder that would be left behind when the selection moves to an element not contained in the placeholder.

5.1.1. Traversal commands and transient placeholders in lists

The traversal commands that are placeholder-inserting commands insert transient placeholders before and after list elements. (A discussion of traversal commands and transient placeholders for optional program elements will come later.) Whenever a traversal command inserts a transient placeholder into the abstract-syntax tree, the new placeholder immediately becomes the new currently selected constituent.

Example. The traversal command **forward-with-optionals** advances the selection to the next template, phrase, or placeholder in a forward-preorder traversal of the tree, but inserts list placeholders as list elements are encountered. (It also inserts placeholders at unexpanded optional elements.) The command **forward-sibling-with-optionals** is just like **forward-with-optionals**, except that it bypasses all resting places contained *within* the current selection and advances directly to the next sibling in the abstract-syntax tree; if there is no next sibling, it ascends to the enclosing resting place and advances to its next sibling, *etc.* To illustrate the action of **forward-sibling-with-optionals**, we will use program fragments from the editor specification that was presented in Chapter 4; however, we will assume that the definition of the While operator is changed to

stmt   :   While(exp stmtList);

so that the body of a while-statement is a list of statements, rather than a single statement. The sequence of display snapshots given in Figure 5.1 illustrates repeated use of **forward-sibling-with-optionals** to advance the selection through a program. When the selection is first advanced from the while-loop's expression in Figure 5.1(a), a transient placeholder is inserted before the first assignment-statement in the loop-body (see Figure 5.1(b)). Repeated use of **forward-sibling-with-optionals** moves the selection through the loop-body. When the selection is advanced from a transient placeholder, as in Figures 5.1(b), 5.1(d), and 5.1(f), the placeholder is deleted from the program. Note carefully the difference between the situations portrayed in Figures 5.1(f) and

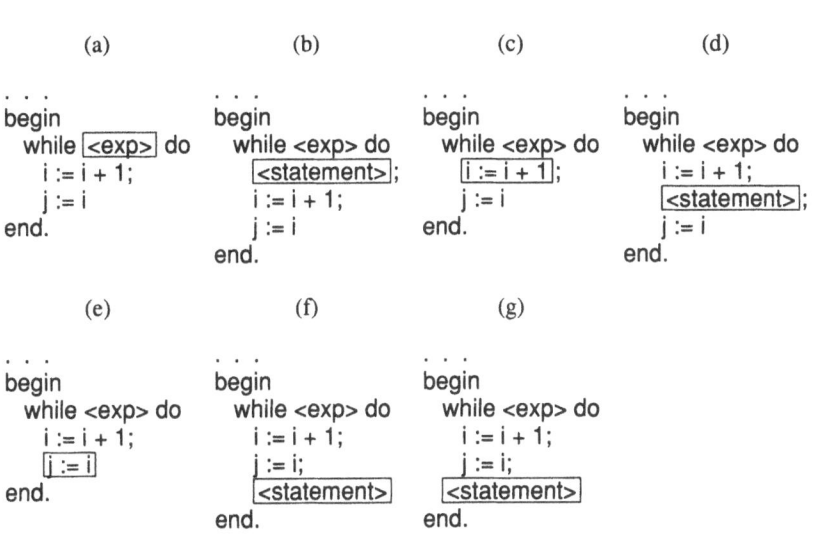

Figure 5.1. Snapshots of the display that illustrate the effect of repeated use of **forward-sibling-with-optionals**. Transient placeholders are inserted before and after list elements ((b), (d), (f), and (g), but are deleted when advancing the selection would leave behind an empty placeholder ((c), (e), and (g)).

5.1(g). In Figure 5.1(f), the <statement> placeholder is located within the loop-body and identifies a location where it is permitted to insert additional statements in the loop; in contrast, the <statement> placeholder in Figure 5.1(g) is a sibling of the while-loop in the enclosing compound-statement. When the selection was advanced from Figure 5.1(f) to 5.1(g), the inner placeholder was removed from the program, and a new placeholder supplied as a sibling of the while-loop.

Other traversal commands never insert placeholders in lists. For example, **forward-sibling** is just like **forward-sibling-with-optionals**, except that it never inserts placeholders in lists (or at optional elements either). The effect on the selection of repeated use of **forward-sibling** is illustrated in Figure 5.2.

Figure 5.1 also illustrates that transient placeholders are automatically deleted from a list when a movement of the selection would leave behind an empty placeholder. In fact, this deletion action is taken by all commands that move the selection, not just placeholder-inserting commands. For example, Figure 5.3 illustrates that if the **forward-sibling** command is invoked when the current

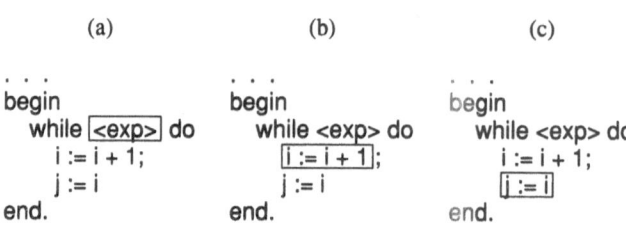

```
        (a)                     (b)                     (c)

. . .                   . . .                   . . .
begin                   begin                   begin
   while <exp> do          while <exp> do          while <exp> do
      i := i + 1;             i := i + 1;             i := i + 1;
      j := i                  j := i                  j := i
end.                    end.                    end.
```

Figure 5.2. Snapshots of the display that illustrate the effect of repeated use of **forward-sibling**.

selection is a transient **<statement>** placeholder, the placeholder is removed from the list.

As shown in Figures 5.1 and 5.3, a command that would leave behind an empty list placeholder ordinarily removes that placeholder from the object; however, this is not always done if the list is otherwise empty, *i.e.* if it has no elements other than a singleton placeholder. Two forms of lists are supported: lists of zero or more elements and lists of one or more elements. In the case of lists of one or more elements, a singleton placeholder remains behind to indicate a location where at least one list element is required. Figure 5.4 illustrates repeated use of **forward-with-optionals** in the two kinds of lists. For lists of zero or more elements, if a traversal placeholder-inserting command advances the selection to the empty list, a singleton placeholder is inserted and made the new selection (see Figure 5.4(b2)).

```
        (a)                     (b)

. . .                   . . .
begin                   begin
   while <exp> do          while <exp> do
      i := i + 1;             i := i + 1;
      <statement>;            j := i
      j := i               end.
end.
```

Figure 5.3. If the command **forward-sibling** is invoked when the currently selected constituent is a transient placeholder (a), the placeholder is removed from the program (b).

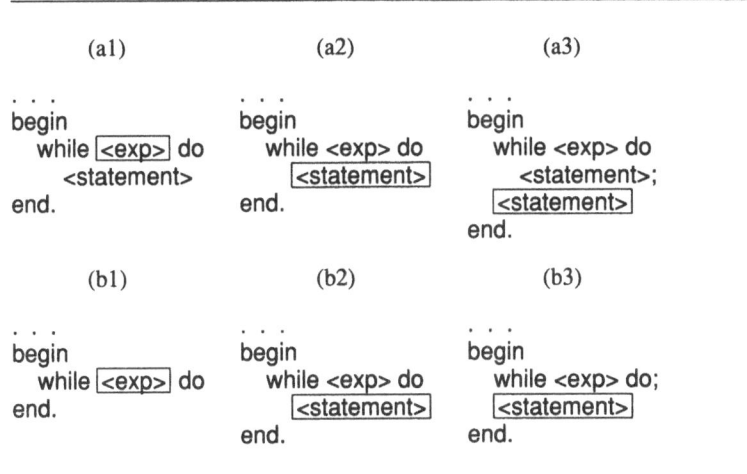

Figure 5.4. Snapshots of the display that illustrate the effect of repeated use of **forward-with-optionals** in empty lists. Sequence (a1) – (a3) illustrates an editor in which statement lists always have at least one element, although the element may be a placeholder. Sequence (b1) – (b3) illustrates a different version of the editor in which statement lists are allowed to have zero elements.

Many placeholders are simply leaves of the derivation tree, with no substructure themselves, such as the placeholders represented by <identifier>, <exp>, and <statement> in Figures 5.1 – 5.4. This is not always the case, for it is possible to have placeholders (including transient placeholders) that have subcomponents. Typically, some of a placeholder's subcomponents are placeholders themselves. In fact, we have already seen an example of a placeholder with substructure in the editor specification presented in Chapter 4. The placeholder for the declList phylum looks like

<identifier> : <type>

and contains two subordinate placeholders, <identifier> and <type>.

When a transient placeholder contains such subcomponents, the transient-placeholder-removal operations that were illustrated earlier are triggered only when the selection is moved entirely outside of the placeholder's scope. For instance, it is possible to move the selection from the position shown in Figure 5.5(a), where the currently selected constituent is the placeholder for declList, to the position shown in Figure 5.5(b), where the selected component is the type component of the declList placeholder's subcomponents.

```
          (a)                         (b)
program <identifier>;       program <identifier>;
var                         var
   i : integer;                i : integer;
   <identifier> : <type>;      <identifier> : <type>;
begin                       begin
    . . .                       . . .
end.                        end.
```

Figure 5.5. Snapshots of the display illustrating that the selection may be moved from a transient placeholder (a) to one of its subordinate components (b).

The kind of action that does trigger a placeholder-removal operation is a movement of the selection to a location entirely outside the scope of the transient placeholder; when this happens, the entire placeholder is removed. Note that this occurs even if the initial selection is a *component* of what needs to be removed. For example, in Figure 5.6(a), the initial selection <type> is a subcomponent of the declList placeholder

<identifier> : <type>

In Figure 5.6(b), the declList placeholder has been removed because the selection was moved out of its scope.

```
          (a)                         (b)
program <identifier>;       program <identifier>;
var                         var
   i : integer;                i : integer;
   <identifier> : <type>;   begin
begin                           . . .
    . . .                   end.
end.
```

Figure 5.6. Effect of moving the selection from a subcomponent of a transient placeholder. Initially, the selection is positioned at a subcomponent of a transient placeholder (a). The placeholder is deleted when the selection is moved outside of its scope (b).

5.1.2. Selection commands and transient placeholders in lists

Selection commands can also cause transient placeholders to be inserted in lists. (Unlike traversal commands, they do not cause placeholders to be inserted at optional elements.) When a selection command is invoked with the locator pointing to the text of a list separator, a placeholder is inserted between the adjacent list elements and is made the currently selected constituent.[1]

Example. Recall that list elements of phylum stmtList are displayed with a semicolon and newline to separate adjacent list elements, as defined by the following unparsing declarations:

stmtList :   StmtListNil   [@ :]
         | StmtListPair   [@ : ^ [";%n"] @]
         ;

As shown in Figure 5.7, when a selection command is invoked with the locator positioned at a semicolon that is a stmtList separator, a transient stmtList placeholder is inserted between the immediately adjacent list elements.

Figure 5.7. Insertion of a transient placeholder when a selection command is invoked with the locator at a list separator. Initially, the locator points to the semicolon separating the two list elements (a). A transient placeholder is inserted between them when a selection command is invoked (b).

---

[1]At present, selection commands cause transient placeholders to be inserted only between list elements; selection commands do not insert placeholders before the first list element or after the last list element. These placeholders appear only through the actions of traversal commands, such as **forward-with-optionals** <˜M> or **backward-with-optionals** <ˆH>.

5.1.3. Transient placeholders for optional elements

Besides inserting transient placeholders before and after list elements, the traversal commands that are placeholder-inserting commands insert transient placeholders at optional elements that happen to be unexpanded. A placeholder is inserted into the tree when an unexpanded optional element is encountered, and the new placeholder immediately becomes the new selection. The placeholder is subsequently deleted if the user moves the selection before making an insertion at the placeholder.

To illustrate this behavior, we again use program fragments based on the editor specification presented in Chapter 4; however, in these examples we assume that the definition of the While operator has been changed to

stmt   :   While(loopname exp stmtList);

where loopname is the phylum of loop names. The full details of how the loopname phylum is specified will be presented in the next section; here it suffices to know that an unexpanded loopname has the property of being an optional program element.

Example. Suppose that the initial situation is as shown in Figure 5.8(a), in which the currently selected constituent is the entire while-loop. When the selection is advanced with the traversal command **forward-with-optionals**, a transient placeholder is inserted for the unexpanded loopname component of the while-loop (see Figure 5.8(b)). At this point, the user could insert a name for the loop. However, if the user leaves the placeholder empty and chooses

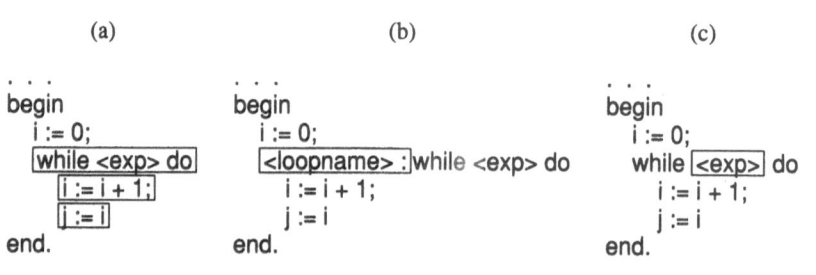

Figure 5.8. A transient placeholder is inserted in the program when **forward-with-optionals** encounters an unexpanded optional element (b). The placeholder is removed when the selection is advanced further (c).

instead to advance the selection to the position shown in Figure 5.8(c), the placeholder is removed from the program.

5.2. Specifying Lists and Optional Elements in SSL

This section describes how to specify lists and optional elements using the facilities that are provided by the Synthesizer Specification Language. The behavior that was described in the previous section, where transient placeholders are automatically inserted and deleted, is enabled by explicit *property declarations* that appear in an editor's specification. SSL property declarations declare that a phylum is either an *optional* phylum, a *list* phylum, or an *optional list* phylum. (Phyla that are not declared as having any of these three properties will be referred to as *ordinary* phyla.) For example, the qualifier list in a phylum's property declaration specifies that placeholder-inserting commands will automatically insert placeholders before and after nonempty elements in that phylum's lists.

The concept of a phylum's "completing term," which was defined in Chapter 4 for ordinary phyla and list phyla, is one of the keys to a discussion of lists, optional elements, and transient placeholders. However, the concept of a transient placeholder is actually defined in terms of a phylum's *placeholder term*, not in terms of the phylum's completing term. The placeholder term and the completing term are two related but slightly different concepts for producing default representatives for a phylum. For an ordinary phylum or a non-optional list phylum, the phylum's placeholder term and its completing term are identical; however, the two concepts differ for optional phyla and optional list phyla. That is, for all phyla that are not declared with the qualifier optional, there is no distinction between a phylum's placeholder term and the phylum's completing term.

The basic relationships among the completing term, the placeholder term, the list property, and the optional property are as follows:

- The qualifier list specifies that placeholder-inserting commands will splice instances of a list phylum's placeholder term before and after elements of that phylum's lists.
- The qualifier optional specifies that whenever the current selection is to be placed at an abstract-syntax tree node from which the phylum's completing term is derived, the completing term is automatically replaced by the phylum's placeholder term.

For optional list phyla, which have both properties, the above characterizations still hold. As will be discussed in detail below, this means that list phyla that are declared to be optional behave as lists of length zero or more, whereas non-optional list phyla behave as lists of length one or more.

To describe these concepts more precisely, we use a notation from SSL's expression language for denoting completing terms and placeholder terms. A phylum's completing term can be denoted by the phylum name enclosed in square brackets; its placeholder term can be denoted by the phylum name enclosed in angle brackets. For example, the completing term of phylum *phy* is denoted by [*phy*], whereas the placeholder term is denoted by <*phy*>.

5.2.1. Placeholders and ordinary phyla

Recall that in Chapter 4 we defined the first operator declared for each phylum to be its *completing operator*. For an ordinary phylum, the completing term is constructed by applying the completing operator to the completing terms of its argument phyla; the placeholder term for an ordinary phylum is identical to the completing term.

Example. Suppose that phylum phy_0 is defined by the following abstract-syntax rules:

$$phy_0 : op_1 (phy_{1,1} \, phy_{1,2} \, \cdots \, phy_{1,k_1})$$
$$| \; op_2 (phy_{2,1} \, phy_{2,2} \, \cdots \, phy_{2,k_2})$$
$$\cdots$$
$$| \; op_n (phy_{n,1} \, phy_{n,2} \, \cdots \, phy_{n,k_n})$$
$$;$$

The completing term of phy_0, as well as its placeholder term, is the term

$$op_1 ([phy_{1,1}], [phy_{1,2}], \ldots, [phy_{1,k_1}]).$$

For an ordinary phylum, a placeholder is an example of a placeholder term supplied at an "unexpanded" node of the abstract-syntax tree. For instance, a placeholder that remains behind when an element of phylum phy_0 is deleted is an instance of the placeholder term for phy_0. Placeholders also appear when insertions are made with template commands – each placeholder in the template is an instance of a placeholder term. (See Section 5.2.5, "Placeholder terms and completing terms in patterns and expressions.")

5.2.2. Placeholders and non-optional list phyla

In Chapter 4, we described the requirement that the abstract-syntax rules for a phylum declared to have the list property must have exactly two operators, one a nullary operator and the other a binary operator that is right recursive. For a non-optional list phylum, the phylum's completing term is defined differently from the way it is defined for an ordinary phylum: it is the singleton list constructed by applying the binary operator to the completing term of its left son and to the list's nullary operator. For non-optional list phyla, the placeholder term is identical to the completing term.

Example. Suppose phylum phy_0 is a typical list phylum declared by:

list phy_0;
$phy_0 : op_1 ( )$
  $| op_2 (phy_1 phy_0)$
  ;

Both the placeholder term and the completing term of phylum phy_0 are the singleton list formed by concatenating the completing term of phy_1 with the nullary operator of phy_0:

$[phy_1] :: op_1$

For list phyla, placeholders are instances of placeholder terms that have been spliced into an existing list. When a placeholder-inserting command inserts a phy_0 placeholder between elements A and B in the list $A :: B :: C :: op_1$, phy_0's placeholder term is spliced into the list. This operation creates the list

$A :: [phy_1] :: B :: C :: op_1$

5.2.3. Placeholders and optional phyla

Thus far, there has been no need to distinguish between a phylum's placeholder term and its completing term; for ordinary phyla and non-optional list phyla, they are identical. We now turn to phyla declared with the optional property: optional phyla and optional list phyla. To discuss how their transient placeholders are defined, we must now distinguish between the phylum's placeholder term and its completing term.

An optional (non-list) phylum can have any number of operators, but one of them must be a nullary operator; the completing term is the term constructed from the first nullary operator of the phylum that is listed in the editor specification. The placeholder term is constructed by "completing" the first operator of the phylum that is not the aforementioned completing-term operator.

Example. Suppose the optional phylum phy_0 is defined by the following abstract-syntax rules:

optional phy_0;
$phy_0 : op_1 (phy_{1,1} \, phy_{1,2} \, \cdots \, phy_{1,k_1})$
  $| \; op_2 (phy_{2,1} \, phy_{2,2} \, \cdots \, phy_{2,k_2})$
  $\cdots$
  $| \; op_j ( )$
  $\cdots$
  $| \; op_n (phy_{n,1} \, phy_{n,2} \, \cdots \, phy_{n,k_n})$
  ;

The completing term of phy_0 is the term op_j, which is constructed from the first nullary operator listed. The placeholder term is the term

$op_1 ([phy_{1,1}], [phy_{1,2}], \ldots, [phy_{1,k_1}])$

Note that the completing term and placeholder term are defined in terms of the first nullary operator listed and the first operator that is not the completing-term operator. Thus, phy_0's placeholder term and completing term would still be the same if we listed the operators in the following order:

$phy_0 : op_j ( )$
  $| \; op_1 (phy_{1,1} \, phy_{1,2} \, \cdots \, phy_{1,k_1})$
  $| \; op_2 (phy_{2,1} \, phy_{2,2} \, \cdots \, phy_{2,k_2})$
  $\cdots$
  $| \; op_{j-1} (phy_{j-1,1} \, phy_{j-1,2} \, \cdots \, phy_{j-1,k_{j-1}})$
  $| \; op_{j+1} (phy_{j+1,1} \, phy_{j+1,2} \, \cdots \, phy_{j+1,k_{j+1}})$
  $\cdots$
  $| \; op_n (phy_{n,1} \, phy_{n,2} \, \cdots \, phy_{n,k_n})$
  ;

The primary use of optional phyla in language-based editors is to specify optional elements of the language. These definitions generally follow the pattern given below:

- The abstract-syntax phylum is declared to have the **optional** property.
- The first nullary operator of the phylum is declared to have the null unparsing declaration. Consequently, an instance of the completing term will contribute nothing to the display representation.
- The operator declarations are ordered so that the placeholder term is a term that displays the desired prompt.

A transient placeholder for an optional phylum is created in the display by a placeholder-inserting command. The command removes an instance of the completing term from the abstract-syntax tree and substitutes an instance of the placeholder term in its place. Because of this substitution, the placeholder term's display representation appears on the screen. This serves as a prompt to the user to insert an appropriate element at that location.

Example. The optional phylum loopname was introduced in the previous section to illustrate the automatic insertion of transient placeholders at unexpanded optional program elements. Its definition follows the pattern outlined above.

```
optional loopname;
loopname:      LoopnameNull( )
       |       LoopnamePrompt( )
       |       Loopname(IDENTIFIER)
       ;
loopname:      LoopnameNull      [ @ : ]
       |       LoopnamePrompt    [ @ ::= "<loopname>: "]
       |       Loopname          [ @ ::= ^ ": "]
       ;
```

Phylum loopname has two nullary operators, LoopnameNull and LoopnamePrompt, as well as the unary operator Loopname. Thus, the completing term of phylum loopname is the term LoopnameNull and the placeholder term is the term LoopnamePrompt. LoopnameNull has the null unparsing declaration, so that an instance of LoopnameNull will be invisible to the user. By contrast, LoopnamePrompt displays the string <loopname>: as a prompt to the user. Recall that in the previous section, the loopname phylum appeared as the first component in our revised definition of the operator While:

```
stmt    :        While(loopname exp stmtList);
```

To describe the way an abstract-syntax tree is modified when a transient placeholder is created, let E be a term of phylum exp and S be a term of phylum stmtList. Before the selection is moved to the loopname, the tree has the subterm

While(LoopnameNull, E, S)

However, when a traversal command that is a placeholder-inserting command encounters the term LoopnameNull, LoopnameNull is replaced by the term LoopnamePrompt to produce

While(LoopnamePrompt, E, S)

The instance of term LoopnamePrompt becomes the new currently selected
constituent of the program after the substitution. If the user makes no insertion,
LoopnamePrompt is again replaced by LoopnameNull when the selection is
moved to another site in the tree.

5.2.4. Placeholders and optional list phyla

The abstract-syntax rules for an optional list phylum are like the ones for a non-
optional list: there must be exactly two operators, one of them nullary, the other
binary and right recursive. The completing term of an optional list phylum is
the constant term constructed from the nullary operator of the phylum. The
placeholder term of an optional list is exactly the same as the completing term
had the phylum not been declared to be optional; that is, the placeholder term is
the singleton list constructed by applying the list's binary operator to the completing term of its left son and to the list's nullary term.

Example. An optional list phylum phy_0 would be defined by abstract-syntax
rules of the form

optional list phy_0;
$phy_0 : op_1 (\ )$
     $| op_2 (phy_1 phy_0)$
     ;

The completing term of phy_0 is the term op_1. The placeholder term is
$[phy_1] :: op_1$.

As is the case for non-optional list phyla, when a placeholder-inserting command inserts a phy_0 placeholder between elements A and B in the list
$A :: B :: C :: op_1$, phy_0's placeholder term is spliced into the list to create

$A :: [phy_1] :: B :: C :: op_1$

The essential difference between an optional list phylum and its non-optional
counterpart is that an optional list phylum behaves as a list of length zero or
more, whereas a non-optional list phylum behaves as a list of length one or
more. The qualifier optional specifies that whenever the current selection is
moved outside the scope of an instance of the phylum's placeholder term, the
placeholder is automatically replaced by an instance of the phylum's completing
term. For example, if phy_0 is an optional list phylum, the term $[phy_1] :: op_1$
would be replaced by the term op_1. In contrast, if phy_0 were a non-optional list
phylum, the subterm would be left as it was.

5.2.5. Placeholder terms and completing terms in patterns and expressions

For expository purposes, in several places we have used the special notation that SSL provides for denoting placeholder terms and completing terms. A phylum's completing term is denoted by the phylum name enclosed in square brackets; its placeholder term is denoted by the phylum name enclosed in angle brackets. This notation can be used in patterns of transformation declarations as well.

Example. Consider the use of the placeholder-term notation in the transformation declarations that declare the template commands for statements in Chapter 4:

```
transform stmt
        on "assign"     <stmt>: Assign(<identifier>, <exp>),
        on "if"         <stmt>: IfThenElse(<exp>, <stmt>, <stmt>),
        on "begin"      <stmt>: Compound(<stmtList>)
        ;
```

Now consider how to define a template command for our revised definition of the While operator, which includes an optional loopname component. One way to define the While template is as follows:

```
transform stmt on "while" <stmt>: While([loopname], <exp>, <stmtList>);
```

This definition causes the loopname element to expand to its completing term when the template is instantiated; because phylum loopname is an optional phylum, the loopname component will be initially hidden from the user.

Using loopname's completing term on the right-hand side of a template is not mandatory. The alternative is to use its placeholder term, as is done in the following declaration:

```
transform stmt on "while" <stmt>: While(<loopname>, <exp>, <stmtList>);
```

The only difference between the revised template definition and the one given previously is that the latter causes a transient placeholder for loopname to appear immediately, when a while-loop is initially created. That is, because the loopname component is expanded to the term LoopnamePrompt when a template is instantiated, the template looks like

```
<loopname> : while <exp> do
    <statement>
```

Thereafter, the loopname placeholder behaves no differently than it does with the original template declaration: once the loopname placeholder becomes the

currently selected component, if it is not filled in immediately it will be automatically removed when the selection is moved to a different location. This is illustrated by the snapshots portrayed in Figure 5.9. When the template is instantiated, it contains a transient loopname placeholder (Figure 5.9(b)). When the
selection is advanced to another location with the loopname left unexpanded,
the transient placeholder is removed from the program in the normal fashion
(Figure 5.9(c)).

5.2.6. Summary of property declarations

We now present two tables that summarize property declarations and the transient placeholders they define. Figure 5.10 lists canonical abstract-syntax rules
for ordinary phyla, list phyla, optional phyla, and optional list phyla, and summarizes the definitions of their completing terms and placeholder terms. Figure
5.11 summarizes the special actions for automatically inserting and deleting
transient placeholders that are enabled by SSL property declarations.

5.3. Sublist Manipulations

The list property carries with it a second characteristic besides the automatic
insertion and deletion of transient placeholders. In addition to the ordinary kind
of selection operations and manipulations, declaring a phylum as a list makes it
possible for the user to select and manipulate arbitrary sublists.

The two selection commands **select-start** and **select-stop** can be used to
select sublists. (Alternatively, **select-transition** <ESC-t> alone is sufficient – it

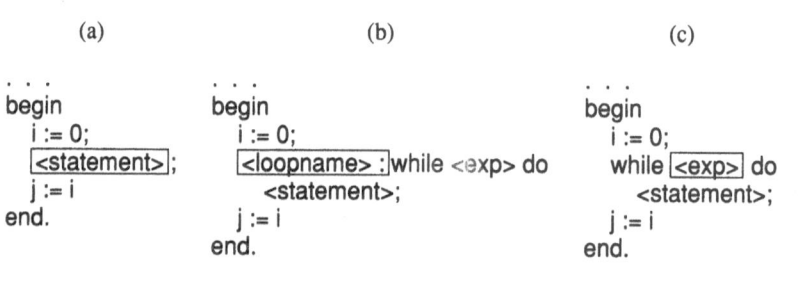

Figure 5.9. A template is instantiated that has a transient placeholder for the loopname
component (b). When the selection is advanced to another placeholder, the loopname
placeholder is removed from the program (c).

Property name	Typical abstract-syntax rules	Completing term	Placeholder term
Ordinary phylum	$phy_0 : op_1 (phy_{1,1} phy_{1,2} \cdots phy_{1,k_1})$ $\mid op_2 (phy_{2,1} phy_{2,2} \cdots phy_{2,k_2})$ ... $\mid op_n (phy_{n,1} phy_{n,2} \cdots phy_{n,k_n})$;	$op_1([phy_{1,1}],$ $[phy_{1,2}],$ $\ldots ,$ $[phy_{1,k_1}]$ $)$	Same as completing term
List phylum	$phy_0 : op_1 ( )$ $\mid op_2 (phy_1 phy_0)$;	$[phy_1] :: op_1$	Same as completing term
Optional phylum	$phy_0 : op_1 (phy_{1,1} phy_{1,2} \cdots phy_{1,k_1})$ $\mid op_2 (phy_{2,1} phy_{2,2} \cdots phy_{2,k_2})$ ... $\mid op_j ( )$ ... $\mid op_n (phy_{n,1} phy_{n,2} \cdots phy_{n,k_n})$;	op_j	$op_1([phy_{1,1}],$ $[phy_{1,2}],$ $\ldots ,$ $[phy_{1,k_1}]$ $)$
Optional list phylum	$phy_0 : op_1 ( )$ $\mid op_2 (phy_1 phy_0)$;	op_1	$[phy_1] :: op_1$

Figure 5.10. Property declarations, abstract-syntax rules, completing terms, and placeholder terms.

Property name	State when unexpanded	Behavior with respect to placeholder-inserting commands
Ordinary phylum	Completing term	No special behavior
List phylum	Completing term (*i.e.* a singleton list with the completing term of the element phylum as the one list element)	A placeholder term is spliced in before or after list elements
Optional phylum	Completing term	The completing term is replaced by a placeholder term
Optional list phylum	Completing term (*i.e.* an empty list)	A placeholder term is spliced in before or after list elements if the list is not empty; otherwise the list is replaced by a singleton placeholder term

Figure 5.11. Property declarations and their characteristics *vis à vis* transient placeholders.

toggles between **select-start** and **select-stop**.) The **select-start** command defines the initial selection point of a *two-point selection* and initiates the process of *dragging*; the locator can then be used to pick the final selection point. During dragging, the current extent of the two-point selection, defined as the least-common ancestor of the initial point and the current locator position, is indicated on the screen by highlighting. If both the initial and final selection point are located in two different elements of the same list, the selection is the sublist containing both list elements as well as all the elements in between.

For example, Figure 5.12 illustrates how to select a sublist that consists of the list's second and third statements. Initially, the locator points to the equal sign of the second statement. A **select-start** command initiates the selection; dragging the locator to the third statement extends the selection to cover the second and third elements; the selection is completed by issuing the **select-stop** command. The resulting selection is the two-element sublist that consists of the list's second and third statements.

When the currently selected constituent is a sublist, the commands for structural editing, such as **cut-to-clipped** <^W> and **paste-from-clipped** <^Y>, are defined to take appropriate actions on the selected sublist. In Figure 5.13, **cut-to-clipped** and **paste-from-clipped** are used to move the sublist selection into the body of a newly instantiated while-loop. First, the sublist is cut to the clip buffer (Figure 5.13(b)) leaving behind a <statement> placeholder. Next, a while-loop is inserted at the placeholder (Figure 5.13(c)). The selection is moved to the loop's body (Figure 5.13(d)), and finally the contents of the clip buffer are inserted (Figure 5.13(e)).

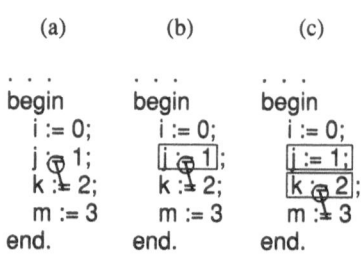

Figure 5.12. Snapshots of the display that illustrate selection of sublists by dragging. Starting with the locator pointing to the equal sign of the second assignment-statement in a four-element list (a), a **select-start** is issued (b). The locator is moved to the third statement, and a **select-stop** is issued, causing a two-element sublist to be selected (c).

(a)	(b)	(c)

```
 . . .                    . . .                    . . .
begin                    begin                    begin
   i := 0;                  i := 0;                  i := 0;
  | j := 1; |             | <statement> |;          while | <exp> | do
  | k := 2 |;               m := 3                      <statement>;
   m := 3                 end.                         m := 3
end.                                                end.
```

(d)	(e)

```
 . . .                    . . .
begin                    begin
   i := 0;                  i := 0;
   while <exp> do           while <exp> do
     | <statement> |;        | j := 1; |
   m := 3                    | k := 2 |;
end.                          m := 3
                           end.
```

Figure 5.13. Snapshots of the display illustrating cut-and-paste operations on sublists. Starting with a selection that is a two-element sublist (a), the selection is cut to the clip buffer (b), a while-loop is inserted (c), the selection is moved to the loop-body (d), and the clip buffer is inserted (e).

5.4. Selections of Singleton Sublists Versus Selections of List Elements

Lists obviously play an important role in generated editors. One of our goals was to streamline the list-manipulation operations to make them as convenient as possible. However, due to the way lists are defined in SSL, the editor-designer must be careful to avoid a few pitfalls that can spoil a design.

The most serious problem that arises concerns selections of singleton sublists versus selections of list elements. For example, consider a selection that is a component of a list, such as

```
 . . .
begin
   i := 0;
   j := 1;
  | k := 2 |;
   m := 3
end.
```

The question is whether the selected constituent is an object of phylum stmt or stmtList. Depending on how the editor specification is written, it could be either. However, if the specification is written to allow selections of individual stmt elements, then there will be annoying "extra resting places" in the abstract-syntax tree.

Example. Consider a sequence of **forward-with-optionals** commands through the following program, assuming that the initial selection is a singleton sublist of phylum stmtList:

(a)	(b)	(c)	(d)

```
. . .          . . .          . . .          . . .
begin          begin          begin          begin
  i := 0;        i := 0;        i := 0;        i := 0;
  j := 1;        j := 1;        j := 1;        j := 1;
 ┌─────┐        ┌─────┐         k := 2;        k := 2;
 │k := 2│;      │k := 2│;     ┌───────────┐  ┌───────────┐
 └─────┘        └─────┘       │<statement>│; │<statement>│;
  m := 3         m := 3       └───────────┘  └───────────┘
end.           end.            m := 3         m := 3
                               end.           end.
```

In this example, the selected constituent is a stmtList in (a) and (c) but is a stmt in (b) and (d). Not only is this undesirable, because the display is ambiguous, but it is also frustrating to have the extra stopping places when advancing the selection through the program with traversal commands.

Because of these considerations, the resting-place definitions in editor specifications are generally defined so that the nodes for individual list elements are invisible to the editor user. That is, they are defined so that they are not resting places in the abstract-syntax tree. With such definitions, the selection never consists of an individual list element; instead, the selection of a single item in a list actually causes a one-element (singleton) sublist to be selected.

The resting-place definitions for lists generally follow the pattern found in the unparsing declarations for the stmtList and stmt phyla shown in Figure 5.14. (These unparsing declarations come from the editor specification presented in Chapter 4.) As used in Figure 5.14, the resting-place symbols prevent the selection of stmt nodes that are elements of stmtLists.

The solution presented above introduces certain problems for other aspects of editor specifications, including transformation declarations, text entry, and cut-and-paste operations. In all three cases, it seemed unnatural to make a distinction between singleton sublists and individual list elements. Consequently, the Synthesizer Generator has a number of features that minimize the distinction between a singleton sublist and an individual list element.

stmtList	:	StmtListNil	[@ :]
	|	StmtListPair	[@ : ˆ [";%n"] @]
	;		
stmt	:	EmptyStmt	[ˆ ::= "<statement>"]
	|	Assign	[ˆ ::= @ error " := " @ assignError]
	|	IfThenElse	[ˆ : "if " @ typeError " then" "%t%n"
			@ "%b%n"
			"else%t%n"
			@ "%b"]
	|	While	[ˆ : "while " @ typeError " do" "%t%n"
			@ "%b"]
	|	Compound	[ˆ : "begin" "%t%n"
			@ "%b%n"
			"end"]
	;		

Figure 5.14. Unparsing declarations for the phyla stmt and stmtList. These declarations illustrate resting-place definitions in which the nodes for the individual list elements are invisible to an editor user.

Transformations

When the current selection of a tree is a singleton sublist, the transformation rules offered by the system as possible transformations include not just ones written as transformations of the list phylum, but ones written as transformations of the list-element phylum, as well. When the user applies one of the latter transformations, the transformation pattern is applied to the list element, and the replacement term computed from the expression on the transformation's right-hand side is automatically converted to a singleton list of the appropriate phylum. The latter term is then used to replace the singleton list selection.

Example. If the current selection is a placeholder in a stmtList, it will be possible to invoke any of the stmt templates to insert an additional stmt in the list.

          (a)   (b)

```
. . .                    . . .
begin                    begin
   i := 0;                  i := 0;
   j := 1;                  j := 1;
   k := 2;                  k := 2;
   <statement> ;           while <exp> do
   m := 3                      <statement>;
end.                        m := 3
                         end.
```

Note that, as defined in Chapter 4, the initial <statement> placeholder represents a stmtList placeholder, whereas the while template is defined to be a stmt transformation.

Text entry

Ordinarily, the text-entry property from the unparsing declaration for the selection's root determines whether text-entry is permitted. However, when the selection is a singleton sublist, the text-entry property for the individual list item is also used (*i.e.* text entry is permitted at a singleton sublist if it is permitted by the text-entry property associated with the list item or the list's binary operator).

Example. In the declarations given in Figure 5.14, text entry is forbidden at StmtListPair operators and at While operators, but is permitted at Assign operators. In the two situations shown below, where in both cases the selection is a singleton sublist, the user will be permitted to enter text in situation (a) but not in (b).

      (a)   (b)

```
. . .             . . .
begin             begin
   j := 1;           j := 1;
   k := 2 ;          k := 2;
   m := 3            while <exp> do
end.                    <statement> ;
                     m := 3
                  end.
```

Note that matters would be slightly different if the text-entry property for StmtListPair were specified with the following unparsing declaration:

stmtList :　　　　StmtListPair　　　　　　[@ ::= ˆ [";%n"] @];

The latter declaration will allow text entry in both cases (a) and (b) above. (It will also allow text entry when a sublist is selected whose length is greater than one, whereas the original one will not.)

Cut-and-paste operations

To further hide the distinction between a singleton sublist and an individual list element, the paste operation is prepared to make automatic conversions from singleton lists to list elements, and *vice versa*.

To illustrate this, note that in Figure 5.14, even though the resting-place definitions hide all stmt nodes that are elements of stmtList lists, it is still possible to select the stmt objects that appear in the second and third components of IfThenElse statements. In the unparsing declaration for IfThenElse, the symbol @ in the operator's second and third components makes these nodes resting places in the tree. Consequently, it will be possible to select stmt nodes in conditional-statements and invoke **cut-to-clipped** to cut them from the program to the clip buffer. However, when **paste-from-clipped** is invoked, certain automatic conversions will be performed, if appropriate. For example, a stmt cut from an IfThenElse operator can be pasted into a stmtList, as shown below:

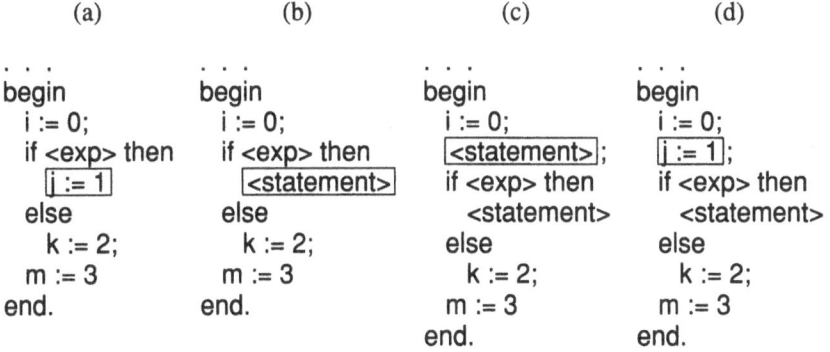

Similarly, a singleton list of phylum stmtList can be pasted as a stmt in an IfThenElse. In both cases, all the necessary conversions will be transparent to the user.

5.5. Parsing Lists

In Chapter 4, the editor specification contained the following rules to define the
syntax of concrete input for phylum stmtList:

```
StmtList { synthesized stmtList t; };
Stmt { synthesized stmt t; };
stmtList  ~  StmtList.t;
StmtList  ::=  (Stmt)                 {StmtList.t = (Stmt.t :: StmtListNil);}
       |    (Stmt ';' StmtList)  {StmtList$1.t = (Stmt.t :: StmtList$2.t);}
       ;
```

These rules define how the input language represented by phylum StmtList is
translated into an element of abstract-syntax phylum stmtList.

Unfortunately, because of the way the Synthesizer Generator is implemented,
these rules have a serious flaw. The parser that is used in a generated editor is a
LALR(1) parser generated using the yacc parser generator [Johnson78]. The
problem lies in the second of the two parse rules given above. Because the production is right recursive, there will be a limit on the number of statements that
can be parsed. As described in [Johnson78], right-recursive grammar rules
cause the parser to scan and push (shift) all list elements onto the stack before
any portion of the list can be reduced. After some fixed number of list elements
are shifted, the stack will overflow.

To avoid stack overflow, parse rules for lists should be written left recursively
to allow reductions to be made on-the-fly as new list elements are encountered.
However, in the Synthesizer Generator, this solution leads to a new problem
because of the Generator's requirement that the abstract-syntax rules for a list
phylum be written right recursively. The problem now is how to build up a
right-recursive abstract list in the attribute equations of left-recursive parse
rules. We could (naively) build up the abstract list with the following rules:

```
StmtList  ::=  (Stmt)                 {StmtList.t = (Stmt.t :: StmtListNil);}
       |    (StmtList ';' Stmt)  {StmtList$1.t = (Stmt.t :: StmtList$2.t);}
       ;
```

However, this has the undesired effect of building up the abstract-syntax list
term in the wrong order – the list's elements would be in the reverse order from
the order in which the input elements were typed by the user!

To build an abstract list in a manner that respects the order of the input elements, we must arrange for the attribution rules to collect the elements of the
abstract list from right to left in the left-recursive input-syntax parse tree. The
solution is to write the attribution rules of the parsing grammar with attributes

whose dependencies are threaded from right to left, as is done in the following input grammar specification:

```
StmtList {
        inherited stmtList tail;
        synthesized stmtList reversed;
        };
Stmt { synthesized stmt t; };
stmtList  ~  StmtList.reversed  { StmtList.tail = StmtListNil; };
StmtList  ::=  (Stmt) { StmtList.reversed = (Stmt.t :: StmtList.tail); }
        |   (StmtList ';' Stmt) {
                StmtList$2.tail = (Stmt.t :: StmtList$1.tail);
                StmtList$1.reversed = StmtList$2.reversed;
                }
        ;
```

Here the attribute equations are written so that phylum StmtList has two attributes, named tail and reversed, both of phylum stmtList. Inherited attribute tail collects the abstract translation of the concrete list elements from right to left; the leftmost production of the parse tree passes the abstract list up as the synthesized attribute reversed. Note the attribute equation associated with the entry declaration:

```
stmtList  ~  StmtList.reversed  { StmtList.tail = StmtListNil; };
```

This equation provides a value for the inherited tail attribute of the StmtList instance at the root of the concrete-syntax parse tree.

5.6. Attribution Rules for a List's Completing Term and Placeholder Term

A final consideration when defining a list phylum (of the abstract syntax) is the effect of the attribution rules for the list's completing term and placeholder term. Placeholder-inserting commands make modifications to the edited object's abstract-syntax tree and thus trigger the change-propagation operation that is used to maintain consistent values for the tree's attributes.

Depending on how the editor's attribute equations are written, these insertions and deletions may be quite costly. Thus, it is usually advisable to define the equations for a list's completing term and placeholder term so that insertions and deletions cause as few attributes as possible to require new values. For example, a frequently used attribution pattern is *left-to-right threading*: each phylum has one inherited and one synthesized attribute, and these attributes are used to pass information through the tree from left to right. It is often the case that a list's completing term or placeholder term can pass the information through unchanged. In such a case, the cost of inserting or deleting a placeholder is essentially zero.

CHAPTER 6

Defining Hybrid Editors with the Synthesizer Generator

The purpose of the Synthesizer Generator is to facilitate the construction of editors that provide powerful synthesis, analysis, and manipulation resources while preventing counterproductive and meaningless transactions. These goals are partially met by structure editors, which furnish a set of commands for instantiating and restructuring objects. Structure editors are based on the premise that the objects being edited are not just strings of text, but are hierarchical compositions of well-formed fragments. Structure editors permit objects to be edited in environments that consistently acknowledge and reinforce this viewpoint. One of their principal advantages is that they place constraints on the user's activities that prohibit many common syntactic mistakes. In addition, the editor can take care of details of secondary importance, such as formatting.

At the same time, objects are also collections of text elements: they must be viewed and manipulated with respect to some concrete textual representation. Some operations are most easily done on the string of characters, not the underlying tree. Thus, there is a need for editors to provide both text-editing and structure-editing capabilities so that the user can use the paradigm – structured object or string of characters – that best fits his needs.

An important concern of editor-designers must be to create a harmonious integration of the structural and textual perspectives. There are many possibilities – an entire spectrum of different ways to integrate textual and structural features. For short, we refer to such editors as *hybrid editors*. This chapter discusses the Synthesizer Generator's mechanisms for creating hybrid editors.

Because the Synthesizer Generator is a tool for creating editors, one of our goals is to offer editor-designers the ability to make their own design decisions about the proper balance of text-editing and structure-editing facilities. Consequently, the Synthesizer Generator allows one to define editors that range between the extremes of a pure structure editor and a pure text editor. In this regard, the Synthesizer Generator's capabilities are in contrast to the capabilities of other editor generators, which offer only pure structure editors [Medina-Mora81] or only one particular (although quite powerful) combination of textual and structural operations that is fixed for all generated editors [Bahlke86].

Some of the Synthesizer Specification Language's mechanisms for defining hybrid editors were illustrated previously in the editor specifications used as examples throughout Chapter 4 and Chapter 5. In this chapter, we discuss these mechanisms in more detail and introduce some additional facilities of SSL that were not utilized in previous examples. In addition, we discuss the rationale for the design decisions that shaped SSL.

We focus on how to write the parts of editor specifications that relate specifically to *editing functions* of generated editors; we are concerned with how an editor-designer uses SSL to specify operations for creating and manipulating objects and with how he or she uses SSL to define a language's display format. Because SSL's mechanisms for defining the concrete input language and the display format are based on the attribution mechanism, we will also discuss certain aspects of writing attribution specifications. The use of attributes and attribute equations for defining *static inferences*, such as name analysis and type checking of programs, as illustrated in Chapter 4, is the subject of Chapter 7.

Section 6.1 addresses matters that must be considered when defining the underlying abstract structure of objects being edited. Section 6.2 discusses the SSL constructs for specifying text-editing and structure-editing operations, as well as how to combine them to specify hybrid editors. Section 6.3 concerns SSL's display language and presents examples of how to use attribute values to specify computed display rules. In SSL, the translation of concrete input to abstract syntax is defined by attribution rules; Section 6.4 discusses an extension of the basic mechanism that permits defining the translation of input text to abstract structure so that the translation varies depending on the context in which the object's currently selected constituent is situated.

6.1. Defining a Language's Underlying Abstract Syntax

The underlying abstract syntax of a language is defined with a collection of rules that define phyla and operators. A *phylum* is a nonempty set of terms. A *term* is the application of a k-*ary operator* to k terms of the appropriate phyla. A k-*ary operator* is a constructor function mapping k terms to a term. Operators are typed; the result, as well as each argument position, has an associated phylum. A rule of the form

$$phy_0 : op\ (\ phy_1\ phy_2\ \cdots\ phy_k\ )\ ;$$

declares membership in phy_0 of all terms constructed by the k-ary operator op with arguments $phy_1, phy_2, \cdots phy_k$.

This phylum/operator formalism is essentially a variant notation for context-free grammars; the rule given above is analogous to the context-free production

$$phy_0 \rightarrow phy_1\ phy_2\ \cdots\ phy_k$$

with the following two differences:

1) The operator name op differentiates this production from all other structurally identical alternatives of phy_0.
2) The given operator op may be a member of other phyla, necessarily with the same arity and arguments.

For defining language-based editors, these differences make the phylum/operator formalism a more suitable notation than the nonterminal/production formalism [Donzeau-Gouge75, Medina-Mora81].

As should be apparent from the examples in this book, the operator names that appear in editor specifications play a key role in SSL. The operator names are used in expressions to express construction operations and selection operations on terms. Operator names are also important for supporting modularity in editor specifications. (See Section 8.2, "Modular Construction of Editor Specifications".)

The ability to have operators that are members of more than one phylum (*intersecting phyla*) gives the phylum/operator formalism certain advantages over the nonterminal/production formalism. In particular, editor definitions written with intersecting phyla have the following two properties:

1) Intersecting phyla eliminate from the specification, and therefore from the abstract-syntax tree, the need for nonterminals that are introduced solely for the purpose of factoring the specification.
2) During editing, the root of a pruned subtree can be identified as an instance of a given operator, not as an instance of a given production. Accordingly, it

may be grafted into the tree as an instance of any of the other phyla containing that operator.

Although we employ the vocabulary of phyla and operators throughout the book, the Synthesizer Generator currently supports only one of the two features that makes the phylum/operator formalism novel. The Synthesizer Generator permits operator names to be supplied for all productions, but does not permit the use of intersecting phyla.

To see how the restriction to disjoint phyla can complicate matters, consider the abstract-syntax rules for the phylum exp, a phylum of integer arithmetic expressions. It is clear that the arithmetic operators should be defined by rules like

```
exp      :      Null( )
         |      Plus, Minus, Times, Div(exp  exp)
         |      Uminus(exp)
         ;
```

The question is how to define the integer constants.

Let us first consider how this definition would be expressed in Metal, the specification language of the MENTOR system [Kahn83], which permits intersecting phyla. Abstract-syntax specifications consist of two parts, one that defines the language's operators and a second that defines the language's phyla. For example, to define the arithmetic expressions, the operators are defined by the rules

```
null     →      ;
plus     →      EXP  EXP;
minus    →      EXP  EXP;
times    →      EXP  EXP;
div      →      EXP  EXP;
uminus   →      EXP;
```

The Metal convention is that operator names are in lower case and phyla names in upper case. Operator names appear to the left of the arrow; the operator's arguments and arity are indicated by the list of phyla on the right-hand side. Phylum EXP is defined by the following rule, which names the operators that generate members of EXP:

```
EXP    ::      null plus minus times div uminus INT;
```

One of the features of Metal that is used in this rule is that a phylum name *phy* may be used on the right-hand side of a phylum definition as a shorthand for the

set of operators that are members of *phy*. In the rule for EXP, the phylum name
INT refers to the predefined, countably-infinite set of 0-ary operators:

{ 0, -1, 1, -2, 2, . . . }

Thus, phylum EXP is generated by the set of all of the INT phylum's operators
together with the operators null, plus, minus, times, div, and uminus. Another
way of putting it is that in a phylum definition, phylum names represent sets of
operators, whereas operator names represent singleton sets; the phylum being
defined is the set of terms generated by the union of all these operator sets. The
definition of EXP is really the statement

EXP = {null} ∪ {plus} ∪ {minus} ∪ {times} ∪ {div} ∪ {uminus} ∪ INT

By contrast, in SSL, the abstract-syntax declaration would be defined by the
rules

exp   :   Null( )
        | Plus, Minus, Times, Div(exp exp)
        | Uminus(exp)
        | Const(INT)
        ;

where operator Const is introduced solely to "mediate" from INT objects to
exp objects. Although this definition of phylum exp introduces an extra level in
the abstract-syntax tree, it is possible to hide this extra level from editor users by
defining the unparsing declarations so that they eliminate one of the levels as a
possible resting place.

For example, consider the following unparsing declarations for the operators
defined above:

exp   :   Null   [^ : "<exp>"]
        | Plus   [^ : "(" @ " + " @ ")"]
        | Minus   [^ : "(" @ " – " @ ")"]
        | Times   [^ : "(" @ " * " @ ")"]
        | Div   [^ : "(" @ " / " @ ")"]
        | Uminus   [^ : "–" @]
        | Const   [^ : ^]
        ;

The salient feature of these rules is the definition of resting places in the rule for
operator Const. In particular, the resting-place symbol ^ for the component INT

prevents that component from ever being selected by the user; the absence of a resting place at component INT effectively conceals its presence.

A final word on terminology: because the phylum/operator formalism coincides with the nonterminal/production formalism when all phyla are disjoint, and because the nonterminal/production vocabulary is more widely known, we shall occasionally refer to phyla as "nonterminals," and refer to an occurrence of a given operator in a phylum as a "production."

6.2. Integration of Text Editing and Structure Editing

This section discusses how an editor-designer uses SSL to define different combinations of text-editing and structure-editing operations in hybrid editors. The question is what to edit, the underlying abstract object or a textual representation of the object?

Conventional text editors can be used to create and modify objects of many different classes, including programs, documents, and data files. However, because their basic primitives are for the manipulation of unstructured text, even the "language modes" of extensible text editors such as EMACS [Stallman81] and Z [Wood81], provide nothing more than typographical assistance.

In contrast, structure editors are tailored for editing objects of a particular language, and they provide special facilities based on the structure of objects. One such special facility is the ability to furnish immediate feedback about syntax errors as an object is being developed [Hansen71]. A structure editor can also furnish a collection of powerful transformations for restructuring objects.

Pure structure editors, such as Emily [Hansen71] and GANDALF [Medina-Mora81, Notkin85], require that every syntactic unit be inserted by command. For example, expressions, even though displayed in infix notation, are entered in prefix order with the operators serving as commands. For instance, to enter the expression $(a*b)**((c+d)/e)$, one would enter its constituents in the following order: $**, *, a, b, /, +, c, d, e$. One of the advantages of this approach is that it is possible to generate automatically the parentheses implied by operator precedence and so reduce the number of errors caused by misconceptions about precedence orderings.

Structure editors present a uniform and consistent conceptual framework to the user. The object being edited is an abstract-syntax tree, and the editor provides two kinds of operations: those that navigate through the tree and those that restructure it. However, there are several drawbacks to structure editors, including the following:

- Prefix-order entry of infix expressions can be awkward, and the zig-zag motion of the cursor in the infix display during prefix-order entry can be distracting or confusing. Despite the observation by proponents of structure editors that the nonstandard order of entry will be accepted by users because "people learn to use and love postfix pocket calculators," this feature does present a barrier to acceptance.

- When inserting a new operator or operand, the need to supply a navigation command to terminate the entry of command input leads to an increase in the number of keystrokes required to enter an object and also to a loss of typing continuity.

- Some modifications are more easily accomplished by editing the textual representation than by manipulating the underlying tree.

To address these concerns, some editing systems compromise and offer a combination of text- and structure-editing operations. For example, editors such as Interlisp [Teitelman78] and MENTOR do allow textual input. However, the text becomes structure as soon as the input is parsed; thereafter, only structural modifications of that part of the object are permitted.

A different compromise of text- and structure-editing operations was adopted in the Cornell Program Synthesizer, which strictly partitioned the language into constructs edited as structure and constructs edited as text. A unit entered as a template remained an abstract structure that had to be manipulated as a whole unit; a unit entered as text remained text and had to be modified as text (*e.g.* through single-character insertions and deletions).

Where does the Synthesizer Generator lie on the spectrum between pure structure editing and traditional text editing? Generated editors need be neither pure structure editors nor pure text editors, but can be a hybrid of both. Most importantly, instead of providing one particular combination of textual and structural operations that is fixed for all generated editors, the Synthesizer Generator gives the editor-designer a great deal of freedom to choose his own combination of text- and structure-editing facilities.

For every phylum of the abstract syntax, the editor-designer may specify text-editing facilities, structure-editing facilities, or both. That is, for any phylum of the underlying abstract syntax, the editor-designer can enable the use of one or more of the following types of operations:

- Template-derivation operations for filling in unexpanded placeholders,
- Text-editing operations for filling in unexpanded placeholders,
- Transformation operations for restructuring existing components, and
- Text-editing operations for reediting existing components.

Because these four kinds of facilities are specified by independent parts of SSL specifications, it is possible to create editors that furnish different combinations of hybrid-editing facilities in different contexts. For example, text-editing operations may be permitted for entering a new component at a phylum's place-holders but not for reediting the component, and *vice versa*. A similar statement can be made about template-insertion operations and transformational restructuring operations.

The table presented in Figure 6.1 summarizes the SSL features that govern which kinds of editing facilities will be furnished in generated editors. In Figure 6.1, the mechanisms for specifying entry operations and modification operations have been listed in separate columns.

It is only fair to point out that there does exist another way, not supported by the Synthesizer Generator, of incorporating text editing in language-based editors: make the editor behave as much like an ordinary text editor as possible, but use an incremental parser to do syntax checking so that syntax errors can be reported to the user.

In editors that use an incremental parser, text is entered character by character, as with an ordinary editor. After completion of each transaction, the incremental parser is applied to determine the syntactic correctness of the modification, in the context given by the rest of the object.[1] One incarnation of this idea is based on an incremental parser that assesses the correctness of the entire object. (Algorithms for this kind of incremental parsing have been described in [Wegman80], [Ghezzi79], [Ghezzi80], and [Jalili82].) A second

	Entry	*Modification*
Structure	Transformations whose patterns are placeholder terms	Construct-to-construct transformations
Text	a) Parse rules b) Entry declarations c) Text-entry property of the completing operator's unparsing declaration	a) Parse rules b) Entry declarations c) Text-entry properties of the operators' unparsing declarations

Figure 6.1. Components of editor specifications that govern text-editing and structure-editing operations for entry and modification.

---

[1] The scope of each transaction varies from system to system. In some systems, each insertion or deletion of an individual character is a transaction; in others, a transaction consists of several insertions and deletions.

approach is based on a much different kind of incremental parser – one that determines only whether the text up to the location of the editing cursor is a prefix of some legal object [Wilcox76, Morris81]. The remainder of the object is allowed to contain syntax errors, so it need not be a suffix that matches the prefix. Text may be inserted or deleted freely at the position of the cursor unless an insertion would violate the correct-prefix condition. The user is notified immediately if this occurs, and the attempted insertion is rejected.

The action of editors that use an incremental parser is substantially different from the way parsing is handled in the Synthesizer Generator. An incremental parser is adaptive, reanalyzing as much or as little of the text and the previous parse tree as necessary to determine the new parse tree. In contrast, parsing that takes place in editors generated with the Synthesizer Generator is exhaustive, but over a limited scope – the current selection – whose extent is known before the parse begins.

To illustrate the Synthesizer Generator's mechanisms for specifying hybrid editors, we develop an example that shows how one specifies an editor for creating and modifying lists of integer expressions. To demonstrate how different varieties of hybrid editors are defined with SSL, this section and later parts of the chapter discuss a number of different versions of the expression-list editor, illustrating the range of variation possible.

Expression lists are a feature common to many languages. For example, in many programming languages, expression lists occur as argument lists of function calls, procedure calls, and output statements. Consequently, the examples also serve as a guide for editor-designers who are writing similar parts of their own editor specifications. A significant portion of many editor specifications can be directly modeled on the examples presented below. However, the reader should keep in mind that some of the versions are included merely to exhibit the Synthesizer Generator's capabilities, not because we are recommending that actual editors be patterned after them.

Although some parts of the expression-list specification vary from example to example, there is a set of declarations that forms a common core for all the different variants. The parts common to all of the examples are shown in Figure 6.2. The abstract-syntax rules given in Figure 6.2 define phylum exp_list to be a list of expressions (*i.e.* a list whose elements are in the exp phylum). The unparsing declaration for ExpListPair specifies that exp_lists are to be displayed with a comma and a space between adjacent list elements. Phylum exp is defined to have six operators: the completing operator Null and the five operators Plus, Minus, Times, Div, and Uminus. The names of the latter five are suggestive of their role in representing the five arithmetic operations of addition, subtraction, multiplication, division, and negation. Phylum WHITE-

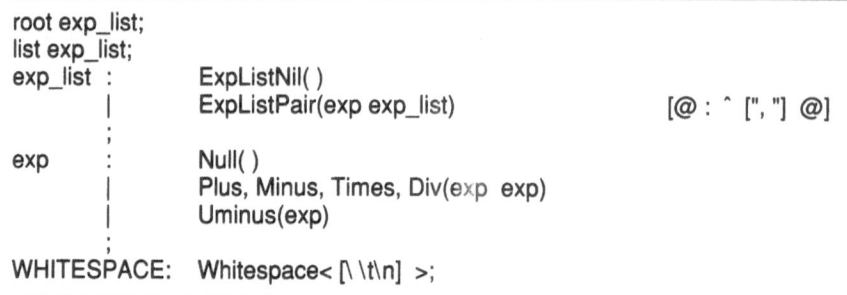

```
root exp_list;
list exp_list;
exp_list :        ExpListNil( )
          |        ExpListPair(exp exp_list)                    [@ : ^ [", "] @]
          ;
exp       :        Null( )
          |        Plus, Minus, Times, Div(exp  exp)
          |        Uminus(exp)
          ;
WHITESPACE:  Whitespace< [\ \t\n] >;
```

Figure 6.2. Abstract-syntax rules and unparsing declarations that are common to all of the versions of the specification of an editor for expression lists that is used in examples throughout the chapter.

SPACE is defined, as usual, to consist of the characters blank, tab, and newline. (The definition of WHITESPACE is not needed for the first variant discussed below because it does not allow text to be entered at any of the grammar's phyla, but WHITESPACE will be needed for all the remaining variants.)

The parts of the specification that vary from example to example consist of (a) declarations for the integer constants, (b) unparsing declarations, which control the way expressions are displayed and specify which operators can be modified with text-editing operations, (c) transformation declarations, and (d) (in some cases) lexical and parsing declarations.

6.2.1. Structural entry

Structure editing is carried out using a set of editor commands that restructure objects. New objects, or new fragments of objects, are created using a subset of the structure-editing commands, called *template* commands. Templates are predefined fragments of objects that may contain additional placeholders. A template's placeholders provide a framework for the insertion of additional elements in an object. Templates permit the user to create objects by deriving them top down.

Structure-editing operations are specified by transformation declarations of the form

transform *phylum* on *transformation-name pattern : expression* ;

This defines a command, with the given *transformation-name*, that means, "If the current selection of the abstract-syntax tree matches *pattern*, replace it by the result of evaluating *expression*."

A template command is a transformation command that transforms a place-holder term or a completing term into the term defined by the expression on the template's right-hand side. Template commands are specified by transformation declarations of a particularly simple form: the left-hand-side pattern is a place-holder term or a completing term. That is, a template command takes one of the following two forms:

transform *phylum* on *transformation-name* *<phylum>* : *expression* ;
transform *phylum* on *transformation-name* *[phylum]* : *expression* ;

Variation 1: A Pure Structure Editor

The first variant of the specification for the expression-list editor that we consider defines the editor so that its only entry operations are template commands: no text-editing operations are allowed at all. Expressions and integer constants must be derived top down, using template commands. To define this editor, the core specification of Figure 6.2 is extended in two ways:

1) Template commands and unparsing declarations are defined for the arithmetic operators.
2) Abstract-syntax rules, template commands, and unparsing declarations are defined for the integer constants.

These different aspects are described in detail below.

Template commands and unparsing declarations for the arithmetic operators

The template commands for the five arithmetic operators are defined with the following transformation declarations:

```
transform exp
        on "+" <exp> : Plus(<exp>, <exp>),
        on "–" <exp> : Minus(<exp>, <exp>),
        on "*" <exp> : Times(<exp>, <exp>),
        on "/" <exp> : Div(<exp>, <exp>),
        on "u–" <exp> : Uminus(<exp>)
        ;
```

These declarations define commands that transform an expression placeholder to a one-level term that contains either one or two additional placeholders itself. For example, the template command defined by the first declaration can be used to transform an expression placeholder (*i.e.* the term Null) into the term

Plus(Null, Null); the latter term contains an additional pair of placeholders.

The unparsing declarations define the display representation of phylum exp to be the conventional infix notation for arithmetic expressions, but with a pair of parentheses enclosing each subexpression whose root is one of the four binary operators.

```
exp      :      Null        [^ : "<exp>" ]
         |      Plus        [^ : "(" @ " + " @ ")" ]
         |      Minus       [^ : "(" @ " – " @ ")" ]
         |      Times       [^ : "(" @ " * " @ ")" ]
         |      Div         [^ : "(" @ " / " @ ")" ]
         |      Uminus      [^ : "–" @ ]
         ;
```

These unparsing declarations specify that an expression will be displayed fully parenthesized. For example, the term Plus(Null, Minus(Uminus(Null), Null)) will be displayed as

(<exp> + (–<exp> – <exp>))

Definitions for integer constants

The remaining declarations of the editor's specification define a phylum of integer constants. The integers are represented by the elements of phylum digitList.

```
list digitList;
digitList : DigitListNull( )
          | DigitListPair(digit digitList)
          ;
digit     : DigitNull, Zero, One, Two, Three, Four, Five, Six,
                       Seven, Eight, Nine( )
          ;
```

The unparsing declaration for DigitListPair specifies that a digitList will be displayed with no separator between adjacent list elements.

```
digitList : DigitListPair        [@ : ^ @];
```

The display representations of the individual operators of phylum digit consist of the appropriate numerals. These are defined by the following unparsing declarations:

digit	:	DigitNull	[^ : "<digit>"]
	|	Zero	[^ : "0"]
	|	One	[^ : "1"]
	|	Two	[^ : "2"]
	|	Three	[^ : "3"]
	|	Four	[^ : "4"]
	|	Five	[^ : "5"]
	|	Six	[^ : "6"]
	|	Seven	[^ : "7"]
	|	Eight	[^ : "8"]
	|	Nine	[^ : "9"]
	;		

A collection of templates for inserting the different operators of phylum digit are defined by the following template declarations:

```
transform digit
        on "0" <digit> : Zero,
        on "1" <digit> : One,
        on "2" <digit> : Two,
        on "3" <digit> : Three,
        on "4" <digit> : Four,
        on "5" <digit> : Five,
        on "6" <digit> : Six,
        on "7" <digit> : Seven,
        on "8" <digit> : Eight,
        on "9" <digit> : Nine
        ;
```

To allow integer constants as components of expressions, a new operator of phylum exp is defined, whose single argument is a digitList.

```
exp    :      Const(digitList) [^ : @ ];
```

It is also necessary to add a new template to permit a Const term with an empty digitList to be inserted at an unexpanded expression. The template is defined by the following transformation declaration:

```
transform exp on "const" <exp> : Const(<digitList>);
```

The editor specified by the rules given above is a rather simple structure editor.[2] It provides template commands for entering each arithmetic operator and each individual digit of integer constants. An example showing the insertion of the integer 12 is presented in the six snapshots in Figure 6.3.

The only editing operations permitted at interior nodes of the abstract-syntax tree are the basic cut-and-paste operations. To see how to define text- and structure-editing operations for modifying expression lists, refer to Section 6.2.3, "Textual modifications," and Section 6.2.4, "Structural modifications," respectively.

6.2.2. Textual entry

The expression-list editor defined in the previous section is a pure structure editor. Anyone who used it would probably be frustrated by it because entering an integer constant is very awkward. As Figure 6.3 illustrates, the editor user is required to derive integer constants one digit at a time, using a template command to insert each digit. Between insertions, the user has to invoke the traversal command **forward-with-optionals** to advance the selection to the next placeholder. We now describe a number of different variations on this expression-list editor.

For the variant discussed next, as well as for the ones presented in the rest of the chapter, it is desirable to change the specification's abstract-syntax rules that define the integer constants. Rather than representing the integer constants by a list of digits (*i.e.* phylum digitList), we alter the declaration of the Const operator so that an integer constant is represented by a value of the built-in phylum INT:

exp   :   Const(INT)   [ˆ : ˆ];

In the discussion that follows, we need to distinguish between the two entry modes allowed in generated editors. We use the terms *text entry* to refer to the process of entering new text at a placeholder and *text editing* to refer to the process of modifying the text representation of an object using operations on the sequence of characters. The term *input text* will refer to the new text that is entered, in the case of text entry, and to the modified text of the current selection, in the case of text editing. The term *command entry* refers to the entry mode used for entering commands, and characters that are entered during command entry will be referred to as *command text*. Command text is echoed in the

---

[2]Some might even say idiotic!

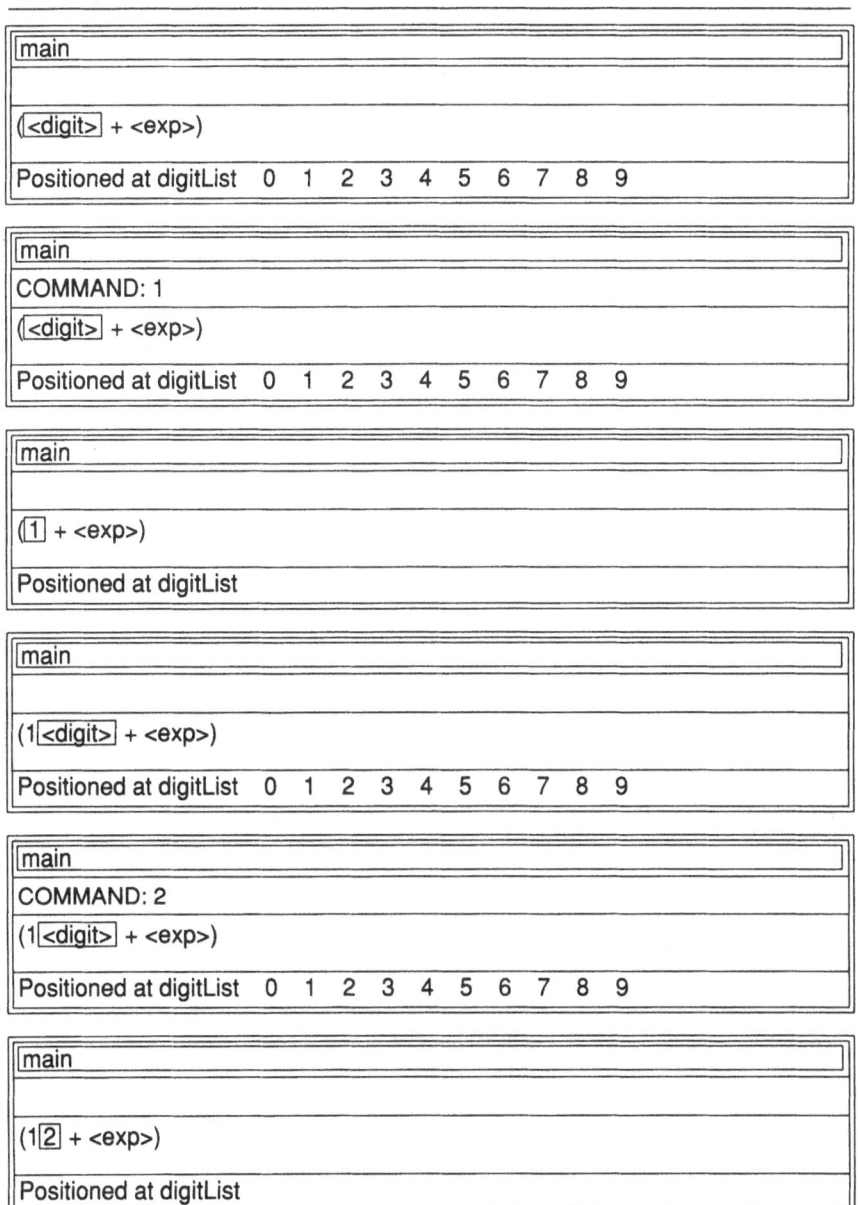

Figure 6.3. Snapshots of the display that illustrate the use of template commands to enter the integer 12.

window's command line, in the top line of the window, whereas input text is echoed in place, at the position of the window's current selection.

We now discuss how to define five different kinds of hybrid editors. For each case, we describe how to specify an expression-list editor that incorporates the desired features.

Variation 2: Text Entry of Integer Constants

The first variant of the expression-list editor permits text entry of integer constants: integers can be entered directly as text whenever the selection is positioned at an expression placeholder.

To enable text entry at unexpanded expressions, we change the text-entry property associated with the operator Null from ::= to :. The unparsing declaration for Null now looks like

exp   :   Null   [ˆ ::= "<exp>"];

The rest of the unparsing declarations remain unchanged:

exp   :   Plus   [ˆ : "(" @ " + " @ ")"]
        | Minus   [ˆ : "(" @ " – " @ ")"]
        | Times   [ˆ : "(" @ " * " @ ")"]
        | Div   [ˆ : "(" @ " / " @ ")"]
        | Uminus   [ˆ : "–" @]
        ;

These declarations permit text-entry operations for entering new expressions, but forbid text-editing for reediting already existing expressions. This is governed by the text-entry symbols of the specification's unparsing declarations. The relevant feature of the unparsing declarations is that the text-entry symbol ::=, which permits text to be entered, appears only in the declaration for the operator Null. In contrast, the symbol :, which forbids text to be entered, appears in the unparsing declarations for all the other operators of phylum exp, thereby forbidding textual reediting of expressions.

A second detail of the unparsing declarations that the reader should not overlook is that the unparsing declaration for ExpListPair still uses the symbol : rather than ::=.

exp_list :   ExpListPair   [@ : ˆ [", "] @];

This apparently disables the ability to enter text at list selections; however, when the selection is a singleton sublist, the text-entry property of the root of the list element is also taken into account when the editor determines whether text editing is permitted. (For further details, see Section 5.4, "Selections of Singleton Sublists Versus Selections of List Elements.") Consequently, the declarations given above allow the user to enter text when the currently selected constituent is a singleton sublist that consists of an expression placeholder; text editing is forbidden for all other kinds of sublist selections.

We now turn to the lexical and parsing declarations that govern the form of the input text that is allowed to be entered. The declaration of token INTEGER defines the syntax of integer constants; INTEGER is specified to be a string of numerals:

INTEGER: Integer< [0–9]+ >;

The parsing rules and their attribution declarations define how Exp-valued and ExpList-valued parse trees are translated to values of phyla exp and exp_list, respectively.

```
Exp { synthesized exp abs; };
Exp  ::=  (INTEGER)   { Exp.abs = Const(STRtoINT(INTEGER)); };
exp   ~   Exp.abs;

ExpList { synthesized exp_list abs; };
ExpList  ::=  (Exp)   { ExpList.abs = Exp.abs :: ExpListNil; };
exp_list  ~   ExpList.abs;
```

Note that the call on the built-in function STRtoINT has the effect of converting the text of the INTEGER token to a value of phylum INT.

To complete the specification of the editor, transformation declarations define templates for the five arithmetic operators:

```
transform exp
        on "+" <exp> : Plus(<exp>, <exp>),
        on "–" <exp> : Minus(<exp>, <exp>),
        on "*" <exp> : Times(<exp>, <exp>),
        on "/" <exp> : Div(<exp>, <exp>),
        on "u–" <exp> : Uminus(<exp>)
        ;
```

These rules are identical to the template declarations used in the pure structure editor specified in Section 6.2.1, "Structural entry," except that because integers are entered directly as text, there is no need to have a template for operator Const.

The version of the expression-list editor specified by the rules given above is a hybrid of a text editor and a structure editor. Arithmetic operators are entered top down using template commands; integer constants are entered by typing the text of the integer directly. Template commands are echoed in the command line, whereas text entered for integer constants is echoed in-place at the position of the window's current selection. Figure 6.4 shows the integer 123 being entered. From top to bottom, the snapshots portray the state of the screen as the characters 1, 2, and 3 are entered, followed by the command **forward-with-optionals**, which terminates entry and advances the selection to the next component of the tree.

Variation 3: Text Entry of Arbitrary Expressions

A second hybrid version of the expression-list editor can be created by extending the editor's specification with additional parsing rules to allow arbitrary expressions to be entered as text. The rules define the translation of the text of an arbitrary expression to a term of the underlying abstract syntax.

```
left '+' '-';
left '*' '/';
Exp  ::=  (Exp '+' Exp)  { Exp$1.abs = Plus( Exp$2.abs, Exp$3.abs); }
     |    (Exp '-' Exp)  { Exp$1.abs = Minus(Exp$2.abs, Exp$3.abs); }
     |    (Exp '*' Exp)  { Exp$1.abs = Times(Exp$2.abs, Exp$3.abs); }
     |    (Exp '/' Exp)  { Exp$1.abs = Div(Exp$2.abs, Exp$3.abs); }
     |    ('-' Exp)      { Exp$1.abs = Uminus(Exp$2.abs); }
     |    ('(' Exp ')')  { Exp$1.abs = Exp$2.abs; }
     ;
```

These rules specify the concrete syntax by ambiguous parsing rules, but precedence declarations are supplied to disambiguate them. (In the example above, the precedence declarations are the lines that begin with the keyword left.)

The LALR(1) parser generator yacc [Johnson78], which is used by the Synthesizer Generator to create an editor's parser, makes use of precedence declarations to resolve ambiguities in the grammar rules. Ambiguities are of two types, corresponding to the following kinds of conflicts that would arise if there were no disambiguation mechanism:

1) A *shift/reduce* conflict arises if there is no way to decide, based on the contents of the stack and the next token α, whether to apply a reduction rule to the stack or to shift α onto the stack, thereby deferring the reduction.

2) A *reduce/reduce* conflict arises when more than one reduction can be applied to the stack.

```
┌─────────────────────────────────────────────────────────┐
│ ┌─────────────────────────────────────────────────────┐ │
│ │main                                                   │ │
│ ├─────────────────────────────────────────────────────┤ │
│ │                                                       │ │
│ ├─────────────────────────────────────────────────────┤ │
│ │(│<exp>│ + 3)                                          │ │
│ ├─────────────────────────────────────────────────────┤ │
│ │Positioned at exp    +    -    *    /    u─             │ │
│ └─────────────────────────────────────────────────────┘ │
└─────────────────────────────────────────────────────────┘
```

```
┌─────────────────────────────────────────────────────────┐
│ ┌─────────────────────────────────────────────────────┐ │
│ │main                                                   │ │
│ ├─────────────────────────────────────────────────────┤ │
│ │                                                       │ │
│ ├─────────────────────────────────────────────────────┤ │
│ │(│1 │    + 3)                                          │ │
│ ├─────────────────────────────────────────────────────┤ │
│ │Positioned at exp    +    -    *    /    u─             │ │
│ └─────────────────────────────────────────────────────┘ │
└─────────────────────────────────────────────────────────┘
```

```
┌─────────────────────────────────────────────────────────┐
│ ┌─────────────────────────────────────────────────────┐ │
│ │main                                                   │ │
│ ├─────────────────────────────────────────────────────┤ │
│ │                                                       │ │
│ ├─────────────────────────────────────────────────────┤ │
│ │(│12 │    + 3)                                         │ │
│ ├─────────────────────────────────────────────────────┤ │
│ │Positioned at exp    +    -    *    /    u─             │ │
│ └─────────────────────────────────────────────────────┘ │
└─────────────────────────────────────────────────────────┘
```

```
┌─────────────────────────────────────────────────────────┐
│ ┌─────────────────────────────────────────────────────┐ │
│ │main                                                   │ │
│ ├─────────────────────────────────────────────────────┤ │
│ │                                                       │ │
│ ├─────────────────────────────────────────────────────┤ │
│ │(│123 │    + 3)                                        │ │
│ ├─────────────────────────────────────────────────────┤ │
│ │Positioned at exp    +    -    *    /    u─             │ │
│ └─────────────────────────────────────────────────────┘ │
└─────────────────────────────────────────────────────────┘
```

```
┌─────────────────────────────────────────────────────────┐
│ ┌─────────────────────────────────────────────────────┐ │
│ │main                                                   │ │
│ ├─────────────────────────────────────────────────────┤ │
│ │                                                       │ │
│ ├─────────────────────────────────────────────────────┤ │
│ │(123 + │3│)                                            │ │
│ ├─────────────────────────────────────────────────────┤ │
│ │Positioned at exp                                      │ │
│ └─────────────────────────────────────────────────────┘ │
└─────────────────────────────────────────────────────────┘
```

Figure 6.4. Snapshots of the display that illustrate text entry to input the integer 123. From top to bottom: the characters 1, 2, and 3 are entered, followed by the command **forward-with-optionals**, which terminates entry and advances the selection to the next component of the tree.

Precedence declarations define precedence levels and associativity for tokens. There are three kinds of associativity: a precedence declaration defines a token to be either left associative, right associative, or nonassociative (according to the respective keywords left, right, and nonassoc). All tokens in a single precedence declaration are assigned the same level and associativity. Precedence levels are assigned lowest to highest in the order the declarations are encountered in the specification. The precedence declarations also define a precedence level and associativity for each parsing rule: a parsing rule is assigned the precedence level and associativity of the final token that appears in the rule.[3]

Using the precedence declarations that are supplied by the editor-designer, conflicts are resolved by the following three rules:

1) In the case of a potential shift/reduce conflict, if both the grammar rule and the look-ahead symbol have an associated precedence and associativity, the conflict is resolved in favor of the action that has the higher precedence. If the precedence levels are identical, then the associativity comes into play: left associativity selects the reduce action, right associativity selects the shift action, and non-associativity raises an error.

2) In the case of a potential shift/reduce conflict that cannot be resolved by the rule above, a parser is still produced with the conflict resolved in favor of the shift action.

3) In the case of a potential reduce/reduce conflict, the conflict is resolved in favor of the rule that is listed earlier in the editor specification.

For cases 2 and 3, the conflicts are reported as editor-generation-time warnings, during the phase when yacc is invoked by sgen.

For the two previous versions of the expression-list editor, the respective editor specifications consisted of the declarations that are listed in Figure 6.2, plus the additional declarations introduced in the course of describing that particular version. Henceforth we shall no longer list the complete specification, but just provide the declarations that make the new version different from one of the previous versions that has been discussed.

Variation 3 of the expression-list editor is created by appending the parsing and precedence declarations given above to all the rules that were used to create Variation 2. Variation 3 permits the user to create new expressions by entering the expression's text at an expression placeholder. Figure 6.5 shows the expression 2 + 4 being entered. From top to bottom, the snapshots of the display that

---

[3]It is possible to assign a different level to a parsing rule using a prec directive. For example, to declare that the rule for parsing unary minus has the same precedence level as the '*' token, one could use the following declaration:

Exp   ::=   ('–' Exp prec '*')   { Exp$1.abs = Uminus(Exp$2.abs); };

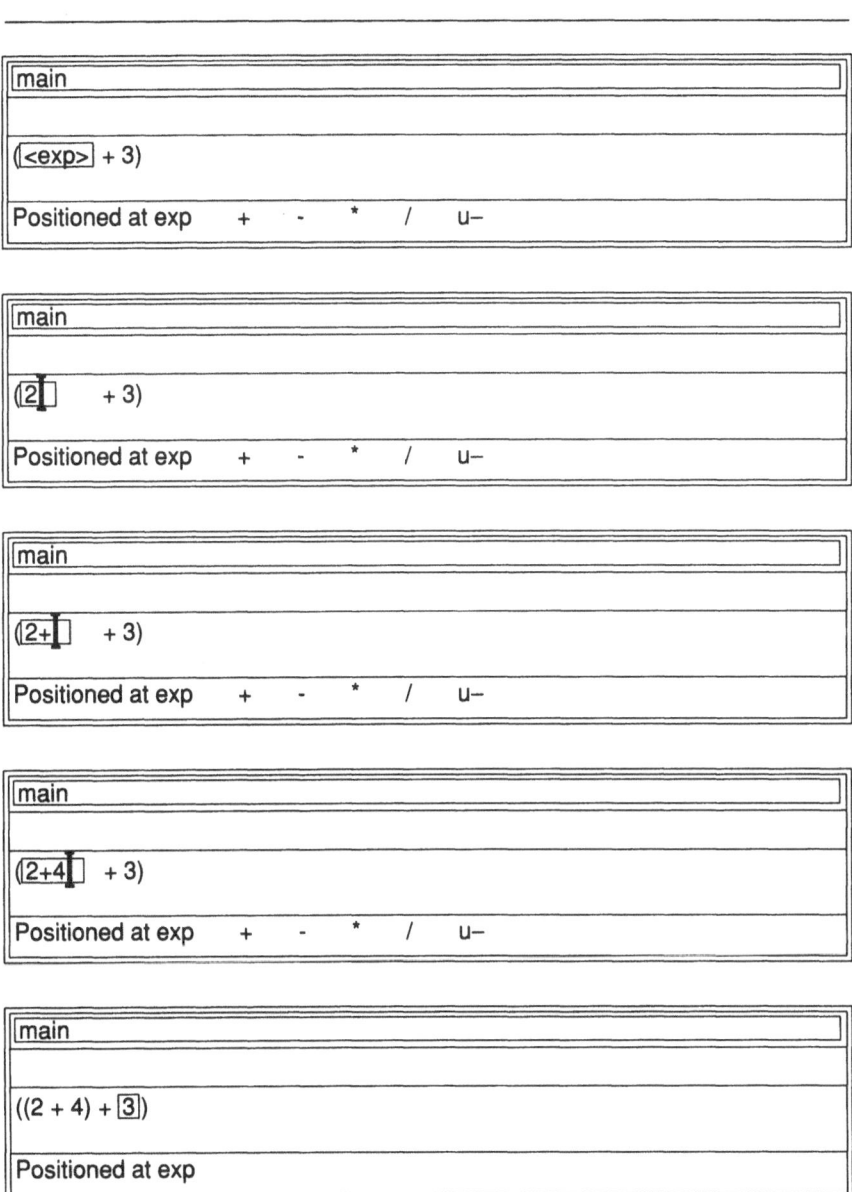

Figure 6.5. Snapshots of the display that illustrate text entry to input the expression 2 + 4. From top to bottom: the characters 2, +, and 4 are entered, followed by the command **forward-with-optionals**, which terminates entry and advances the selection to the next component of the tree.

are depicted show the characters 2, +, and 4 being entered, followed by a command to terminate text entry and advance the selection to the next component.

The editor defined by this version of the editor specification will exhibit the hybrid-editing characteristics of the Interlisp and MENTOR editors; input that the user types as text gets turned into structure that can only be re-edited by structural cut-and-paste operations.

In our opinion, it is usually a mistake to define such an editing interface, for it gives an inconsistent treatment of entry and modification operations. The object is entered as text, not according to its structure, so it is not obvious what the underlying structure is when the user reedits it. Although this is not really a problem in the Interlisp editor because Lisp has a trivial abstract syntax, the inconsistency is likely to be a real problem for a language with a more complicated syntax, such as languages in the Algol family.

One of our design goals was to give editor-designers as much freedom as possible to design whatever user interface deemed desirable. Thus, although we felt the user interface incorporated in the version of the expression-list editor that is described above is not a particularly desirable combination of text editing and structure editing, we felt that SSL had to be expressive enough to allow its specification.

Variation 4: Text Entry of Expression Lists

A drawback of Variation 3 is that it permits only a single expression to be entered at an expression placeholder, even when the current selection is a singleton sublist of exp_list. The fourth version of the editor rectifies this so that several expressions can be entered at once.

To permit the input of multiple expressions, we must replace the parsing rules for concrete phylum ExpList. The rules that follow provide a new definition of the translation of ExpList to abstract phylum exp_list. With the rules given below, input is permitted to be a comma-separated list of expressions.

```
ExpList {
        inherited exp_list tail;
        synthesized exp_list reversed;
        };
exp_list ~        ExpList.reversed  { ExpList.tail = ExpListNil; };
ExpList ::=        (Exp) { ExpList.reversed = Exp.abs :: ExpList.tail; }
        |        (ExpList ',' Exp) {
                        ExpList$2.tail = Exp.abs :: ExpList$1.tail;
                        ExpList$1.reversed = ExpList$2.reversed;
                        }

        ;
```

Figure 6.6 shows the last step of entering the list 2 + 3, 4 + 5; command
forward-with-optionals terminates text entry and advances the selection to a
new expression placeholder.

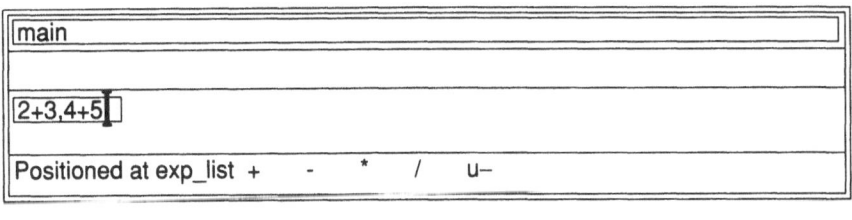

Figure 6.6. Snapshots of the display that illustrate text entry to input the expressions 2 +
3 and 4 + 5. From top to bottom: the character string 2+3,4+5 is entered, followed by
command **forward-with-optionals**, which terminates entry and advances the selection to
a new expression placeholder.

Variation 5: Expressions as Phrases

Yet another version of the expression-list editor implements expressions that are *phrases*, or units that can be selected and modified only as an entire unit. This version can be obtained by replacing the unparsing declarations that were given previously by

exp	:	Null	[^ ::= "<exp>"]
	|	Plus	[^ : "(" ^ " + " ^ ")"]
	|	Minus	[^ : "(" ^ " – " ^ ")"]
	|	Times	[^ : "(" ^ " * " ^ ")"]
	|	Div	[^ : "(" ^ " / " ^ ")"]
	|	Uminus	[^ : "–" ^]
	|	Const	[^ : ^]
	;		

The use of ^ for the resting-place properties of the phylum occurrences in these operators means that it will not be possible to select arbitrary subexpressions of an expression; it will only be possible to make selections of sublists – including singleton sublists – of the expression list. For example, if a selection is made with the locator pointing to a character that is within an expression e, the operation will actually cause the selection to be set to the singleton sublist that contains e.

Variation 6: Defining a Structural Interface Where Commands are Typed in Place

In the editors illustrated thus far, whenever a command is entered, the characters of the command are echoed in the command line (the top line of the window) rather than "in-place" at the location of the currently selected constituent. In contrast, when generated editors permit the user to enter fragments of objects directly as text, the characters that the user types are echoed in-place. (To see examples that illustrate the differences in the two modes of entry, refer back to Figures 6.3 – 6.6.)

In this section, we show how to define an editor that acts like an ordinary structure editor, except that the user is able to type commands in-place in the window rather than in the window's command line.

The use of the attribution mechanism for translating input text to an abstract-syntax tree provides an editor-designer with a powerful formalism that can be used to define textual and structural interfaces in whatever balance is desired. The editor-designer is free to define parsing rules to recognize whatever input language he feels is appropriate; in particular, the definition of the concrete-input language that is accepted need not be restricted to legal fragments of the object's display representation. The attribute equations that the editor-designer supplies with the parsing rules define the translation of the input text to the corresponding term of the abstract syntax. To create a structure editor in which the user is allowed to type his commands in-place, the editor-designer defines the concrete-input language to consist of simple command strings, and specifies attribution rules that translate each string to an appropriate template term (*i.e.* to the kind of one-level term that appears in the usual template declarations).

Variation 6 is defined with all the rules for Variation 2, except that the transformation declarations that define the five templates of Variation 2 are replaced by the parsing rules given below. With these rules, a string prefaced by a period (.) acts like an in-place "command" for template-style insertion of the arithmetic operators. For instance, the input text .+ is translated either to the term Plus(Null, Null) or to the term Plus(Null,Null) :: ExpListNil, depending, respectively, on whether the current selection is an exp or an exp_list.

```
ExpCommand { synthesized exp abs; };
exp  ~  ExpCommand.abs;
ExpCommand
        ::= ('.' '+')     { ExpCommand.abs = Plus(<exp>, <exp>); }
         |  ('.' '–')     { ExpCommand.abs = Minus(<exp>, <exp>); }
         |  ('.' '*')     { ExpCommand.abs = Times(<exp>, <exp>); }
         |  ('.' '/')     { ExpCommand.abs = Div(<exp>, <exp>); }
         |  ('.' 'u' '–') { ExpCommand.abs = Uminus(<exp>); }
        ;
```

```
ExpListCommand { synthesized exp_list abs; };
exp_list  ~  ExpListCommand.abs;
ExpListCommand ::= (ExpCommand)
        { ExpListCommand.abs = ExpCommand.abs :: ExpListNil; };
```

Because these rules are parsing rules, and not transformation declarations, they apply only to input text and not to command text. Obviously, we also have to modify Variation 2 to allow input text to be entered at exp placeholders. This is governed by the unparsing declaration for the Null operator, which must make use of the ::= text-entry property. The appropriate unparsing declaration, shown earlier, is repeated for emphasis:

```
exp    :       Null              [^ ::= "<exp>" ];
```

The rules given above define a set of editing commands that implement a structural interface; it differs from the structural interface incorporated in Variation 2 in that the user is allowed to type his commands as input text, which means that they are echoed in-place, at the currently selected constituent, rather than in the window's command line.

Figure 6.7 shows a sequence of snapshots of the display that illustrate a template being inserted using Variation 6. Note that the input text .+ is echoed in-place. In the last snapshot, the text has parsed successfully by the rules for phylum ExpCommand; the resulting template term, Plus(Null, Null), computed by the attribution rules of the ExpCommand grammar, has been inserted in the tree and the selection has been advanced to the next placeholder.

```
┌────────────────────────────────────────────┐
│ main                                         │
├────────────────────────────────────────────┤
│                                              │
│ (⌊<exp>⌋ + 3)                                │
├────────────────────────────────────────────┤
│ Positioned at exp                            │
└────────────────────────────────────────────┘

┌────────────────────────────────────────────┐
│ main                                         │
├────────────────────────────────────────────┤
│                                              │
│ (.+□    + 3)                                 │
├────────────────────────────────────────────┤
│ Positioned at exp                            │
└────────────────────────────────────────────┘

┌────────────────────────────────────────────┐
│ main                                         │
├────────────────────────────────────────────┤
│                                              │
│ ((⌊<exp>⌋ + <exp>) + 3)                      │
├────────────────────────────────────────────┤
│ Positioned at exp                            │
└────────────────────────────────────────────┘
```

Figure 6.7. Snapshots of the display that, from top to bottom, illustrate text input that is interpreted as a command to insert a template.

6.2.3. Textual modifications

In all the versions of the expression-list editor discussed in the previous two sections, there are only two ways to modify an existing expression: either reorganize it using the basic cut-and-paste operations or replace it entirely by first deleting the old expression and then entering the new one in its entirety.

SSL also allows the editor-designer to define operations for reediting objects. In this section, we discuss how to change the specification of the expression-list editor to allow text editing of expressions. Section 6.2.4 discusses how to define construct-to-construct transformations that permit the user to make structural modifications of expressions.

Text editing is controlled by the text-entry symbol that appears in an operator's unparsing declaration. In the previous section, which discussed how to specify textual operations for creating new objects, the relevant text-entry symbol was the one for the operator Null because Null is the operator that appears at the root of the placeholder term. To allow textual modifications of terms other than the placeholder term, the unparsing declarations for the other operators of the specification are changed to use the text-entry symbol ::= in place of :.

Variation 7: Textual Reediting of Expressions

In the unparsing declarations given below, the text-entry property of each operator is ::=, rather than :, as in the unparsing declarations that have appeared earlier.

```
exp    :    Null         [ ^ ::= "<exp>" ]
       |    Plus         [ ^ ::= "(" ^ " + " ^ ")" ]
       |    Minus        [ ^ ::= "(" ^ " – " ^ ")" ]
       |    Times        [ ^ ::= "(" ^ " * " ^ ")" ]
       |    Div          [ ^ ::= "(" ^ " / " ^ ")" ]
       |    Uminus       [ ^ ::= "–" ^ ]
       |    Const        [ ^ ::= ^ ]
       ;
```

These rules define an editor in which expressions are treated as phrases. Because there are no resting places at interior nodes of expressions, it is not possible to make selections of subexpressions, so it will not be possible to restructure expressions by cutting and pasting subexpressions. In this variation, expressions can only be modified by applying text-editing operations to their textual representation.

An editor specification that permits textual reediting really only makes sense if text can be reparsed, and in particular only if slightly modified text can be reparsed. What this means for the editor-designer is that the display image of an object, generated from the unparsing declarations, should be a subset of the input language that is defined by the parsing rules. For example, for this version of the editor, we want to incorporate parsing rules that allow arbitrary expressions to be parsed. The rules for Exp have been given earlier, but are repeated below for emphasis; the rules for ExpList are written so that only a singleton sublist can be parsed:

```
Exp { synthesized exp abs; };
exp      ~ Exp.abs;
left '+' '–';
left '*' '/';
INTEGER: Integer< [0–9]+ >;
Exp  ::=   (INTEGER)    { Exp.abs = Const(STRtoINT(INTEGER)); }
       |   (Exp '+' Exp) { Exp$1.abs = Plus( Exp$2.abs, Exp$3.abs); }
       |   (Exp '–' Exp) { Exp$1.abs = Minus(Exp$2.abs, Exp$3.abs); }
       |   (Exp '*' Exp) { Exp$1.abs = Times(Exp$2.abs, Exp$3.abs); }
       |   (Exp '/' Exp) { Exp$1.abs = Div(Exp$2.abs, Exp$3.abs); }
       |   ('–' Exp)     { Exp$1.abs = Uminus(Exp$2.abs); }
       |   ('(' Exp ')') { Exp$1.abs = Exp$2.abs; }
       ;
```

```
ExpList { synthesized exp_list abs; };
exp_list ~ ExpList.abs;
ExpList ::=     (Exp)             { ExpList.abs = Exp.abs :: ExpListNil; };
```

Note that the parsing declarations and the unparsing declarations given in this section are mutually compatible in the sense that the display image generated by the unparsing declarations will always be a subset of what is parsable by the parsing rules.

Figure 6.8 shows a sequence of snapshots of the display that illustrate the expression $((2 + 3) + 4)$ being reedited. From top to bottom, they portray the state of the screen as the character 3 is replaced by 6. In the final image, the modified text has been successfully re-parsed, the new term Plus(Plus(2, 6), 4) has been inserted, and the selection has been advanced to the next placeholder.

This version of the expression-list editor defines essentially the same mix of hybrid-editing operations that was permitted by the Cornell Program Synthesizer's editor. By permitting only one editing style for each syntactic

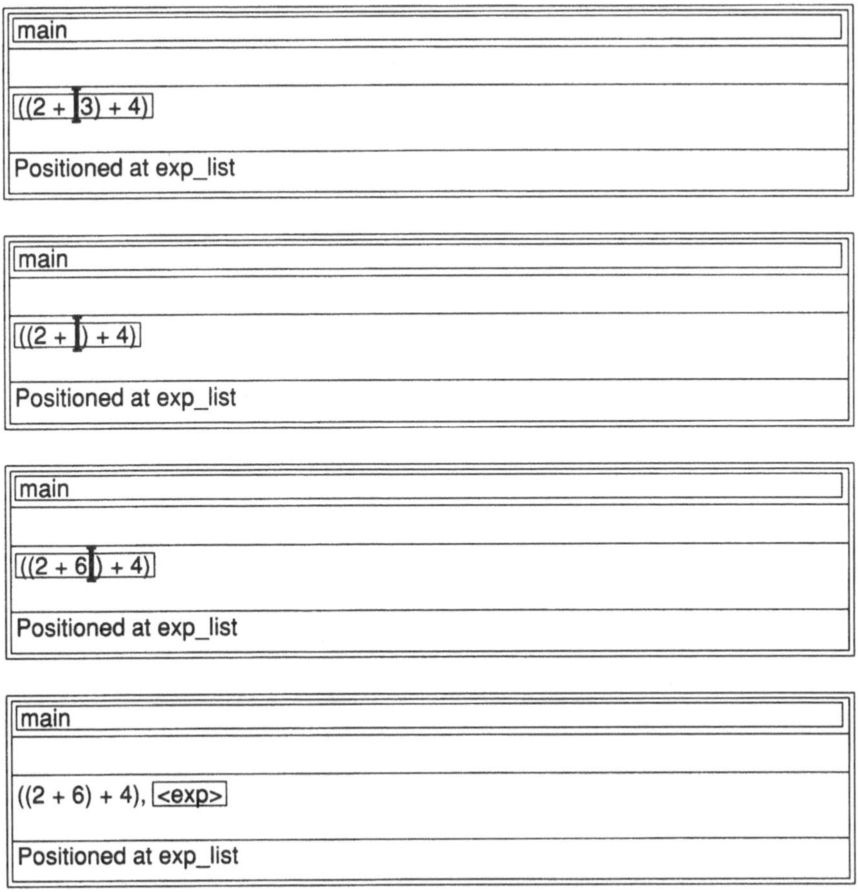

Figure 6.8. Snapshots of the display that, from top to bottom, illustrate textual reediting of the expression ((2 + 3) + 4).

unit, the Cornell Program Synthesizer promoted a consistent conceptual viewpoint. Although it did not provide any transformation operations for restructuring expressions, this particular hybrid of text and structure sacrificed little, since most expressions are short and have relatively simple structure.

Variation 8: Textual Reediting of Sublists

Variation 7 permits textual modification only when the selection is a *singleton* sublist. A simple change to the specification permits text-editing operations when the selection is an arbitrary sublist of the expression list. The text-entry properties are changed to the following rules:

```
exp_list :       ExpListPair    [@ ::= ^ [", "] @];
exp      :       Null           [^ : "<exp>" ]
         |       Plus           [^ : "(" ^ " + " ^ ")" ]
         |       Minus          [^ : "(" ^ " − " ^ ")" ]
         |       Times          [^ : "(" ^ " * " ^ ")" ]
         |       Div            [^ : "(" ^ " / " ^ ")" ]
         |       Uminus         [^ : "−" ^ ]
         |       Const          [^ : ^ ]
         ;
```

Note the use of ::= in the rule for ExpListPair. The choice between : and ::= in the rules for Null, Plus, *etc.* is irrelevant.

We also must add the parsing rules from Variation 4 that permit the textual input of exp_lists in the form of comma-separated lists of expressions:

```
ExpList {
        inherited exp_list tail;
        synthesized exp_list reversed;
        };
exp_list ~      ExpList.reversed { ExpList.tail = ExpListNil; };
ExpList ::=     (Exp) { ExpList.reversed = Exp.abs :: ExpList.tail; }
        |       (ExpList ',' Exp) {
                        ExpList$2.tail = Exp.abs :: ExpList$1.tail;
                        ExpList$1.reversed = ExpList$2.reversed;
                        }
        ;
```

Variation 9: Full Hybrid Editing

There are usually advantages to be gained by having subexpressions be select-able. This is allowed by the following unparsing declarations, which, in con-junction with the parsing declarations given previously, implement full hybrid editing:

exp	:	Null	[^ ::= "<exp>"]
	|	Plus	[^ ::= "(" @ " + " @ ")"]
	|	Minus	[^ ::= "(" @ " – " @ ")"]
	|	Times	[^ ::= "(" @ " * " @ ")"]
	|	Div	[^ ::= "(" @ " / " @ ")"]
	|	Uminus	[^ ::= "–" @]
	|	Const	[^ ::= ^]
	;		

6.2.4. Structural modifications

Editor commands that restructure objects are defined with transformation declarations that have the form

transform *phylum* on *transformation-name pattern* : *expression* ;

A transformation declaration defines a command *transformation-name* that means: "If the current selection of the abstract-syntax tree matches *pattern*, replace it by the result of evaluating *expression*." The patterns allowed are exactly those allowed in with-expressions. Recall that if no pattern variable is desired in a given argument position, it can be replaced by an asterisk (*); however, a transformation so defined will lose information when it is applied.

Variation 10: Transformation Commands for Restructuring Expressions

The following transformation declarations define commands for restructuring expressions according to the distributive and commutative laws of arithmetic:

transform exp
    on "factor-left" Plus(Times(a,b),Times(a,c)): Times(a,Plus(b,c)),
    on "factor-left" Minus(Times(a,b),Times(a,c)): Times(a,Minus(b,c)),
    on "factor-right" Plus(Times(b,a),Times(c,a)): Times(Plus(b,c),a),
    on "factor-right" Minus(Times(b,a),Times(c,a)): Times(Minus(b,c),a),
    on "distribute-left" Times(a,Plus(b,c)) : Plus(Times(a,b),Times(a,c)),
    on "distribute-left" Times(a,Minus(b,c)) : Minus(Times(a,b),Times(a,c)),
    on "distribute-right" Times(Plus(b,c),a) : Plus(Times(b,a),Times(c,a)),
    on "distribute-right" Times(Minus(b,c),a) : Minus(Times(b,a),Times(c,a)),
    on "commute" Plus(a,b) : Plus(b,a),
    on "commute" Times(a,b) : TImes(b,a)
    ;

To illustrate the application of these transformations, suppose the current selection is the expression $((3 * 4) + (3 * 2))$. Only two of the transformation patterns match this expression: the one in the first factor-left transformation and the one in the first commute transformation. Thus, these two commands and none of the others are displayed in the help pane.

| main |
| |
| $[((3 * 4) + (3 * 2))]$ |
| |
| Positioned at exp_list   factor-left   commute |

If we apply the factor-left transformation, pattern-variable a is bound to the term 3, b is bound to 4, and c is bound to 2. The term computed from the transformation's right-hand-side expression Times(a, Plus(b, c)) is Times(3, Plus(4, 2)), so the selection is restructured as shown below:

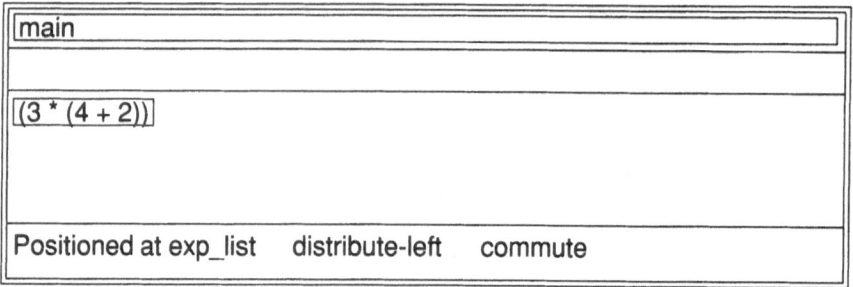

For this term, the only transformations that apply are distribute-left and commute. Next, we apply the commute transformation.

```
┌─────────────────────────────────────────────────────────────┐
│┌─────────────────────────────────────────────────────────────┐│
││main                                                            ││
│├─────────────────────────────────────────────────────────────┤│
││                                                                ││
││⌈((4 + 2) * 3)⌉                                                ││
││                                                                ││
││                                                                ││
││                                                                ││
│├─────────────────────────────────────────────────────────────┤│
││Positioned at exp_list    distribute-right  commute            ││
│└─────────────────────────────────────────────────────────────┘│
└─────────────────────────────────────────────────────────────┘
```

Finally, we apply distribute-right.

```
┌─────────────────────────────────────────────────────────────┐
│┌─────────────────────────────────────────────────────────────┐│
││main                                                            ││
│├─────────────────────────────────────────────────────────────┤│
││                                                                ││
││⌈((4 * 3) + (2 * 3))⌉                                          ││
││                                                                ││
││                                                                ││
││                                                                ││
│├─────────────────────────────────────────────────────────────┤│
││Positioned at exp_list    factor-right      commute            ││
│└─────────────────────────────────────────────────────────────┘│
└─────────────────────────────────────────────────────────────┘
```

We could get back to the original expression by selecting each of the summands individually and applying the commute transformation to them.

Order dependences in transformation declarations

It is possible to have more than one transformation with the same command name. For example, the two transformations defined above for commuting expressions are both associated with the command name commute:

transform exp
        on "commute" Plus(a,b) : Plus(b,a),
        on "commute" Times(a,b) : Times(b,a),
        ;

Because the root operator is different for the patterns that appear in the two transformations, it happens that they can never both match the current selection; thus, at most one of the transformations ever applies. In general, however, the current selection may match the pattern of several transformations that have the same command name. In this case, invoking the command causes the transformation that appears earliest in the specification to be applied.

128   Chapter 6. Defining Hybrid Editors with the Synthesizer Generator

Example. To illustrate this feature, consider the following transformation declarations that define commands for restructuring expressions that involve the Plus, Minus, and Uminus operators:

transform exp
        on "form-subtraction" Plus(a,Uminus(b)) : Minus(a,b),
        on "form-subtraction" Plus(a,b) : Minus(a,Uminus(b)),
        on "form-addition" Minus(a,Uminus(b)) : Plus(a,b),
        on "form-addition" Minus(a,b) : Plus(a,Uminus(b))
        ;

Using these transformations, it is possible to restructure expressions according to the laws of arithmetic. In each of the pairs with identical command names, the transformation declarations have been ordered so that the rule with the more specific pattern appears first. For example, a term of the form Plus(a, Uminus(b)) is also of the form Plus(a, b), but the converse does not always hold. Because the transformation whose pattern is Plus(a, Uminus(b)) is defined earlier than the one whose pattern is Plus(a, b), the first transformation takes precedence over the second. For instance, suppose the initial situation is the one displayed below:

```
main

(3 + 2)



Positioned at exp_list    form-subtraction        commute
```

When the form-subtraction transformation is invoked, the second transformation is applied because (3 + 2), which corresponds to the term Plus(Const(3), Const(2)), is of the form Plus(a, b) but not of the form Plus(a, Uminus(b)). The result of applying the transformation appears below:

```
┌──────────────────────────────────────────────────────────────┐
│┌────────────────────────────────────────────────────────────┐│
││ main                                                        ││
│├────────────────────────────────────────────────────────────┤│
││                                                              ││
││ ┌─────────┐                                                  ││
││ │(3 − −2)│                                                   ││
││ └─────────┘                                                  ││
││                                                              ││
││                                                              ││
│├────────────────────────────────────────────────────────────┤│
││ Positioned at exp_list     form-addition                    ││
│└────────────────────────────────────────────────────────────┘│
└──────────────────────────────────────────────────────────────┘
```

In contrast, if the initial situation is the one pictured below, the current selection, (3 + −2), corresponds to the term Plus(Const(3), Uminus(Const(2))). This term is of the form Plus(a, Uminus(b)), which matches the pattern of the first of the two form-subtraction transformations.

```
┌──────────────────────────────────────────────────────────────┐
│┌────────────────────────────────────────────────────────────┐│
││ main                                                        ││
│├────────────────────────────────────────────────────────────┤│
││                                                              ││
││ ┌─────────┐                                                  ││
││ │(3 + −2)│                                                   ││
││ └─────────┘                                                  ││
││                                                              ││
││                                                              ││
│├────────────────────────────────────────────────────────────┤│
││ Positioned at exp_list     form-subtraction       commute   ││
│└────────────────────────────────────────────────────────────┘│
└──────────────────────────────────────────────────────────────┘
```

Invoking form-subtraction causes the first version of the transformation to be applied:

```
┌──────────────────────────────────────────────────────────────┐
│┌────────────────────────────────────────────────────────────┐│
││ main                                                        ││
│├────────────────────────────────────────────────────────────┤│
││                                                              ││
││ ┌────────┐                                                   ││
││ │(3 − 2)│                                                    ││
││ └────────┘                                                   ││
││                                                              ││
││                                                              ││
│├────────────────────────────────────────────────────────────┤│
││ Positioned at exp_list     form-addition                    ││
│└────────────────────────────────────────────────────────────┘│
└──────────────────────────────────────────────────────────────┘
```

6.3. Defining Computed Display Representations

For most purposes, the rather simple features of the display language used in unparsing declarations are satisfactory. The formatting features that are provided in the display language control line breaks and indentation, as discussed in Chapter 4, as well as optional line breaks, unparsing groups, tab stops, and column-control directives. (For details, see the *The Synthesizer Generator Reference Manual.*)

In addition, the Synthesizer Generator's display language incorporates a further mechanism providing the ability to define computed display schemes. This mechanism provides editor-designers with an extremely powerful method for defining an object's display representation.

As illustrated by the example specification in Chapter 4, SSL furnishes a notation based on attribute grammars to express the annotation of objects with attribute values. As the editor specification in Chapter 4 illustrated, attribution rules can be used to define static inferences about objects, such as name analysis and type checking of programs.[4] To define computed display schemes, the results computed by the Synthesizer Generator's attribution facility are made accessible in SSL's unparsing declarations. When used to define computed display representations, the attributes carry information about how the object is to be displayed, rather than, for example, sets of declared names and their types.

To define computed display representations, the specification's unparsing declarations are parameterized by attribute occurrences. Any of an operator's attribute occurrences can appear as a component of the operator's unparsing declaration. When the display image is generated, the value of the corresponding attribute instance is displayed on the screen. The attributes that contribute to the display are defined by attribute equations, and thus can depend on the values of other attributes in the tree.

The use of the attribution mechanism to define the object's display representation means that the image displayed on the screen depends on values of attributes in the tree. The display algorithm relies on the incremental attribute-updating algorithm to decorate the underlying tree with correct (*i.e.* consistent) attribute values before the display image is generated.

To illustrate how attribution rules may be used to define computed display representations, we present two final variations of the expression-list editor.

---

[4]Additional material concerning the use of attribute equations in editor specifications also appears in later chapters of the book.

Suppose we wish to display expressions in infix format, but using only the minimal number of parentheses needed to represent the underlying expression tree. In determining an expression's minimal parenthesization, we assume the standard precedence rules for the arithmetic-operation symbols – Times and Div have higher precedence than Plus and Minus, and unparenthesized terms at the same level associate to the left. For instance, the term $\text{Times}(\text{Plus}(a, b), c)$ should be displayed as $(a + b) * c$, and $\text{Plus}(a, \text{Times}(b, c))$ should be displayed as $a + b * c$. In addition, there should be no redundant parentheses: *i.e.* $((a + b)) * c$ and $(a + b * c)$ are forbidden. Figure 6.9 lists the minimally parenthesized infix representations for all terms of the form $Op_1(a, Op_2(b, c))$ and $Op_2(Op_1(a, b), c)$.

Note that the use here of the term "precedence level" is separate and distinct from its use in Section 6.2. In Section 6.2, "precedence level" was used in connection with precedence declarations for disambiguating parsing rules. The precedence levels discussed in this section are introduced for computing the minimal use of parentheses in an expression's infix display representation. The latter precedence levels are defined with SSL's attribution mechanism; different precedence levels are represented by different values of certain attributes. In contrast, precedence declarations used for disambiguating parsing rules are a

Op_1	Op_2	$Op_1(a, Op_2(b, c))$	$Op_2(Op_1(a, b), c)$
Plus	Plus	$a + (b + c)$	$a + b + c$
Plus	Minus	$a + (b - c)$	$a + b - c$
Plus	Times	$a + b * c$	$(a + b) * c$
Plus	Div	$a + b / c$	$(a + b) / c$
Minus	Plus	$a - (b + c)$	$a - b + c$
Minus	Minus	$a - (b - c)$	$a - b - c$
Minus	Times	$a - b * c$	$(a - b) * c$
Minus	Div	$a - b / c$	$(a - b) / c$
Times	Plus	$a * (b + c)$	$a * b + c$
Times	Minus	$a * (b - c)$	$a * b - c$
Times	Times	$a * (b * c)$	$a * b * c$
Times	Div	$a * (b / c)$	$a * b / c$
Div	Plus	$a / (b + c)$	$a / b + c$
Div	Minus	$a / (b - c)$	$a / b - c$
Div	Times	$a / (b * c)$	$a / b * c$
Div	Div	$a / (b / c)$	$a / b / c$

Figure 6.9. Minimally parenthesized infix representations for all terms of the form $Op_1(a, Op_2(b, c))$ and $Op_2(Op_1(a, b), c)$.

feature that is built into SSL; tokens are assigned different precedence levels depending on the order in which the precedence declarations are encountered.

Variation 11: Minimal Parenthesization of Expressions

An expression's parentheses are specified in terms of two STR-valued attributes, lp and rp, which are declared as local attributes associated with the operators Plus, Minus, Times, and Div, as follows:

```
exp     :        Plus, Minus, Times, Div {
                     local STR lp;
                     local STR rp;
                     }
        ;
```

The equations that define the values of attributes lp and rp, given below, define them to be either the null string or a parenthesis-valued string – (in the case of lp,) in the case of rp. The lp and rp values are incorporated as components of the unparsing declarations, thereby placing parentheses or null strings around each subexpression, as shown below:

```
exp     :        Null         [^ ::= "<exp>" ]
        |        Plus         [^ : lp @ " + " @ rp ]
        |        Minus        [^ : lp @ " – " @ rp ]
        |        Times        [^ : lp @ " * " @ rp ]
        |        Div          [^ : lp @ " / " @ rp ]
        |        Uminus       [^ : "–" @ ]
        |        Const        [^ : ^ ]
        ;
```

   The parenthesization rules are expressed in terms of two precedence levels. One of the levels is the operator's local precedence level, represented by local attribute localLevel of the operators Plus, Minus, Times, and Div. The other level is that of the enclosing operator, which is available from the left-hand-side occurrence of phylum exp as the value of the inherited attribute exp$1.precedence. The two levels are compared to determine whether the subexpression needs to be enclosed in parentheses; parentheses are needed if the precedence level of the subexpression's root is less than the precedence level of its parent.

   The rules for when a subexpression needs to be enclosed in parentheses are captured by the following attribute definitions and equations:

```
exp { inherited INT precedence; };
exp_list :          ExpListPair { exp.precedence = 0; };

exp       :          Plus, Minus, Times, Div {
                          local STR lp;
                          local STR rp;
                          local INT localLevel;
                          exp$2.precedence = localLevel;
                          exp$3.precedence = localLevel + 1;
                          lp = (exp$1.precedence > localLevel) ? "(" : "";
                          rp = (exp$1.precedence > localLevel) ? ")" : "";
                          }
          |          Plus, Minus { localLevel = 1; }
          |          Times, Div { localLevel = 2; }
          |          Uminus { exp$2.precedence = 3; }
          ;
```

In the equations given above, note how the precedence value passed down to the right child of a binary operator is made one greater than the local precedence level. Artificially raising the precedence level in this fashion causes parentheses to be generated for terms like Times(a, Div(b, c)) and Div(a, Times(b,c)), which are displayed as $a * (b / c)$ and $a / (b * c)$, respectively. It also causes parentheses to be supplied around the second component of a term that involves associative operators but is not a "left association." For example, the term Plus(a, Plus(b, c)) is displayed with parentheses to indicate that the term is grouped to the right: $a + (b + c)$; by contrast, the term Plus(Plus(a, b), c) is displayed without any parentheses: $a + b + c$.

Variation 12: Minimal Parenthesization of Expressions that are Phrases

The equations given above would be appropriate for an editor that allows structural editing of subexpressions. For example, the resting-place symbols in the unparsing declarations for Variation 11 make it possible to select subexpressions and edit the substructure of an expression directly. Under these conditions, it is desirable to generate parentheses that indicate the true grouping of terms involving associative operators. For example, the parentheses in $a + (b + c)$ but not in $a + b + c$ allow one to determine that the former corresponds to the term Plus(a, Plus(b, c)) and the latter to Plus(Plus(a, b), c).

However, an editor specification could use an alternative set of unparsing declarations to specify that expressions have no internal resting places, such as the ones given below:

exp	:	Null	[^ ::= "\<exp\>"]
	|	Plus	[^ ::= lp ^ " + " ^ rp]
	|	Minus	[^ ::= lp ^ " − " ^ rp]
	|	Times	[^ ::= lp ^ " * " ^ rp]
	|	Div	[^ ::= lp ^ " / " ^ rp]
	|	Uminus	[^ ::= "−" ^]
	|	Const	[^ ::= ^]
	;		

The absence of any resting-places in these declarations means that the internal structure of an expression is inaccessible, which forces expressions to be treated as textual phrases. For these editing conditions, if a term can associate either way without affecting the expression's value, we would like to make an expression's internal structure completely invisible to the user. In particular, the three associative laws

$$(a + b) + c = a + (b + c)$$
$$(a * b) * c = a * (b * c)$$
$$(a + b) - c = a + (b - c)$$

say that the respective terms for these expressions have the same value no matter what the association. Accordingly, we would like parentheses to be left out of the display representation of such terms. For example, the terms Plus(Plus(a, b), c) and Plus(a, Plus(b, c)) should both be displayed as $a + b + c$. (We are assuming that the symbol / denotes the operation of integer division, which means that $*$ and / are not associative; in general, for these operations $(a * b) / c \neq a * (b / c)$. Consequently, the term Div(Times(a, b), c) should be displayed as $a * b / c$, but Times(a, Div(b, c)) should be displayed as $a * (b / c)$.)

Figure 6.10 lists our revised notion of the minimally parenthesized infix representation for the terms of the form $Op_1(a, Op_2(b, c))$ and $Op_2(Op_1(a, b), c)$. Note the absence of parentheses in the lines marked with a dagger (†).

One way to express the parenthesization scheme listed in Figure 6.10 is given in Figure 6.11. The declarations in Figure 6.11 use four precedence levels to capture the revised parenthesization requirements, rather than just three as in the previous version. The main difference is that the local level of operator Div is 2, whereas Times has precedence level 3; the use of different levels for Div and Times makes it possible to write rules that distinguish between them.

Op_1	Op_2	$Op_1(a, Op_2(b, c))$	$Op_2(Op_1(a, b), c)$	
Plus	Plus	$a + b + c$	$a + b + c$	(†)
Plus	Minus	$a + b - c$	$a + b - c$	(†)
Plus	Times	$a + b * c$	$(a + b) * c$	
Plus	Div	$a + b / c$	$(a + b) / c$	
Minus	Plus	$a - (b + c)$	$a - b + c$	
Minus	Minus	$a - (b - c)$	$a - b - c$	
Minus	Times	$a - b * c$	$(a - b) * c$	
Minus	Div	$a - b / c$	$(a - b) / c$	
Times	Plus	$a * (b + c)$	$a * b + c$	
Times	Minus	$a * (b - c)$	$a * b - c$	
Times	Times	$a * b * c$	$a * b * c$	(†)
Times	Div	$a * (b / c)$	$a * b / c$	
Div	Plus	$a / (b + c)$	$a / b + c$	
Div	Minus	$a / (b - c)$	$a / b - c$	
Div	Times	$a / (b * c)$	$a / b * c$	
Div	Div	$a / (b / c)$	$a / b / c$	

Figure 6.10. Minimally parenthesized infix representations for all terms of the form $Op_1(a, Op_2(b, c))$ and $Op_2(Op_1(a, b), c)$. Note the absence of any parentheses in the lines marked with a dagger (†).

```
exp     :          Plus, Minus, Times, Div {
                        local STR lp;
                        local STR rp;
                        local INT localLevel;
                        lp = (exp$1.precedence > localLevel) ? "(" : "";
                        rp = (exp$1.precedence > localLevel) ? ")" : "";
                        }
        |       Plus {
                        localLevel = 1;
                        exp$2.precedence = 1;
                        exp$3.precedence = 1;
                        }
        |       Minus {
                        localLevel = 1;
                        exp$2.precedence = 1;
                        exp$3.precedence = 2;
                        }
        |       Times {
                        localLevel = 3;
                        exp$2.precedence = 2;
                        exp$3.precedence = 3;
                        }
        |       Div {
                        localLevel = 2;
                        exp$2.precedence = 2;
                        exp$3.precedence = 4;
                        }
        |       Uminus {
                        exp$2.precedence = 4;
                        }
        ;
```

Figure 6.11. Attribute equations that express the minimal parenthesization scheme given in Figure 6.10.

6.4. Context-Sensitive Translations and Transformations

To provide additional power to editor-designers, the basic mechanisms for translation and transformation were extended to permit *context-sensitive translations* and *context-sensitive transformations* to be defined.

6.4.1. Context-sensitive translations

Recall that any declared phylum, including the phyla used to represent the abstract syntax of editable objects, is a valid attribute type. Hence, attribute computations can construct terms of the phyla that represent the abstract syntax of editable objects. By making available the full power of the attribution mechanism for defining the translation of input text to a term of the abstract syntax, the Synthesizer Generator provides editor-designers with a powerful and flexible facility. To specify an input interface, productions are supplied to define the concrete syntax of the input language, along with attribution rules that define a translation of input text to a term of the abstract syntax.

To permit context-sensitive translations to be defined, SSL allows attributes at the root of the abstract-syntax tree's current selection to be passed into the parse tree as the inherited attributes of the parse tree's root. In essence, this provides a method for parameterizing the translation of the input text by the values of the selection's attributes. Attribute values may contain information about the contents of the current selection as well as the contents of the rest of the object. Thus, the extended translation mechanism makes it possible to define translation schemes where the abstract-syntax term produced varies depending on the component of the object that is currently selected, on the surrounding context provided by the rest of the object, or both.

Context-sensitive translations can be used for many purposes in programming-language editors. In particular, they can be used to define specialized insertion commands where the component that gets inserted depends on information derived from a program's type declarations or procedure declarations. For example, it is possible to define a context-sensitive translation where a piece of input text, say .p, gets translated to a call on procedure p expanded with the correct number of expression placeholders for the arguments to p. In this case, the translation scheme would be designed to extract the appropriate information from the selection's symbol-table attribute.

Example. A similar, but less involved example, will be used to demonstrate context-sensitive translation. Suppose we wish to extend the expression-list editor with a simple abbreviation facility that permits the binding of names to expressions; the definition of an abbreviation is an expression of the form

define <*name*> = <*exp$_1$*> in <*exp$_2$*> ni

Such an expression binds the given <*name*> to <*exp$_1$*>. The scoping of names is block structured, so that each exp will be associated with an appropriate set of local name bindings provided by an inherited attribute (named env). The second part of the extension is to define a context-sensitive translation that interprets input of the form .*name* to mean "insert, at the current selection, the expression that is bound to *name* in the selection's env attribute."

The first step is to define a new operator of phylum exp and define a template for it.

```
exp     :          Abbrev(identifier exp exp)
                     [^ : "define " @ " = " @ " in " @ " ni" ];
transform exp
       on "abbreviation" <exp>: Abbrev(<identifier>, <exp>, <exp>);
```

Second, we define phylum identifier and give rules for translating textual input
to an identifier.

```
IDENTIFIER:    IdentLex< [a–zA–Z][a–zA–Z_0–9]* >;
identifier:     IdentifierNull( )              [@ ::= "<identifier>"]
        |       Identifier(IDENTIFIER)  [^ ::= ^]
        ;
Ident    {synthesized identifier t;};
identifier  ~    Ident.t;
Ident    ::=     (IDENTIFIER)   {Ident.t = Identifier(IDENTIFIER);};
```

Third, we define phylum ENV, to be used for the environment of bindings of
names to expressions.

```
list ENV;
ENV     :          NullEnv( )
        |          EnvConcat(BINDING  ENV)        [@ : ^ [",%n"] @]
        ;
BINDING:        Binding(IDENTIFIER  exp)          [^ : ^ ": " @];
```

The recursive function lookup returns the binding for a given IDENTIFIER if it
exists in a given environment, or returns the term Null if the IDENTIFIER does
not exist.

```
exp lookup(IDENTIFIER id, ENV env) {
     with (env) (
          NullEnv( ): Null,
          EnvConcat(Binding(s, e), tail): (id == s) ? e : lookup(id, tail)
          )
     };
```

Next, we supply a declaration attaching the inherited ENV-valued attribute env
to phylum exp and give attribute equations to pass the environment to each
operator's right-hand-side exp phyla.[5]

---

[5]It is also necessary to supply an attribute equation for the exp.env attribute in the Binding operator,
although this attribute is never actually given a value:

```
BINDING:Binding { exp.env = NullEnv; };
```

```
exp { inherited ENV env; };
exp      :   Abbrev {
                exp$2.env = exp$1.env;
                exp$3.env = with(identifier) (
                        IdentifierNull: exp$1.env,
                        Identifier(i): Binding(i, exp$2) :: exp$1.env
                        );
             }
         |   Plus, Minus, Times, Div {
                exp$2.env = exp$1.env;
                exp$3.env = exp$1.env;
             }
         |   Uminus { exp$2.env = exp$1.env; }
         ;
exp_list :   ExpListPair { exp.env = NullEnv; };
```

Finally, we define the desired context-sensitive translation, which interprets text of the form *.name* as a command to insert the expression that is bound to *name* in the selection's env attribute.

```
ExpCommand {
        inherited ENV env;
        synthesized exp abs;
        };
exp    ~        ExpCommand.abs { ExpCommand.env = exp.env; };
ExpCommand ::= ('.' IDENTIFIER) {
        ExpCommand.abs = lookup(IDENTIFIER, ExpCommand.env);
        };
```

In the entry declaration above, exp.env refers to the environment attribute of the exp node that is the root of the selection when the input is typed.

Figure 6.12 shows a sequence of snapshots of the display that illustrate the effect of the context-sensitive translation. The input text .a is translated to the expression to which the identifier a is bound in the context that encloses the currently selected expression placeholder. In the example shown, a is bound to the expression (2 + 5).

```
┌─────────────────────────────────────────────────────────┐
│┌─────────────────────────────────────────────────────────┐│
││main                                                      ││
│├─────────────────────────────────────────────────────────┤│
││                                                          ││
│├─────────────────────────────────────────────────────────┤│
││define a = 2 + 5 in  <exp>  ni                            ││
│├─────────────────────────────────────────────────────────┤│
││Positioned at exp      +    -    *    /    u–    abbreviation││
│└─────────────────────────────────────────────────────────┘│
└─────────────────────────────────────────────────────────┘

┌─────────────────────────────────────────────────────────┐
│┌─────────────────────────────────────────────────────────┐│
││main                                                      ││
│├─────────────────────────────────────────────────────────┤│
││                                                          ││
│├─────────────────────────────────────────────────────────┤│
││define a = 2 + 5 in .[]      ni                           ││
│├─────────────────────────────────────────────────────────┤│
││Positioned at exp      +    -    *    /    u–    abbreviation││
│└─────────────────────────────────────────────────────────┘│
└─────────────────────────────────────────────────────────┘

┌─────────────────────────────────────────────────────────┐
│┌─────────────────────────────────────────────────────────┐│
││main                                                      ││
│├─────────────────────────────────────────────────────────┤│
││                                                          ││
│├─────────────────────────────────────────────────────────┤│
││define a = 2 + 5 in .a[]      ni                          ││
│├─────────────────────────────────────────────────────────┤│
││Positioned at exp      +    -    *    /    u–    abbreviation││
│└─────────────────────────────────────────────────────────┘│
└─────────────────────────────────────────────────────────┘

┌─────────────────────────────────────────────────────────┐
│┌─────────────────────────────────────────────────────────┐│
││main                                                      ││
│├─────────────────────────────────────────────────────────┤│
││                                                          ││
│├─────────────────────────────────────────────────────────┤│
││define a = 2 + 5 in 2 + 5 ni,  <exp>                      ││
│├─────────────────────────────────────────────────────────┤│
││Positioned at exp_list      +    -    *    /    u–    abbreviation││
│└─────────────────────────────────────────────────────────┘│
└─────────────────────────────────────────────────────────┘
```

Figure 6.12. Snapshots of the display that, from top to bottom, illustrate the use of an abbreviation. By a context-sensitive translation, the input text .a is translated to the expression to which the identifier a is bound, *i.e.* (2 + 5).

6.4.2.　Context-sensitive transformations

By permitting *context-sensitive transformations* to be defined, the transformation mechanism provides an additional facility for defining context-sensitive manipulations of the currently selected constituent. This extension relies on the fact that the currently selected constituent of a buffer is not merely a term but an attributed term, so the pattern variables of a transformation's pattern are necessarily bound to attributed terms. Context-sensitive transformations can be defined by referring to these attributes in the transformation's expression. That is, if *p* is a pattern variable that has been bound to a subterm of a phylum with synthesized or inherited attribute a, then the expression $p.a$ is legal within the transformation's expression and denotes the value of the corresponding attribute instance.

Example. To illustrate the definition of a context-sensitive transformation, let us extend the expression-list editor to permit the use of abbreviation names in expressions:

```
exp     :        Use(IDENTIFIER);
Exp     ::=      (IDENTIFIER) { Exp.abs = Use(IDENTIFIER);};
```

We now define a transformation, named expand-abbreviation, whose effect is to expand an identifier to the expression to which it is bound in the nearest enclosing abbreviation:

```
transform exp on "expand-abbreviation" e : with(e) (
                                     Use(i): lookup(i, e.env),
                                     default: e
                                     );
```

Note the use of e.env as the second argument of the call on lookup; e.env denotes the value of the env attribute of the root of the term to which pattern variable e is bound. In other words, e.env refers to the value of the env attribute of the root of the currently selected expression.

Figure 6.13 shows a sequence of snapshots of the display that illustrate the effect of a context-sensitive transformation. The invocation of the expand-abbreviation transformation in Figure 6.13 causes identifier a to be replaced by the expression 2 + 5.

```
┌────────────────────────────────────────────────────────────────┐
│ ┌──────────────────────────────────────────────────────────────┐ │
│ │ main                                                           │ │
│ ├──────────────────────────────────────────────────────────────┤ │
│ │                                                                │ │
│ ├──────────────────────────────────────────────────────────────┤ │
│ │ define a = 2 + 5 in ⬚a⬚ ni                                     │ │
│ ├──────────────────────────────────────────────────────────────┤ │
│ │ Positioned at exp     +     -     *     /     u−     abbreviation │ │
│ │ expand-abbreviation                                            │ │
│ └──────────────────────────────────────────────────────────────┘ │
└────────────────────────────────────────────────────────────────┘

┌────────────────────────────────────────────────────────────────┐
│ ┌──────────────────────────────────────────────────────────────┐ │
│ │ main                                                           │ │
│ ├──────────────────────────────────────────────────────────────┤ │
│ │ COMMAND: expand-abbreviation                                   │ │
│ ├──────────────────────────────────────────────────────────────┤ │
│ │ define a = 2 + 5 in ⬚a⬚ ni                                     │ │
│ ├──────────────────────────────────────────────────────────────┤ │
│ │ Positioned at exp     +     -     *     /     u−     abbreviation │ │
│ │ expand-abbreviation                                            │ │
│ └──────────────────────────────────────────────────────────────┘ │
└────────────────────────────────────────────────────────────────┘

┌────────────────────────────────────────────────────────────────┐
│ ┌──────────────────────────────────────────────────────────────┐ │
│ │ main                                                           │ │
│ ├──────────────────────────────────────────────────────────────┤ │
│ │                                                                │ │
│ ├──────────────────────────────────────────────────────────────┤ │
│ │ define a = 2 + 5 in ⬚2 + 5⬚ ni                                 │ │
│ ├──────────────────────────────────────────────────────────────┤ │
│ │ Positioned at exp     +     -     *     /     u−     abbreviation │ │
│ │ expand-abbreviation                                            │ │
│ └──────────────────────────────────────────────────────────────┘ │
└────────────────────────────────────────────────────────────────┘
```

Figure 6.13. Snapshots of the display that illustrate the expansion of an identifier to the expression to which it is bound in an enclosing abbreviation. This transformation is defined with a context-sensitive transformation rule.

CHAPTER 7

Performing Static Inferences with Attributes

When an editor-designer creates an editor, a substantial part of the specification consists of attribute declarations and attribute equations. This chapter illustrates some of the considerations that influence the way an editor specification's attribution schemes are written.

In addition to being one of the Synthesizer Generator's most distinctive features, the attribution mechanism is also one of its most pervasive features. For this reason, there has already been a good deal of discussion of the attribution mechanism in earlier chapters. For instance, in Chapter 6, we described how to define hybrid text/structure editors with the Synthesizer Generator, using SSL's facilities for specifying a language's display format and concrete syntax for textual input. Both of these facilities make use of the Synthesizer Generator's attribution mechanism – in the former case to incorporate results computed by the attribution facility, in the latter case for translating text to abstract syntax.

The most innovative aspect of the Synthesizer Generator's attribution mechanism is its facility for incremental attribute updating. As an object is developed with a generated editor, it is represented as a derivation tree that is consistently attributed in accordance with the specification's equations. When an object is modified by restructuring the derivation tree, some of the tree's attribute instances may no longer have consistent values. However, each time a restructuring operation introduces such inconsistencies, the editor applies an algorithm that incrementally reestablishes consistent attribute values throughout the tree.

The incremental attribution mechanism serves as the basic inference facility in editors that perform static inferences as objects are created and modified. To create such an editor, one specifies the inference method as an attribute computation on the terms of the phyla of edited objects. As illustrated in Chapter 4, one application of this facility is in detecting violations of a programming language's context conditions. (Many languages have such non-context-free syntactic constraints, which require widely separated parts of a program to be interrelated.) In a programming-language editor, it is possible to perform static inferences that detect violations of such constraints. By analyzing a program during editing for violations of such constraints and displaying the results of these computations on the screen, the editor can provide feedback to the programmer about mistakes while the program is still being developed.

Example. The use of the Synthesizer Generator's attribution mechanism to perform name analysis and type checking was illustrated in Chapter 4. In the editor described there, warnings are supplied for multiple declarations of variables, uses of undeclared variables, and type mismatches. To review the different kinds of warnings furnished by this editor, consider the following code fragment:

```
main

program <identifier>;
var
    b : integer;
    a : boolean;
    c : integer;
begin
    b := c;
    while a do
        <statement>
end.

Positioned at identifier
```

In this example, the single modification of changing the declaration of variable b to a declaration for a introduces all three kinds of errors into the program: after the change, a is declared twice, b is not declared at all, and, because the declaration of a as an integer variable precedes its declaration as a boolean, the loop-condition has the wrong type. Each error is signaled to the user by attaching an appropriate comment.

```
┌────────────────────────────────────────────────────────────────┐
│ ┌──────────────────────────────────────────────────────────────┐│
│ │main                                                          ││
│ └──────────────────────────────────────────────────────────────┘│
│                                                                  │
│ program <identifier>;                                            │
│ var                                                              │
│     [a] { MULTIPLY DECLARED } : integer;                         │
│     a { MULTIPLY DECLARED } : boolean;                           │
│     c : integer;                                                 │
│ begin                                                            │
│     b { NOT DECLARED } := c;                                     │
│     while a { BOOLEAN EXPRESSION NEEDED } do                     │
│         <statement>                                              │
│ end.                                                             │
│ ┌──────────────────────────────────────────────────────────────┐│
│ │Positioned at identifier                                      ││
│ └──────────────────────────────────────────────────────────────┘│
└────────────────────────────────────────────────────────────────┘
```

For the Synthesizer Generator to be used successfully to create editors that perform static inferences, it is essential to know how to make effective use of the attribution mechanism. There are often several possible approaches to checking and reporting violations of a given context-sensitive condition. Such alternatives correspond to different static-inference problems specified using different attribute declarations and attribute equations. One of the objectives of this chapter is to articulate some of the issues to be considered when designing attribution schemes. To illustrate the issues, we discuss several attribution schemes for name analysis and type checking that are alternatives to the one that was presented in Chapter 4.

The primary consideration is the issue of aggregating information and passing it to where it is needed. Although a language's context conditions require widely separated parts of an object to be consistent, the Synthesizer Generator's attribution mechanism does not provide a way for *enforcing* consistency, only for *checking* consistency. Checking consistency requires that information be passed between potentially inconsistent sites. However, whereas an unbounded number of sites can be inconsistent, there are only a fixed number of attribute instances per tree node through which information can be passed. The solution is to aggregate information in a compound data structure and pass the entire aggregate around the tree.

When an editor-designer creates an editor with the Synthesizer Generator, the primary issue in the design of the attribution scheme is deciding what informa-

tion needs to be aggregated and in what manner these aggregates will be passed
to the locations that need them. At the same time, it is often possible to formu-
late different attribution schemes to implement the same aggregation strategy.
For example, to collect information that is distributed throughout an object,
left-to-right threading and right-to-left threading are sometimes both possible.

Additional considerations arise when implementing a given design. There are
implementation choices to be made similar to those that arise with any programming language, such as the choice among different implementations of a given
abstract data type (*e.g.* the choice between using a list versus using an AVL-tree
to implement a dictionary). The data types available in SSL and the techniques
for manipulating them will be familiar to those acquainted with other functional
programming languages.[1]

These issues are illustrated using two examples that represent alternatives to
the design presented in Chapter 4 for an editor that performs name analysis and
type checking. Instead of annotating each occurrence of an undeclared variable
with a warning, the editor discussed in Section 7.1 collects the names of undeclared variables and lists them at the beginning of the declaration section.
Instead of requiring an identifier to be used in a way that is consistent with its
declaration, the editor discussed in Section 7.2 infers a type for each variable
from its uses and generates an appropriate declaration.

7.1. Aggregation and Information-Passing Strategies

This section describes several aggregation and information-passing strategies
and discusses their use in an editor that performs name analysis and type checking. As in Chapter 4, the names that appear in a program's declarations must be
consistent with the uses of names in the program's statements.

For this problem, there are three possible aggregation strategies:

1) Aggregate information from the declarations; broadcast or thread the aggregate through the statements.
2) Aggregate information from the statements; broadcast or thread the aggregate through the declarations.
3) Aggregate information from the declarations; aggregate information from
   the statements; compare the two aggregates.

---

[1]We anticipate that future releases of the Synthesizer Generator will have some additional built-in
data types for aggregates in order to provide more efficient updating of aggregate-valued attributes
using the techniques described in [Hoover87].

The editor described in Chapter 4 uses the first of these strategies, although it uses an indirect method of aggregation in which the aggregate is "created" by a syntactic reference. Recall that a syntactic reference permits attribute equations to refer to and to perform computations on syntactic components. In Chapter 4, the program's declList component serves as the aggregated declaration information. The declarations given below, which are repeated from Chapter 4, establish a local attribute, named env, whose value is the program's declList component:

```
program:        Prog(identifier declList stmtList) {
                    local declList env;
                    env = declList;
                }
            ;
```

Broadcast of the aggregate is specified by equations that make use of an upward remote attribute set:

```
identifier:  IdentifierNull { identifier.type = EmptyTypeExp; }
          |  Identifier { identifier.type = LookupType(identifier, {Prog.env}); }
          ;
```

The expression {Prog.env} in the second equation refers to the instance of attribute env attached to the nearest enclosing Prog operator; in this case there can only be one such operator, the one at the root of the program tree.

Direct use of component declList via a syntactic reference is by no means the only way of aggregating information from the declarations. For example, it would be possible to attach explicit env attributes to each phylum and write appropriate attribute equations to define their values, as done in Chapter 3 in Figure 3.2.

In the editor described in Chapter 4, violations of the constraint that a declaration be supplied for each variable used in a program are reported by annotating each use of an undeclared variable with a warning message. An alternative way to report that a program contains undeclared variables would be to collect the names of the undeclared variables and list them at the beginning of the program's declaration section. For instance, in the example program shown below, the fact that a declaration has not been provided for variables a and b is reported on the second line:

```
┌─────────────────────────────────────────────────────────┐
│ ╔═══════════════════════════════════════════════════════╗ │
│ ║ main                                            ═══ ══ ║ │
│ ╠═══════════════════════════════════════════════════════╣ │
│ │                                                        │ │
│ ├────────────────────────────────────────────────────────┤ │
│ │ program <identifier>;                                  │ │
│ │ var a, b : UNDECLARED;                                 │ │
│ │    │<identifier>│ : integer;                           │ │
│ │ begin                                                  │ │
│ │    a := b                                              │ │
│ │ end.                                                   │ │
│ ├────────────────────────────────────────────────────────┤ │
│ │ Positioned at identifier                               │ │
│ └─────────────────────────────────────────────────────────┘ │
```

When a declaration for variable a is inserted, the message on the second line would change to reflect the fact that variable b is the lone remaining variable without a declaration:

```
┌─────────────────────────────────────────────────────────┐
│ ╔═══════════════════════════════════════════════════════╗ │
│ ║ main                                            ═══ ══ ║ │
│ ╠═══════════════════════════════════════════════════════╣ │
│ │                                                        │ │
│ ├────────────────────────────────────────────────────────┤ │
│ │ program <identifier>;                                  │ │
│ │ var b : UNDECLARED;                                    │ │
│ │    │a│ : integer;                                      │ │
│ │ begin                                                  │ │
│ │    a := b                                              │ │
│ │ end.                                                   │ │
│ ├────────────────────────────────────────────────────────┤ │
│ │ Positioned at identifier                               │ │
│ └─────────────────────────────────────────────────────────┘ │
```

We now describe how to write an attribution scheme that achieves this effect. The attribute equations use the third aggregation strategy outlined above: the equations aggregate information from the declarations, aggregate additional information from the statements, and compare the two aggregates. In particular, the attribution scheme collects the set of declared variables, the set of used variables, and takes their set difference.

The two collections of identifiers are represented by phylum IdSet, which is defined in Figure 7.1 along with several operations on IdSets. An IdSet is a list of identifiers; the IdSet operations given in Figure 7.1 implement the data type "set of identifiers," maintaining each IdSet value as a sorted list.

To determine which identifiers lack a declaration, we use two synthesized IdSet attributes, named **declared** and **used**. The **declared** attribute is a syn-

```
list IdSet;
IdSet    :          IdSetNil( )                                    [ @ : ]
         |          IdSetPair(identifier IdSet)                    [ @ : ^ [ "," ] @ ]
         ;
IdSet NullIdSet( ) { IdSetNil };
BOOL IsNull(IdSet s) { s == IdSetNil };
BOOL IsElement(identifier i, IdSet s) {
        with (s) (
                IdSetNil: false,
                IdSetPair(id, t): i==id ? true : IsElement(i, t)
                )
        };
IdSet SingletonIdSet(identifier i) { i :: IdSetNil };
IdSet IdSetUnion(IdSet s1, IdSet s2) {
        with (s1) (
                IdSetNil: s2,
                IdSetPair(i1, t1): with (s2) (
                        IdSetNil: s1,
                        IdSetPair(i2, t2): i1 < i2  ?  i1 :: IdSetUnion(t1, s2)
                                         : i1 == i2 ? i1 :: IdSetUnion(t1, t2)
                                         :            i2 :: IdSetUnion(s1, t2)
                        )
                )
        };
IdSet IdSetDifference(IdSet s1, IdSet s2) {
        with (s1) (
                IdSetNil: s1,
                IdSetPair(i1, t1): with (s2) (
                        IdSetNil: s1,
                        IdSetPair(i2, t2): i1 < i2  ?  i1 :: IdSetDifference(t1, s2)
                                         : i1 == i2 ? IdSetDifference(t1, t2)
                                         :            IdSetDifference(s1, t2)
                        )
                )
        };
```

Figure 7.1. Definition of the module IdSet, which implements the data type "set of identifiers." The operations given above maintain an identifier set as a sorted list.

thesized attribute of phyla declList and decl; it is used to compute the set of identifiers declared in the program. The used attribute is a synthesized attribute of phyla exp, stmtList, and stmt; it is used to compute the set of identifiers that occur in the program's statements and expressions. The attribute declarations and equations that define declared and used are given in Figure 7.2.

The set of undeclared identifiers that are used in a program is determined by taking the set difference of the declList.declared and stmtList.used attribute occurrences of the Prog operator. The following attribute equations and

```
declList, decl { synthesized IdSet declared; };
declList : DeclListNil  { declList.declared = NullIdSet; }
         | DeclListPair { declList$1.declared = IdSetUnion(decl.declared,
                                                    declList$2.declared); }
         ;
decl     : Declaration { decl.declared = (identifier==IdentifierNull) ? NullIdSet
                                        : SingletonIdSet(identifier); }
         ;
exp, stmtList, stmt { synthesized IdSet used; };
stmtList : StmtListNil  { stmtList.used = NullIdSet; }
         | StmtListPair { stmtList$1.used = IdSetUnion(stmt.used,
                                                    stmtList$2.used); }
         ;
stmt     : EmptyStmt  { stmt$1.used = NullIdSet; }
         | Assign     { stmt$1.used = IdSetUnion(SingletonIdSet(identifier),
                                                    exp.used); }
         | IfThenElse, While
                      { stmt$1.used = IdSetUnion(exp.used, stmt$2.used); }
         | Compound   { stmt.used = stmtList.used; }
         ;
exp      : EmptyExp, IntConst, True, False
                      { exp.used = NullIdSet; }
         | Id         { exp.used = SingletonIdSet(identifier); }
         | Equal, NotEqual, Add
                      { exp$1.used = IdSetUnion(exp$2.used, exp$3.used); }
         ;
```

Figure 7.2. Attribution scheme to determine which identifiers lack a declaration. The declared attribute computes the set of identifiers declared in a program; the used attribute computes the set of identifiers that occur in the program's statements and expressions.

unparsing declarations cause an appropriate message to appear if the set difference is nonempty:

```
program: Prog {
            local IdSet undeclared;
            local STR error;
            undeclared = IdSetDifference(stmtList.used,declList.declared);
            error = IsNull(undeclared) ? "" : " : UNDECLARED;";
            }
            [ @ : "program "  @    ";%n"
                   "var "  undeclared error "%t%n"
                     @ ";"         "%b%n"
                   "begin"         "%t%n"
                     @             "%b%n"
                   "end."
            ]
            ;
```

The only other changes that must be made to the unparsing declarations presented in Figure 4.5 are to the ones for operators Assign and Id so that they no longer display a message indicating the presence of an undeclared variable:

```
stmt    :     Assign          [^ ::= @ " := " @  assignError];
exp     :     Id              [^ ::= ^ ];
```

7.2. Using the Attribution Mechanism to Perform Type Inference

The Synthesizer Generator's attribution mechanism provides a way to check that widely separated parts of an object are consistent. The specifications presented in the previous section and in Chapter 4 make use of this mechanism to check the consistency of variable declarations and variable uses. In this section, we consider an alternative strategy in which a *type-inference* scheme is employed to *generate* all variable declarations. A type-inference scheme examines the ways in which variables are used in a program and deduces a type that is consistent with the different uses [Tenenbaum74, Milner78].

This approach to finding and reporting type mismatches between declarations and uses is a bit different from the kind of consistency checking that has been illustrated earlier. In particular, a program will no longer contain a group of (editable) declarations that may be inconsistent with the uses. Note, however, that two or more uses may be inconsistent with each other.

Although declarations will no longer be editable constituents of a program,[2] declarations will still appear in the program's display representation. Instead of being an editable component of the abstract syntax, the declarations will be attribute values – the results of the type-inference computation performed via the attribution mechanism. Each generated declaration represents a derived view of how variables are used in the program body.

For example, in the program shown below it can be deduced that variable c must be an integer variable (assuming there is no automatic type coercion). Variables a and b, on the other hand, may be either boolean or integer, although a and b must both have the same type. The declarations shown below are consistent with these observations:

```
main

program <identifier>;
var
    a, b: <type>;
    c: integer;
begin
    a := b;
    c := 1;
    while <exp> do
        <statement>
end.

Positioned at exp
```

Continuing with this example, when the expression b = c is inserted in the program, variables b and c must have the same type. Because of the presence of the assignment-statement c := 1, c (and hence b) must be of type integer. Because the assignment a := b forces a and b to have the same type, variable a must also be of type integer.

---

[2]The language's abstract syntax is redesigned to eliminate the declaration component from programs entirely:

program: Prog(identifier stmtList);

```
┌─────────────────────────────────────────────────────────────┐
│┌───────────────────────────────────────────────────────────┐│
││main                                                         ││
│└───────────────────────────────────────────────────────────┘│
│                                                              │
├──────────────────────────────────────────────────────────────┤
│program <identifier>;                                          │
│var                                                            │
│    a, b, c: integer;                                          │
│begin                                                          │
│    a := b;                                                    │
│    c := 1;                                                    │
│    while [(b = c)] do                                         │
│        <statement>                                            │
│end.                                                           │
├──────────────────────────────────────────────────────────────┤
│Positioned at exp                                              │
└──────────────────────────────────────────────────────────────┘
```

By changing the one statement that forces the type of variable c to be integer from c := 1 to c := true, the inferred type for all three variables changes to boolean:

```
┌─────────────────────────────────────────────────────────────┐
│┌───────────────────────────────────────────────────────────┐│
││main                                                         ││
│└───────────────────────────────────────────────────────────┘│
│                                                              │
├──────────────────────────────────────────────────────────────┤
│program <identifier>;                                          │
│var                                                            │
│    a, b, c: boolean;                                          │
│begin                                                          │
│    a := b;                                                    │
│    c := [true];                                               │
│    while (b = c) do                                           │
│        <statement>                                            │
│end.                                                           │
├──────────────────────────────────────────────────────────────┤
│Positioned at exp                                              │
└──────────────────────────────────────────────────────────────┘
```

A program has a type conflict when the program's constituents require a variable to have more than one type. For example, there are type conflicts for variables a, b, and c if we insert the statement a := 1, which requires that a be of type integer (hence b and c are also of type integer). The type conflicts are reported by generating a declaration that assigns them the type inconsistent.

```
┌────────────────────────────────────────────────────────────────┐
│┌────────────────────────────────────────────────────────────┐ │
││ main                                                         │ │
│└────────────────────────────────────────────────────────────┘ │
│                                                                  │
│ program <identifier>;                                            │
│ var                                                              │
│     a, b, c: inconsistent;                                       │
│ begin                                                            │
│     a := b;                                                      │
│     c := true;                                                   │
│     while (b = c) do                                             │
│         ┌──────┐                                                 │
│         │a := 1│                                                 │
│         └──────┘                                                 │
│ end.                                                             │
│                                                                  │
├──────────────────────────────────────────────────────────────┤
│ Positioned at stmt  (begin                                       │
└────────────────────────────────────────────────────────────────┘
```

To implement the type-inference scheme illustrated above, phylum **typeExp** is extended with an additional operator **NoTypeExp**, to represent the inconsistent type.

typeExp: NoTypeExp( )   [@ : "inconsistent"];

The four operators of **typeExp** are treated as the elements of a four-element lattice. The top element of the lattice, **EmptyTypeExp**, stands for the unknown, or most general, type; the bottom element of the lattice, **NoTypeExp**, stands for the inconsistent type.

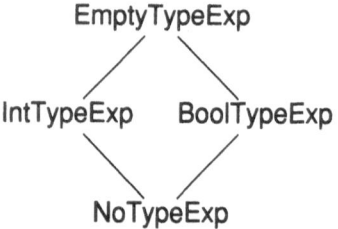

To infer types for a program's variables, a type environment, which associates types with variables, is threaded through the program left to right. When a variable is initially encountered in this threading, it is associated with the most general type, **EmptyTypeExp**. As subsequent occurrences of the variable are encountered, the variable's type is narrowed by taking the meet of the previously inferred type (found in the type environment) with the type implied by the new context for the variable. For example, if a variable is used as an integer in one context and as a boolean in another, the final type inferred for the variable is NoTypeExp, the meet of IntTypeExp and BoolTypeExp. NoTypeExp represents the inconsistent type, which indicates a conflict in how the variable is used in the program.

The meet operation for the type lattice is implemented by the function Meet, given in Figure 7.3.

Assignment-statements of the form a := b do not necessarily cause further narrowing of the types of a and b. However, assuming coercion is not a feature of the language, the presence of such a statement requires that a and b be of the same type. Thus, in addition to associating variables with types, the type environment must partition variables into equivalence classes of variables with the same types.

Program variables in the same type class are represented by phylum TypedSet, which consists of an IdSet together with a typeExp, representing the type common to all of the variables in the IdSet.

TypedSet: TypedSetOp(IdSet typeExp)   [@ : @ ":" @];

A type environment is a collection of TypedSets; type environments are represented by phylum TypeEnv, defined in Figure 7.4 along with several

```
typeExp Meet(typeExp t1, typeExp t2) {
        with (t1) (
                EmptyTypeExp: t2,
                IntTypeExp:
                        with (t2) (
                                EmptyTypeExp:   IntTypeExp,
                                IntTypeExp:     IntTypeExp,
                                BoolTypeExp:    NoTypeExp,
                                NoTypeExp:      NoTypeExp
                                ),
                BoolTypeExp:
                        with (t2) (
                                EmptyTypeExp:   BoolTypeExp,
                                IntTypeExp:     NoTypeExp,
                                BoolTypeExp:    BoolTypeExp,
                                NoTypeExp:      NoTypeExp
                                ),
                NoTypeExp: NoTypeExp
                )
        };
```

Figure 7.3. The function Meet implements the meet operation for the four element lattice of types.

```
list TypeEnv;
TypeEnv:         TypeEnvNil( )                              [@ : ]
        |        TypeEnvPair(TypedSet TypeEnv)   [@ : ^ [ ";%n" ] @ ]
        ;
TypeEnv NullTypeEnv( ) { TypeEnvNil };
TypeEnv TypeEnvUnion(TypeEnv c, identifier i1, identifier i2) {
    with (c) (
        TypeEnvNil:
            TypedSetOp(IdSetUnion(SingletonIdSet(i1), SingletonIdSet(i2)),
                        EmptyTypeExp) :: TypeEnvNil,
        TypeEnvPair(ts as TypedSetOp(s, tp), tail):
            IsElement(i1, s)
                ? IsElement(i2, s)
                    ? c
                    : TypeEnvUnion2(tail, s, tp, i2)
                : IsElement(i2, s)
                    ? TypeEnvUnion2(tail, s, tp, i1)
                    : ts :: TypeEnvUnion(tail, i1, i2)
    )
};
TypeEnv TypeEnvUnion2(TypeEnv c, IdSet s1, typeExp tp1, identifier i2) {
    with (c) (
        TypeEnvNil:
            TypedSetOp(IdSetUnion(s1, SingletonIdSet(i2)), tp1) :: TypeEnvNil,
        TypeEnvPair(ts2 as TypedSetOp(s2, tp2), tail):
            IsElement(i2, s2)
                ? TypedSetOp(IdSetUnion(s1, s2), Meet(tp1, tp2)) :: tail
                : ts2 :: TypeEnvUnion2(tail, s1, tp1, i2)
    )
};
TypeEnv MeetType(TypeEnv c, identifier i, typeExp t) {
    with (c) (
        TypeEnvNil: TypedSetOp(SingletonIdSet(i), t) :: TypeEnvNil,
        TypeEnvPair(ts, tail): with(ts) (
            TypedSetOp(s, tp): IsElement(i, s)
                ? TypedSetOp(s, Meet(t, tp)) :: tail
                : ts :: MeetType(tail, i, t)
        )
    )
};
```

Figure 7.4. Definition of module TypeEnv.

operations on TypeEnvs. A TypeEnv is a list of TypedSets, where each TypedSet represents program variables in the same equivalence class. The TypeEnv operations maintain a TypeEnv so that a given identifier is a member of exactly one TypedSet.

The operation TypeEnvUnion(TypeEnv c, identifier i1, identifier i2) creates a TypeEnv value that is identical to c except for the TypedSets that contain i1 and i2. In place of two separate TypedSets, in the new TypeEnv i1 and i2 are grouped in the same TypedSet; the IdSet element is the union of the IdSets for i1 and i2 and the typeExp element is the meet of the typeExps for i1 and i2.

The operation MeetType(TypeEnv c, identifier i, typeExp t) creates a TypeEnv value that is identical to c except that the TypedSet that contains i, which in c is associated with some type tp, is associated with type Meet(t, tp) in the new TypeEnv.

The attribute computation for inferring types in a program is expressed using two attributes, named typeEnvBefore and typeEnvAfter, which are threaded left to right through the instances of phyla exp, stmtList, and stmt in a program tree as shown in Figures 7.5 and 7.6.

The equations for the operators of stmt and exp make use of two additional functions on phylum TypeEnv:

PossibleUnion(TypeEnv c, exp e1, exp e2)

and

```
exp {
      inherited TypeEnv typeEnvBefore;
      synthesized TypeEnv typeEnvAfter;
      };
exp : EmptyExp, IntConst, True, False, Id  {
      exp.typeEnvAfter = exp.typeEnvBefore;
      }
   | Equal, NotEqual  {
      exp$2.typeEnvBefore =
            PossibleMeetType(exp$1.typeEnvBefore, exp$2, exp$3.type);
      exp$3.typeEnvBefore =
            PossibleMeetType(exp$2.typeEnvAfter, exp$3, exp$2.type);
      exp$1.typeEnvAfter = PossibleUnion(exp$3.typeEnvAfter, exp$2, exp$3);
      }
   | Add  {
      exp$2.typeEnvBefore =
            PossibleMeetType(exp$1.typeEnvBefore, exp$2, IntTypeExp);
      exp$3.typeEnvBefore =
            PossibleMeetType(exp$2.typeEnvAfter, exp$3, IntTypeExp);
      exp$1.typeEnvAfter = exp$3.typeEnvAfter;
      }
   ;
```

Figure 7.5. Attribution rules for inferring types in expressions. The two attributes typeEnvBefore and typeEnvAfter are threaded left to right to collect a TypeEnv that is consistent with the ways variables are used in the expression.

```
stmtList, stmt {
        inherited TypeEnv typeEnvBefore;
        synthesized TypeEnv typeEnvAfter;
        };
program : Prog { stmtList.typeEnvBefore = NullTypeEnv; };
stmtList : StmtListNil { stmtList.typeEnvAfter = stmtList.typeEnvBefore; }
        | StmtListPair {
          stmt.typeEnvBefore = stmtList$1.typeEnvBefore;
          stmtList$2.typeEnvBefore = stmt.typeEnvAfter;
          stmtList$1.typeEnvAfter = stmtList$2.typeEnvAfter;
          }
        ;

stmt      : EmptyStmt { stmt.typeEnvAfter = stmt.typeEnvBefore; }
        | Assign {
          exp.typeEnvBefore =
               PossibleMeetType(MeetType(stmt.typeEnvBefore,
                                               identifier, exp.type),
                               exp, identifier.type);
          stmt.typeEnvAfter =
               PossibleUnion(exp.typeEnvAfter, Id(identifier), exp);
          }
        | IfThenElse {
          exp.typeEnvBefore =
               PossibleMeetType(stmt$1.typeEnvBefore, exp, BoolTypeExp);
          stmt$2.typeEnvBefore = exp.typeEnvAfter;
          stmt$3.typeEnvBefore = stmt$2.typeEnvAfter;
          stmt$1.typeEnvAfter = stmt$3.typeEnvAfter;
          }
        | While {
          exp.typeEnvBefore =
               PossibleMeetType(stmt$1.typeEnvBefore, exp, BoolTypeExp);
          stmt$2.typeEnvBefore = exp.typeEnvAfter;
          stmt$1.typeEnvAfter = stmt$2.typeEnvAfter;
          }
        | Compound {
          stmtList.typeEnvBefore = stmt.typeEnvBefore;
          stmt.typeEnvAfter = stmtList.typeEnvAfter;
          }
        ;
```

Figure 7.6. Attribution rules for inferring types in a program. The two attributes typeEnvBefore and typeEnvAfter are threaded left to right to collect a TypeEnv that is consistent with the ways variables are used in the program.

PossibleMeetType(TypeEnv c, exp e, typeExp t).

These functions, defined in Figure 7.7, are used in the equations given in Figures 7.5 and 7.6 to create a TypeEnv that is a narrowing of TypeEnv c when the arguments of phylum exp are identifiers (as opposed to other kinds of expressions). For example, PossibleMeetType is used in the equations for an

```
TypeEnv PossibleUnion(TypeEnv c, exp e1, exp e2) {
        with (e1) (
                Id(i1): with (e2) (
                                        Id(i2): TypeEnvUnion(c, i1, i2),
                                        default: c
                                        ),
                default: c
                )
        };
TypeEnv PossibleMeetType(TypeEnv c, exp e, typeExp t) {
        with (e) (
                Id(i): MeetType(c, i, t),
                default: c
                )
        };
```

Figure 7.7. Declarations of the auxiliary functions PossibleUnion and PossibleMeet-Type.

IfThenElse operator so that, for a fragment such as

if x then <statement> else <statement>

the TypedSet for variable x gets narrowed by taking the meet of its type with BoolTypeExp. When the condition of a conditional-statement consists of something other than a lone identifier (*e.g.* x <> 100), additional narrowing at the IfThenElse operator is unnecessary.

The value of attribute stmtList.typeEnvAfter in operator Prog that is produced by the equations in Figure 7.6 is a TypeEnv that is consistent with the ways variables are used in the program. The following unparsing declaration causes it to be displayed as the program's (generated) declarations:

```
program:        Prog    [ @ : "program " @       ";%n"
                                "var "  "%t%n"
                                   stmtList.typeEnvAfter ";" "%b%n"
                                "begin"    "%t%n"
                                    @           "%b%n"
                                "end."]

        ;
```

CHAPTER 8

Practical Advice

This chapter furnishes practical advice to prospective editor-designers about a range of topics. Section 8.1 gives recommendations about the steps a novice editor-designer should take when starting to develop a new editor. Section 8.2 discusses how to organize an editor specification in a modular fashion to make it easier to re-use editor specifications. Section 8.3 contains two case studies of commonly arising editor features: the first concerns the facilities in a programming-language editor for writing comments in programs; the second concerns error messages.

To make the chapter cohesive, Sections 8.1 and 8.2 both make use of the same running example, the definition of a simple, screen-oriented desk calculator. The desk calculator allows one to create and modify a list of expressions, during which time each expression's value is incrementally computed and displayed.

The operations permitted are integer addition, subtraction, multiplication, and division. Each expression is displayed fully parenthesized. If the value of a divisor is 0, the error message

<—DIVISION BY ZERO—>

appears in the display and the value of the dividend is used as the value of the quotient. For example:

```
┌────────────────────────────────────────────────┐
│ main                                           │
├────────────────────────────────────────────────┤
│                                                │
│ (1 + 2)                                        │
│ VALUE = 3;                                     │
│                                                │
│ (2 / <—DIVISION BY ZERO—> (7 – 7))             │
│ VALUE = 2                                      │
│                                                │
├────────────────────────────────────────────────┤
│ Positioned at calc                             │
└────────────────────────────────────────────────┘
```

Expressions and subexpressions can be entered either textually or by template insertion. The command strings +, −, *, and / insert templates for the corresponding constructs. In textual input, parentheses are optional and the operation symbols * and / take precedence over + and −.

The desk calculator's "let-expressions" permit the binding of names to values. A let-expression has the form:

let <name > = <exp₁> in
    <exp₂>
ni

The value of a let-expression is the value of <exp₂>, as computed in an environment in which the given <name > is bound to the value of <exp₁>. In computing the value of <exp₁>, the given <name > either is unbound or has the value defined in an enclosing let construct. For example, the expression shown below has the value 5:

```
┌────────────────────────────────────────────────┐
│ main                                           │
├────────────────────────────────────────────────┤
│                                                │
│ let a = 1 in                                   │
│     let b = 2 + a in                           │
│         let a = a + a in                       │
│             a + b                              │
│         ni                                     │
│     ni                                         │
│ ni                                             │
│ VALUE = 5                                      │
│                                                │
├────────────────────────────────────────────────┤
│ Positioned at calc                             │
└────────────────────────────────────────────────┘
```

If an unbound *<name>* occurs in an expression, the error message

<—UNDEFINED SYMBOL

is printed after the name, and the value associated with the name is 0.

8.1. How to Begin Developing an Editor

Because there are so many aspects of an editor to be specified, a novice editor-designer may be confused as to how to begin. In this section we outline a recommended order of development and illustrate the steps to follow to develop the desk calculator.

To get started, it is usually advantageous to begin implementing a subset of the full language. We follow this practice here and begin by specifying an editor for a subset of the desk calculator language that consists of the integer constants and the arithmetic operators, omitting the constructs for let-expressions and the use of bound names in expressions. Extensions to support the full desk-calculator language are presented in Section 8.2.

8.1.1. Define abstract syntax

The first step in implementing the editor is to define the abstract syntax of the objects to be edited.

A context-free or BNF grammar for the given language, if available, may provide a convenient starting point. Bear in mind, however, that such grammars have usually been designed to serve a different purpose. Concrete syntax defines the strings of a language, and has often been fashioned to serve as input to a parser generator. In order to make the grammar unambiguous, extra syntactic categories may have been introduced; in order that left-to-right parsing be deterministic, the grammar may have been factored unnaturally.

Such parsing considerations are not relevant in designing abstract syntax for an editor. What is essential is that the structure of the abstract-syntax trees be convenient for editing. The hierarchical decomposition of an edited object must make sense to editor users, for the subtrees of this hierarchy, and not arbitrary substrings of the object's textual representation, will be selected, edited, cut, and pasted.

As a rule, minimize unnecessary syntactic distinctions. Generated editors enforce context-free syntactic correctness by restricting the insertion of subtrees with root symbol X to contexts where an X is permitted. However, a poorly written abstract syntax can turn this advantage into a weakness; inappropriate categories or excessive refinement will impede rather than assist editing. For example, whereas a parsing grammar may distinguish between expressions, terms, factors, and primaries, such distinctions are both unnecessary and cumbersome for editing. Because appropriate parentheses can be generated from the nesting structure of operations and their known precedence, a separate production for parenthesized expressions is also unnecessary.

Example. Such considerations lead to the following abstract syntax for the desk calculator:

```
root calc;
list calc;
calc    :       CalcNil( )
        |       CalcPair(exp calc)

        ;

exp     :       Null( )
        |       Sum, Diff, Prod, Quot(exp  exp)
        |       Const(INT)

        ;
```

In designing abstract syntax, omit all terminal characters that are merely syntactic sugar; the operator of a production is sufficient to distinguish it from the other alternatives of the left-hand-side phylum. The only terminal symbols that should be retained in abstract-syntax trees are identifiers, numerals, and other lexemes that carry semantic information.

The use of abstract-syntax trees as the sole intermediate representation of objects necessarily results in textually distinct expressions being represented by one and the same tree. Because the display of an object is generated from this tree alone, the abstract syntax imposes a canonical form not only on the structure of objects being edited, but on their textual representation as well.

In the abstract syntax, one should retain precisely the distinctions worth keeping and discard inessential differences in favor of a canonical representation and display format. Note that a construct that is omitted from the abstract syntax, such as redundant parentheses, may be included in the parsing grammar. In this case, one has the effect that the construct is translated to canonical form on input.

Example. In the desk calculator, only the number represented by a numeral is stored, which results in some loss of information from the original input text. For instance, the numerals 007 and 7 will both be translated to the INT value 7, which is displayed as the numeral 7. If numerals are to be displayed exactly as they are entered, they should appear in the abstract-syntax tree as lexemes, *i.e.* strings. In other words, if the distinction between 007 and 7 is to be preserved, then the last alternative of exp's phylum declaration should have been exp   :   Const(INTEGER);

where INTEGER is the phylum of integer lexemes:

INTEGER   :   Integer< [0–9]+ >;

An additional factor that influences the design of a language's abstract syntax is the design of attribution schemes on the language's terms. Lexically indistinguishable phrases are often used for distinct purposes. For example, in Pascal, an identifier may be a constant, a type, a variable, or a procedure name, and the required static-semantic analysis depends on the context in which the identifier is used. If a common syntax is employed for all usages of a phrase, then the context must be passed down in an inherited attribute in order to select the appropriate analysis. Alternatively, if a different phylum is used for each distinct usage, the context is implicit in the phylum's operators, and the appropriate attribute equations for static-semantic analysis are selected automatically; however, moving such phrases from one context to another would then require a syntactic coercion. Be resigned to the fact that the abstract syntax may need to be changed when attribution rules are addressed.

8.1.2. Define a display representation

The second step in implementing the editor is to provide an initial set of unparsing declarations. It is pointless to devote much effort to fancy pretty-printing until the abstract syntax has been firmly settled. At this stage, define only enough syntactic sugar to debug the abstract syntax. Defer consideration of alternative unparsing schemes, optional line breaks, context-dependent display formats, and special fonts. However, line breaks and simple indentation rules are advisable at this stage. At locations where attribute values will ultimately be displayed, either provide some temporary indication of the value or omit the reference entirely.

Unparsing declarations also specify permissible resting places for the selection. Start with a maximal number of resting places, since this will allow full exploration of syntax trees while debugging the abstract syntax and the attribute equations. Plan to eliminate undesirable resting places later.

Occurrences of primitive phyla are an exception to the rule – they should *not* be resting places. To see why, imagine that the selection is positioned on an instance of INT in one of the desk calculator's expressions. Executing **delete-selection** would replace the selection with 0, the placeholder term of INT. In contrast, by making INT a non-resting place the selection is forced one node higher in the tree, to the entire Const(INT) subterm. In this case, executing

delete-selection would replace the selection with Null, the placeholder term of exp, whose display representation is the string <exp>. In general, the textual representation of a placeholder term of a primitive phylum is not mnemonic, whereas that of a user-defined phylum can be made so.

Example. The following unparsing declarations specify that the desk calculator's expressions are displayed fully parenthesized, on separate lines, followed by their values (temporarily represented by ??), and separated by semicolons:

```
calc    :       CalcPair   [@ ::= @ "%nVALUE = ??" [";%n%n"] @];
exp     :       Null       [@ ::= "<exp>" ]
        |       Sum        [@ ::= "(" @ " + " @ ")" ]
        |       Diff       [@ ::= "(" @ " – " @ ")" ]
        |       Prod       [@ ::= "(" @ " * " @ ")" ]
        |       Quot       [@ ::= "(" @ " / " @ ")" ]
        |       Const      [@ ::= ^ ]
        ;
```

It is a good idea to adopt some convention for displaying placeholders and stick to it. Enclosing the phylum name in angle brackets, as we have done above, seems as good as any.

Note that if occurrences of primitive phyla are not resting places, then in operators of arity two or more, they will not be individually selectable. For example, suppose we had included integer pairs in the desk calculator:

```
exp     :       Pair(INT  INT) [ @ ::=  "<" ^ "," ^ ">" ];
```

Then, an entire pair would be selectable, but not the components separately. An extra syntactic level is required if the components are to be individually selectable:

```
exp       :     Pair(component component) [ @ ::= "<" @ "," @ ">" ];
component:      ComponentNull( )          [ @ ::= "<integer>" ]
          |     Component(INT)            [ @ ::= ^ ]
          ;
```

The omission of such extra syntactic levels is a common mistake.

8.1.3. Define template transformations

The third step in creating the editor specification is to provide a set of transformations that will permit the top-down derivation of an object. Complex
transformations for restructuring objects may be added later; for now, define.
only transformations that correspond directly to productions of the grammar.
Such transformations are called *template transformations*, because invoking one
has the effect of providing a template into which additional components may be
inserted.

The template transformation associated with a production of the form

$$X_0 : operator \ (\ X_1 \ \cdots \ X_n \ )$$

should normally be:

transform X_0 on *transformation-name* $<X_0>$: *operator* $(<X_1>, \ . \ . \ . \ , \ <X_n>)$;

Any of the $<X_i>$ in the replacement expression may instead be $[X_i]$, with the
choice affecting whether or not a placeholder for X_i appears in the resulting
template. (When X_i is neither an optional phylum nor an optional list phylum,
the distinction between $<X_i>$ and $[X_i]$ is irrelevant, since the placeholder and
completing terms for X_i are the same.)

Example. The following transformations permit the derivation of expression
trees in the desk calculator:

transform exp
        on "+" <exp> : Sum (<exp>, <exp>),
        on "–" <exp> : Diff (<exp>, <exp>),
        on "*" <exp> : Prod (<exp>, <exp>),
        on "/" <exp> : Quot (<exp>, <exp>)
        ;

Template transformations are normally not required for list phyla and optional
phyla, since adequate transformations are already built into some of the commands that move the selection (*e.g.* **forward-with-optionals** and **forward-
sibling-with-optionals**). Template transformations are also not appropriate for
productions corresponding to lexemes; the mechanism for inserting lexemes will
be defined later when the concrete syntax for textual input is defined.

8.1.4. Generate and debug the editor

The partial editor specification that has been written up to this point defines enough of the editor's structure-editing functions that it is usually worthwhile to create an editor from the specification and test the editor's characteristics. Generate an editor by invoking the sgen command on the specification files; by default, the editor that sgen creates is placed in file syn.out. This editor should be able to derive any term, except for token leaves.

8.1.5. Define concrete input syntax

The next step in implementing the editor is to define the concrete syntax for text input. As a first cut, provide only enough rules to permit lexemes and simple expressions to be entered. The parser can be elaborated later to permit additional language constructs to be entered as text. Ultimately it may be desirable to implement a parser for the entire language so that users of the editor can read in objects from existing text files.

Example. The following rules permit the user of the desk calculator to enter an integer constant at an expression. The rules designate phylum Exp to be an entry point to the parser when the selection is positioned at an exp in the abstract-syntax tree; the rules define the concrete syntax for expression input to be the strings of phylum Exp, which, by the declarations shown below, consists only of the INTEGER lexemes:

```
INTEGER:      Integer< [0–9]+ >;
Exp { synthesized exp abs; };
Exp      ::=      (INTEGER)   { $$.abs = Const(STRtoINT(INTEGER)); };
exp      ~        Exp.abs;
```

Note that, as in the declaration of the INTEGER phylum, a blank must precede the closing angle bracket of a lexeme declaration.

Do not forget to provide appropriate entry declarations; if an entry declaration is lacking for a phylum X, the editor has no way to parse text entered when the selection is positioned at an X-node. (In such a case, the user is forbidden from even entering text at an X-node.)

It is a good idea to put in the rule for scanning whitespace now, so that it is not left out later, by accident, when additional rules are added to the editor specification to permit more elaborate phrases to be parsed.

```
WHITESPACE: Whitespace< [\ \t\n] >;
```

Once we have provided rules for parsing lexemes, the specification defines an editor that can be used to derive any term of the language. In many cases these rules are sufficient for the purposes of development. However, some editor-designers may find it desirable to provide a few additional rules to permit simple phrases to be entered as text.

Example. The declarations given below augment the previous definition of phylum Exp to consist of the arithmetic expressions with optional parentheses; the precedence declarations specify that * and / take precedence over + and −.

```
left '+' '−';
left '*' '/';
Exp  ::=  (Exp '+' Exp)   { $$.abs = Sum( Exp$2.abs, Exp$3.abs); }
      |   (Exp '−' Exp)   { $$.abs = Diff(Exp$2.abs, Exp$3.abs); }
      |   (Exp '*' Exp)   { $$.abs = Prod(Exp$2.abs, Exp$3.abs); }
      |   (Exp '/' Exp)   { $$.abs = Quot(Exp$2.abs, Exp$3.abs); }
      |   ('(' Exp ')')   { $$.abs = Exp$2.abs; }
      ;
```

With these rules, the user can now enter all arithmetic expressions when the selection is positioned at an exp node of the abstract-syntax tree.

For now, write the productions for parsing lists as right-recursive rules rather than as left-recursive rules. Although right-recursive rules have the disadvantage that it will not be possible to parse more than some fixed number of list elements (because the parser stack overflows at some point), right-recursive rules are somewhat more straightforward to write. The rules can be changed later to use left recursion. (See Section 5.5, "Parsing Lists".)

Example. The following right-recursive rules permit the user to enter a list of expressions when the current selection is positioned at a calc node:

```
VALUE :        Value < "VALUE" >;
Calc { synthesized calc abs; };
Calc   ::=    (Exp)            { Calc.abs = Exp.abs :: CalcNil; }
       |      (Exp ';' Calc)   { Calc$1.abs = Exp.abs :: Calc$2.abs; }
       |      (Exp VALUE '=' INTEGER)
                               { Calc.abs = Exp.abs :: CalcNil; }
       |      (Exp VALUE '=' INTEGER ';' Calc)
                               { Calc$1.abs = Exp.abs :: Calc$2.abs; }
       ;
calc   ~      Calc.abs;
```

Phylum calc in the example above is a (non-optional) list phylum. The list property is used when a phylum is to be treated as a sequence whose minimum length is one; consequently, the rules for parsing the corresponding concrete phylum (*i.e.* phylum Calc) should be written, as above, so that a sequence of *one* or more elements is accepted. By contrast, the parsing rules that should be supplied for a concrete phylum that corresponds to an optional-list phylum are slightly different; they should be written to accept a sequence of *zero* or more elements.

Example. If calc were declared to be an optional list, the rules for the desk calculator's concrete input syntax would be written as follows:

```
Calc    ::=    ( )              { Calc.abs = CalcNil; }
        |      (Exp)            { Calc.abs = Exp.abs :: CalcNil; }
        |      (Exp ';' Calc)   { Calc$1.abs = Exp.abs :: Calc$2.abs; }
        |      (Exp VALUE '=' INTEGER)
                                { Calc.abs  = Exp.abs :: CalcNil; }
        |      (Exp VALUE '=' INTEGER ';' Calc)
                                { Calc$1.abs = Exp.abs :: Calc$2.abs; }
        ;
```

At this point, a new version of the editor should be generated to test and debug the rules for parsing textual input.

Once the (preliminary version of the) editor's concrete input syntax is settled, it is a good idea to use sgen's −r option whenever a new version of the editor is generated. The −r option directs sgen to attempt to bypass unnecessary calls on some of the subsidiary tools that are invoked as part of editor generation, such as yacc, lex, and cc. (When the −r option is employed, sgen compares the new versions of the intermediate files it generates with any previously generated intermediate files that are in the local directory; if certain files are identical, some of the steps of generating an editor are skipped. The new intermediate files are retained for future comparisons.)

8.1.6. Define attribution rules

The fifth step in implementing the editor is to define the attribution schemes that will be incorporated in the editor. Decide what information needs to be passed around the syntax tree, and write the attribute equations that cause the right information to be passed to the right locations. Ultimately, some of the information collected in attributes will be used to annotate the display, for example, to inform the user of inconsistencies and possible errors or to perform context-sensitive pretty-printing. However, during development it is often better to concentrate on the attribute equations by themselves and to postpone modifying the unparsing declarations to incorporate attributes in the display.

Example. The following attribute declarations and attribute equations define the v attribute of each exp in the syntax tree to be the value of the arithmetic subexpression with root exp. As specified by the equations of operator Quot, if a divisor is 0, the local attribute error is defined to have the value

<—DIVISION BY ZERO—>

and the value of the quotient is taken to be the value of the dividend; if the value of the dividend is not 0, the value of error is the empty string.

```
exp { synthesized INT v; };
exp : Null   { exp.v = 0; }
    | Sum    { exp$1.v = exp$2.v + exp$3.v; }
    | Diff   { exp$1.v = exp$2.v – exp$3.v; }
    | Prod   { exp$1.v = exp$2.v * exp$3.v; }
    | Quot   { local STR error;
                error = (exp$3.v == 0) ? "<—DIVISION BY ZERO—> " : "";
                exp$1.v = (exp$3.v == 0) ? exp$2.v : (exp$2.v / exp$3.v);
             }
    | Const { exp$1.v = INT; }
    ;
```

At this point, a new version of the editor should be generated to test and debug the specification's attribute declarations and attribute equations.

To examine a syntax tree's attribute values when debugging the attribution rules, use the commands **dump-on**, **show-attribute**, and **write-attribute**.[1] Because all three commands generate the textual representation of one or more attribute values, it is worth spending the effort to provide unparsing declarations for the phyla used to represent attribute values. This should be done for *all* attribute phyla, not just the ones whose members will annotate the display in the finished editor.

---

[1]The **dump-on** command creates a textfile buffer that is thereafter associated with the buffer that is the current buffer at the time of the command. In the new buffer, the editor displays the current values of all attribute instances associated with the apex of the editing buffer's selection; the dump-buffer's contents are updated whenever the selection in the editing buffer changes position. The **show-attribute** command writes to a given buffer the textual representation of the value of an attribute instance of the current selection's apex. The **write-attribute** command writes to a file the textual representation of the value of an attribute instance of the current selection's apex.

8.1.7. Putting the finishing touches on (an initial version of) the editor

A few steps remain to complete an initial version of the editor.

First, the unparsing declarations should be changed so that information collected in attributes annotates the display in the appropriate places.

Example. In the desk-calculator specification, two unparsing declarations need to be changed: the unparsing declaration for the operator CalcPair needs to be altered as shown below so that each expression in a calc is displayed with the value of attribute exp.v (*i.e.* the value computed for the expression).

calc   :   CalcPair [@ ::= @ "%nVALUE = " exp.v [";%n%n"] @];

The unparsing declaration for operator Quot needs to be altered so that each quotient is displayed together with the value of the local attribute error. This change causes occurrences of operator Quote where the denominator has the value 0 to be annotated with the message <—DIVISION BY ZERO—>.

exp   :   Quot [@ ::= "(" @ " / " error @ ")"];

Earlier, we suggested writing the unparsing declarations with a maximal number of resting places so that the editor-designer would be able to explore syntax trees fully while debugging the specification. It is now time to eliminate undesired resting places by changing some of the @ selection symbols to ˆ. Because selections in lists are handled specially, be sure to define the selection symbols in lists to follow the pattern given below:

```
list listType;
listType :      ListTypeNull( )
         |      ListTypePair(listElementType listType) [@ ::= ˆ @ ]
         ;
listElement:    ListElementNull [ˆ ::= "<listElement>" ];
```

Example. The desk calculator's unparsing declarations need to be changed as follows:

```
calc    :       CalcPair [@ ::= ^ "%nVALUE = " exp.v [";%n%n"] @];
exp     :       Null      [^ ::= "<exp>" ]
        |       Sum       [^ ::= "(" @ " + " @ ")" ]
        |       Diff      [^ ::= "(" @ " - " @ ")" ]
        |       Prod      [^ ::= "(" @ " * " @ ")" ]
        |       Quot      [^ ::= "(" @ " / " error @ ")" ]
        |       Const     [^ ::= ^ ]
        ;
```

One last step needs to be taken to complete an initial version of the editor: check that the editing-mode symbols that appear in the specification's unparsing declarations (*i.e.* the ::= and : symbols) specify the desired text-editing properties for the various operators. For consistency, we recommend that textual reediting be permitted for exactly those elements that can be entered as text.

Example. Suppose the desk calculator's parsing rules permit text entry only of lexemes, but not full expressions, as outlined at the beginning of Section 8.1.5. The entry-mode symbols of the operators of phylum exp should be changed to forbid textual reediting of the arithmetic operators:

```
exp     :       Null      [^ ::= "<exp>" ]
        |       Sum       [^ : "(" @ " + " @ ")" ]
        |       Diff      [^ : "(" @ " - " @ ")" ]
        |       Prod      [^ : "(" @ " * " @ ")" ]
        |       Quot      [^ : "(" @ " / " error @ ")" ]
        |       Const     [^ ::= ^ ]
        ;
```

8.2. Modular Construction of Editor Specifications

For more experienced editor-designers, the most effective approach to building an editor is often not to start writing the specification from scratch, as illustrated in Section 8.1, but to adapt parts of already existing specifications. The declarative nature of SSL facilitates such re-use of existing specifications. In particular, an editor specification for language L_1 can be employed in the specification for a language L_2 that has L_1 as a sublanguage. Thus, an important aspect of writing an editor specification is the organization of the specification in a modular fashion.

It must be recognized that modularity in editor specifications is supported in rather crude ways. In fact, the notion of a module in SSL is only an informal one. There is no such thing as a module declaration, and modularity is supported only by two rather simple facilities that permit different parts of an editor specification to be contained in different source files:

1) All argument files passed to the sgen command (*i.e.* files with suffix .ssl) are concatenated together in the order found on the command line.

2) SSL permits new attributes, operators, and equations to be attached to an existing phylum and new attribute equations to be attached to existing operators.

Despite the primitiveness of these mechanisms, there are significant benefits to be gained by taking advantage of them to help organize a specification.

There are two main advantages of a modular organization. First, it enhances the comprehensibility of editor specifications. Second, it permits the same "module" to be used in several editors; in particular, it facilitates the creation of collections of related editors – both upward-compatible editors for extensions of a base language as well as different editors for the same language that perform different kinds of static inferencing or display the language in different formats.

Organizing an editor specification or editor extension in a modular fashion involves placing closely related aspects of the specification in the same file and less related aspects of the specification in different files. We recommend organizing each layer of a specification in six files containing the following elements:

1) abstract-syntax declarations,
2) lexical declarations,
3) concrete-input syntax declarations,
4) attribute-domain declarations and operations on the attribute domain,
5) attribute declarations and equations, and
6) unparsing declarations.

In the remainder of this section, we describe and illustrate some guidelines for organizing the specification's various files. To illustrate the conventions that we have found to be useful, we augment the desk-calculator specification of Section 8.1 to extend the editor with additional constructs for let-expressions and the use of bound names in expressions. The declarations from Section 8.1 are extended by the declarations presented below.

Abstract-syntax specification file

Additional language constructs require new phyla and operators to be defined to represent their abstract syntax. Transformations on these constructs should also be placed in the abstract-syntax specification file.

Example. Two new operators, Let and Use, are added to the existing phylum exp to represent let-expressions and uses of bound names, respectively. A new phylum, symb, is also required, to represent the *<name >* component in a let-expression.

```
exp      :        Let(symb exp exp)
         |        Use(ID)
         ;
symb     :        DefNull( )
         |        Def(ID)
         ;
```

A transformation declaration is needed to define a template for inserting a let-expression:

```
transform exp on "let" <exp>: Let(<symb>, <exp>, <exp>);
```

Lexical specification file

New lexemes should be declared in a file of lexeme declarations. Unfortunately, one sometimes finds that precedence conflicts in lexical definitions disrupt the modular organization of editor specifications. Because the order in which lexeme declarations are given is important, it is sometimes necessary to disregard "module boundaries" and merge new lexeme declarations with previously given ones.

Example. To parse let-expressions and uses of names, four lexical phyla are introduced. The first three are keywords in let-expressions; the fourth is a phylum of identifiers.

```
LET      :        LetLex< "let" >;
IN       :        InLex< "in" >;
NI       :        NiLex< "ni" >;
ID       :        IdLex< [a–zA–Z][a–zA–Z0–9]*|[?] >;
```

Note that an ID is either an alphanumeric string or a question mark, the latter being used to represent an undefined name. For this extension of the desk calculator, the new lexeme declarations do not conflict with any of the previous ones, so it is possible to place them in a file of their own. However, if a further extension introduced additional keywords, to avoid a conflict their declarations would have to be placed before the declaration of ID.

Parsing specification file

As with lexeme declarations, conflicts with previous parsing rules sometimes arise that interfere with the modular organization of editor specifications. For example, ordering conflicts can arise between new and old precedence declarations. The introduction of new parsing rules can also introduce ambiguities in the concrete-input language.

Example. A new phylum, Symb, defines the concrete input syntax of identifiers in the binding clause of a let-expression. Phylum Symb is designated as the entry point to the parser when the selection is positioned at a symb element. Phylum Exp is extended with rules for parsing let-expressions and identifiers that appear in expressions. No conflicts with previous rules arise in this example.

```
Symb   { synthesized symb abs; };
Symb   ::= (ID)  { Symb.abs = Def(ID); };
symb   ~  Symb.abs;
Exp    ::= (LET Symb '=' Exp IN Exp NI) {
             Exp$1.abs = Let(Symb.abs, Exp$2.abs, Exp$3.abs);
             }
       |   (ID) { Exp$1.abs = Use(ID); }
       ;
```

Attribute-domain specification file

Some phyla are used exclusively to represent attribute values and never to represent a subterm of an abstract-syntax tree. That is, they are are not derivable from the root phylum, so their members can never appear as editable components of a buffer. The declarations for such a phylum, together with associated operations on the phylum, should be encapsulated in a file as an abstract data type.

Example. The scoping of names in let-expressions is block-structured, so each exp must be evaluated in an environment of appropriate local name bindings provided by an inherited environment attribute. One possible representation for such environment attributes is as a list of identifier-value pairs, as defined by the following declarations for phyla BINDING and ENV:

```
list ENV;
ENV      :        NullEnv( )                          [ @ : ]
         |        EnvConcat(BINDING ENV)        [ @ : ^ [",%n"] @ ]
         ;
BINDING:          Binding(ID INT)                      [ ^ : ^ "=" ^ ];
```

Three functions are defined to manipulate environments: EnvEmpty( ), which returns an empty environment, EnvInsert(ID id, INT v, ENV env), which returns an ENV that is identical to env except that in the new ENV id is bound to v, and EnvLookup(ID id, ENV env), which returns the binding for id if it exists in env and returns Binding("?", 0) if it does not. These functions are defined as follows:

```
ENV EnvEmpty( ) { NullEnv };
```

```
ENV EnvInsert(ID id, INT v, ENV env) { Binding(id, v) :: env };
```

```
BINDING EnvLookup(ID id, ENV env) {
  with (env) (
    NullEnv( ): Binding("?", 0),
    EnvConcat(b as Binding(s, *), e): (id == s) ? b : EnvLookup(id, e)
    )
};
```

Attribution specification file

New attribute declarations and their associated attribute equations should be placed in a separate attribution specification file. In some situations, for example when the "module" extends an existing phylum with new operators, it is necessary to add additional attribute equations to previously defined operators.

Example. To the previously defined phylum exp, we add an additional declaration for an inherited environment attribute env of type ENV.

```
exp     { inherited ENV env; };
symb    { synthesized ID id; };
```

The attribution rules to build up the environment are as follows:

```
calc : CalcPair { exp.env = EnvEmpty( ); };
exp : Let {
        exp$2.env = exp$1.env;
        exp$3.env = EnvInsert(symb.id, exp$2.v, exp$1.env);
        }
     ;
symb  DefNull { symb.id = "?"; }
    | Def { symb.id = ID; }
     ;
```

The attribution rules of the existing arithmetic operators must also be extended by adding attribute equations to pass the inherited environment to both the left and right operands.

```
exp      :      Sum, Diff, Prod, Quot {
                        exp$2.env = exp$1.env;
                        exp$3.env = exp$1.env;
                        }
         ;
```

It is also necessary to define attribute equations for attribute v of the left-hand-side occurrence of exp in the Let and Use productions. Finally, if an unbound identifier is detected at a Use, a local attribute of the Use production, named error, is given the value <—UNDEFINED SYMBOL. These declarations are shown below:

```
exp : Let { exp$1.v = exp$3.v; }
    | Use { local BINDING b;
            local STR error;
            b = EnvLookup( ID, exp.env);
            error = with(b)(
                    Binding(s, *):
                      (s == "?") ? "<—UNDEFINED SYMBOL" : ""
                    );
            exp.v = with(b)( Binding(*, i): i );
            }
    ;
```

Unparsing specification file

The remaining component contains the unparsing declarations for the new productions declared in the abstract-syntax specification file.

Example. The unparsing declarations for let-expressions specify that all four
kinds of operators are editable and that operator Use is annotated by the value
of its error attribute.

```
exp   : Let      [^ ::= "let %t" @ " = " @ " in%n" @ "%b%nni" ]
      | Use      [^ ::= ^ error ]
      ;
symb  : DefNull  [@ ::= "<name>" ]
      | Def      [@ ::= ^ ]
      ;
```

As defined above, the attribution specification file and the unparsing
specification file are closely coupled; attributes that appear in the unparsing
declarations are declared and defined by equations in the attribution
specification file. This coupling prevents one from generating a syntax-only editor for the language (*i.e.* an editor that does not make use of the attribution
mechanism).

It is possible to de-couple the attribution specification file and the unparsing
specification file by the following means: in place of each attribute name
appearing in an unparsing declaration, use a macro name; to create a version of
the editor that employs the attribution mechanism, provide a macro definition
that expands the macro to the appropriate attribute name; to create a syntax-only
editor, provide a definition that expands the macro to the null string.

Example. In our running example, the unparsing declaration for operator
Use would be changed to the following rule:

```
exp   :         Use    [^ ::= ^ ERROR ];
```

To generate an editor that provides warnings for uses of unbound variables,
ERROR would be declared to expand as the name of the error attribute:

```
# define ERROR error
```

For a syntax-only editor, ERROR would be defined as:

```
# define ERROR
```

8.3. Problems That Frequently Arise

In handling certain common features of different languages, a handful of problems crop up repeatedly. This section contains two case studies: the first concerns the facilities in a programming-language editor for commenting programs; the second concerns error messages.

8.3.1. Comments

The chief problem with comments stems from the fact that, in many programming languages, comments serve no linguistic purpose (other than to delimit tokens) and consequently are permitted to appear in arbitrary places in program text. In a conventional compiler, the scanner skips over the comment-delimiter characters and the comment text at the same time that it skips over the "white-space" characters that can also appear between tokens (*e.g.* blanks, tabs, and newline characters).

By contrast, in editors generated with the Synthesizer Generator, comments can appear only at certain selected places designated by the editor-designer. A basic requirement is that the comment text must be preserved among the components of a program's underlying abstract-syntax tree. Thus, comments can only appear in the program display at the places where the editor's unparsing declarations specify that these components appear. Even in user-typed input, comments can only appear at certain selected places; any editor-designer would find it very tedious work to try to create an input grammar that permitted comments to appear between each pair of tokens.

Comments in the Synthesizer Generator

Because the existing features of the Synthesizer Generator do not support comments located in arbitrary places in the text of a program, an editor-designer is restricted to providing more controlled ways of annotating programs with comments. To illustrate some of the kinds of constructions that can be supported, we describe below how to extend the programming-language editor from Chapter 4 so that programs can be annotated with several classes of comments. In these examples, a comment consists of a list of text lines enclosed in curly braces, such as the following one:

{Now is the time
 for all good men
 to come to the aid
 of the party.}

To represent comment text in a program's abstract-syntax tree, we introduce three phyla: commentLines, commentLine, and CLINE. Phylum comment-Lines is a list of elements of phylum commentLine; phylum CLINE, which will be defined shortly, represents a single line of comment text. The first two of these phyla are defined by the following declarations:

```
list commentLines;
commentLines : CommentLinesNil( )      [ @ : ]
             | CommentLinesPair(commentLine  commentLines)
                                        [ @ ::= ˆ ["%n "] @ ]

             ;
commentLine  : CommentLineNil( )       [ ˆ : "<comment>" ]
             | CommentLine(CLINE)      [ ˆ : ˆ ]
             ;
```

For comments to be represented as elements of abstract-syntax trees, it is necessary to alter the phylum declarations introduced in Chapter 4 to represent a program's abstract syntax. For example, to require a comment to appear at the head of each program, we would alter the declaration for the Prog operator to include an additional commentLines component:

```
program:        Prog(commentLines identifier  declList  stmtList)
                   [ @ :    "{" @ "}%n"
                            "program " @  ";%n"
                            "var"          "%t%n"
                                @ ";"      "%b%n"
                            "begin" "%t%n"
                                @          "%b%n"
                            "end."]

      ;
```

When using the editor generated with this declaration, exactly one comment appears in each buffer at the head of the program, as in the following example:

```
┌──────────────────────────────────────────────────────────────┐
│┌──────────────────────────────────────────────────────┐       │
││main                                                    │       │
│└──────────────────────────────────────────────────────┘       │
│                                                                │
│ ┌────────────────┐                                             │
│ │Now is the time │                                             │
│  ┌──────────────┐                                              │
│  │for all good men│                                            │
│   ┌───────────────┐                                            │
│   │to come to the aid│                                         │
│    ┌─────────────┐                                             │
│    │of the party.│}                                            │
│ program <identifier>;                                          │
│ var                                                            │
│     <identifier> : <type>;                                     │
│ begin                                                          │
│     <statement>                                                │
│ end.                                                           │
│                                                                │
│ Positioned at commentLines                                     │
└──────────────────────────────────────────────────────────────┘
```

A more useful addition to the language involves defining an optional phylum
that is added as an element of each construct to which a comment may be
attached. For example, the following phylum declarations define the optional
phylum optionalComment:

optional optionalComment;
optionalComment
        : OptionalCommentNil( )   [^ :]
        | OptionalComment(commentLines)   [@ ::= " {" @ "}"]
        ;

To permit a comment to be attached to each variable declaration, the declaration
for the operator Declaration is altered to have an additional optionalComment
component:

decl   :   Declaration(identifier typeExp optionalComment)
                   [^ : @ error " : " @ "%t%t" @ "%b%b"];

The following example shows a comment attached to an empty declaration:

```
┌─────────────────────────────────────────────────────────────┐
│ ┌───────────────────────────────────────────────────────────┐ │
│ │ main                                                        │ │
│ └───────────────────────────────────────────────────────────┘ │
│                                                               │
│ {<comment>}                                                   │
│ program <identifier>;                                         │
│ var                                                           │
│     <identifier> : <type> {Now is the time                    │
│                         for all good men                      │
│                         to come to the aid                    │
│                         of the party.};                       │
│ begin                                                         │
│    <statement>                                                │
│ end.                                                          │
│                                                               │
│ Positioned at commentLines                                    │
└─────────────────────────────────────────────────────────────┘
```

As a further addition to aid the insertion of comments in declarations, it is useful to provide the following transformation command, which will insert a placeholder for the hidden optional comment:

```
transform decl on "comment-part"
    Declaration(i, t, [optionalComment]):
    Declaration(i, t, <optionalComment>);
```

By use of this transformation, it becomes easy to add a comment to an uncommented declaration. For example, suppose the transformation is invoked when the selection is as shown below:

```
┌─────────────────────────────────────────────────────────────┐
│ ┌───────────────────────────────────────────────────────────┐ │
│ │ main                                                        │ │
│ └───────────────────────────────────────────────────────────┘ │
│ COMMAND: comment-part                                         │
│ {<comment>}                                                   │
│ program <identifier>;                                         │
│ var                                                           │
│     a : integer;                                              │
│ begin                                                         │
│    <statement>                                                │
│ end.                                                          │
│                                                               │
│ Positioned at declList    comment-part                        │
└─────────────────────────────────────────────────────────────┘
```

This command causes a placeholder for optionalComment to be inserted in the declaration and advances the current selection to it.

```
┌─────────────────────────────────────────────────────┐
│ ┌───────────────────────────────────────────────┐   │
│ │main                                            │   │
│ └───────────────────────────────────────────────┘   │
│                                                       │
│ {<comment>}                                           │
│ program <identifier>;                                 │
│ var                                                   │
│     a : integer  {<comment>} ;                        │
│ begin                                                 │
│     <statement>                                       │
│ end.                                                  │
│                                                       │
│ Positioned at optionalComment                         │
└─────────────────────────────────────────────────────┘
```

In the two extensions described above, we took an *existing* operator and added an additional component to it. An alternative way to add comments to the language is to declare some entirely *new* operators for existing phyla. For example, the operator StmtComment declared below pairs an element of phylum commentLines with an element of phylum stmt:

stmt   :   StmtComment(commentLines stmt)
                 [ˆ : "{" @ "}%t%n" @ "%b"];

An example of a statement-comment is given below:

```
┌─────────────────────────────────────────────────────┐
│ ┌───────────────────────────────────────────────┐   │
│ │main                                            │   │
│ └───────────────────────────────────────────────┘   │
│                                                       │
│ {<comment>}                                           │
│ program <identifier>;                                 │
│ var                                                   │
│     <identifier> : <type>;                            │
│ begin                                                 │
│     {Now is the time                                  │
│      for all good men                                 │
│      to come to the aid                               │
│      of the party.}                                   │
│         <statement>                                   │
│ end.                                                  │
│                                                       │
│ Positioned at commentLines                            │
└─────────────────────────────────────────────────────┘
```

The two components commentLines and stmt are part of one operator. The intention is that stmt be the implementation of the specification provided in the comment part; to indicate the subordinate status of the implementation, the stmt part is indented one level deeper than the comment text.

In conjunction with the Synthesizer Generator's alternate-unparsing facility, statement-comments can be used to provide a mechanism for suppressing details of a file. By furnishing an alternate unparsing scheme that elides the stmt component of a StmtComment, an editor-designer can provide a mechanism for hiding the refinement of a comment. For example, we could define the following alternate unparsing scheme for the StmtComment operator, which would display the body of a comment as the string . . . :

```
stmt    :        StmtComment  [^ : "{" @ "} ... " .. ];
```

By switching to the alternate unparsing scheme, the user could hide implementation details and, at the same time, cause more of the program to be displayed on the screen.

One way of inserting statement-comments would be to have a template-insertion command for them, which would be declared as follows:

```
transform stmt on "comment"
    <stmt>: StmtComment(<commentLines>, <stmt>);
```

A more general facility can be provided to make it possible to enclose an existing statement, or group of statements, within a statement-comment. This is done by extending the editor specification with the following two transformations commands:

```
transform stmt on "comment" s: StmtComment(<commentLines>, s);
transform stmtList on "comment"
        s: StmtComment(<commentLines>, Compound(s)) :: StmtListNil;
```

For example, consider what happens when the comment command is invoked in the program shown below:

```
┌────────────────────────────────────────────────────────┐
│ main                                                     │
├────────────────────────────────────────────────────────┤
│ COMMAND: comment                                         │
├────────────────────────────────────────────────────────┤
│ {<comment>}                                              │
│ program <identifier>;                                    │
│ var                                                      │
│    a : integer;                                          │
│ begin                                                    │
│    a := 1;                                               │
│    ┌───────┐                                             │
│    │a := 2;│                                             │
│    ├───────┤                                             │
│    │a := 3;│                                             │
│    ├───────┤                                             │
│    │a := 4│;                                             │
│    └───────┘                                             │
│    a := 5                                                │
│ end.                                                     │
├────────────────────────────────────────────────────────┤
│ Positioned at stmtList    comment                        │
└────────────────────────────────────────────────────────┘
```

The transformation causes the selected sublist to be enclosed in a compound-statement, which, in turn, is contained in a statement-comment.

```
┌────────────────────────────────────────────────────────┐
│ main                                                     │
├────────────────────────────────────────────────────────┤
│                                                          │
├────────────────────────────────────────────────────────┤
│ {<comment>}                                              │
│ program <identifier>;                                    │
│ var                                                      │
│    a : integer;                                          │
│ begin                                                    │
│    a := 1;                                               │
│    ┌────────────┐                                        │
│    {│<comment>  │}                                       │
│    └────────────┘                                        │
│       begin                                              │
│          a := 2;                                         │
│          a := 3;                                         │
│          a := 4                                          │
│       end;                                               │
│    a := 5                                                │
│ end.                                                     │
├────────────────────────────────────────────────────────┤
│ Positioned at commentLines                               │
└────────────────────────────────────────────────────────┘
```

Textual input of comments

Clearly, comment text itself (as opposed to an entire comment in the context of some larger program construct) has to be entered and reedited textually, not structurally. In the Synthesizer Generator, all text that is typed in by the user is parsed to determine whether it is syntactically correct in the context of the current selection, so comment text is parsed, even though it has a trivial syntactic structure. (For most programming languages, comment text is a regular set.)

This requirement causes some slight inconveniences for the editor-designer, because to parse comment text properly, it is necessary to treat the input text in such a way that the ordinary whitespace lexemes defined by phylum **WHITESPACE** go unrecognized. In particular, it is necessary to override the normal consumption of whitespace that is enabled by the usual declaration of phylum **WHITESPACE**. This is accomplished by means of (left-) context sensitive scanning, specified with directives to shift the scanner to a different scanning state.

The regular expression of a lexeme declaration is enabled only when the current scanning state of the scanner matches the start-state of the declaration; if a declaration has no start-state or has the start-state **INITIAL**, the declaration is enabled in *all* scanner states. At the beginning of parsing, the scanner is a state that only recognizes the **INITIAL**-state lexemes. The scanner's state can be changed in two ways: by a start-state directive in an entry declaration and by a final-state directive in a lexeme declaration.

Example. We now illustrate how to cause comment text to be treated as a sublanguage separate from the rest of the editor's concrete-input language, shielded by the scanner state **NO_WHITESPACE**. We will suppose that phylum **WHITESPACE** is defined in the usual way:

WHITESPACE :   WhitespaceLex< [\ \t\n] >;

The two kinds of lexemes that make up comment text – individual newline characters and single lines of comment text, which are represented by phyla **CLINEBREAK** and **CLINE**, respectively – are declared to be recognizable only when the scanner is in scanner state NO_WHITESPACE:

CLINEBREAK :   CLinebreakLex< <NO_WHITESPACE>[\n] >;
CLINE   :   CLineLex< <NO_WHITESPACE>[^\n\}]+ >;

The use of the scanner state in these declarations ensures that these tokens, which are used only in the limited context of parsing comment text, do not conflict with any of the other tokens employed in the editor's concrete input syntax. However, it is also necessary to ensure the converse, namely that other tokens, such as WHITESPACE, do not interfere with CLINEBREAK and CLINE. Thus, the CLINEBREAK and CLINE declarations should precede any lexeme declaration that is not shielded by some scanner state.

The context-free syntax of comments is specified in a straightforward manner by the following declarations:

```
yCommentLine { synthesized commentLine a; };
yCommentLine ::= (CLINE)   { $$.a = CommentLine(CLINE); }
      |          ()        { $$.a = CommentLine(" "); }
      ;
yCommentLines       {
      inherited commentLines tail;
      synthesized commentLines reversed;
      };
yCommentLines
      ::= (yCommentLine) {
         yCommentLines.reversed =
            yCommentLine.a :: yCommentLines.tail;
         }
      |  (yCommentLines CLINEBREAK yCommentLine) {
         yCommentLines$2.tail =
            yCommentLine.a :: yCommentLines$1.tail;
         yCommentLines$1.reversed = yCommentLines$2.reversed;
         }
      ;
```

The changeover from the INITIAL scanner state to the NO_WHITESPACE state is specified in the entry declaration for commentLines:

```
commentLines ~ <NO_WHITESPACE>yCommentLines.reversed {
                yCommentLines.tail = CommentLinesNil;
                };
```

A second place where it is necessary to have the scanner state change from INITIAL to NO_WHITESPACE is when a left curly bracket is recognized; this change is triggered by the final-state component of the token declaration. The state then stays as NO_WHITESPACE until a right curly bracket, whose final-state component triggers the resetting of the scanner state to the INITIAL state:

```
LCURLY    :    LCurly< [\{] <NO_WHITESPACE> >;
RCURLY    :    RCurly< [\}] <INITIAL> >;
```

Because the transition to state NO_WHITESPACE is handled in the lexeme declarations, there is no initial-state declaration in the entry declaration for optionalComment.

```
yOptionalComment        { synthesized optionalComment a; };
yOptionalComment
        ::= ( )   { $$.a = OptionalCommentNil; }
        |   (LCURLY yCommentLines RCURLY) {
                $$.a = OptionalComment(yCommentLines.reversed);
                yCommentLines.tail = CommentLinesNil;
                }
        ;
optionalComment  ~  yOptionalComment.a;
```

In conjunction with the above declarations, the final change needed is to alter the parsing rules for textual input of declarations so that the user can type in a comment with each declaration:

```
Decl::=(Ident ':' INTKW yOptionalComment) {
        Decl.t = Declaration(Ident.t, IntTypeExp, yOptionalComment.a);
        }
    |  (Ident ':' BOOLKW yOptionalComment) {
        Decl.t = Declaration(Ident.t, BoolTypeExp, yOptionalComment.a);
        }
    ;
```

8.3.2. Error messages

When an editor-designer creates an editor with the Synthesizer Generator, part of the editor specification consists of attribute equations for computing derived information from the abstract-syntax tree. As an object is developed with the generated editor, its attributes are maintained so as to be consistent with the grammar's defining equations; that is, the editor's derived information is always up to date.

Derived information about an object being edited can be displayed in the object's display representation. In programming-language editors, it is possible to use the attribution mechanism to perform static analysis of the program and have the results of this computation reported in the form of messages about static-semantic errors that exist in a program (see Chapters 2, 4, and 7).

Selective display of error messages

Instead of having errors reported continually as programs are created or modified (as happens with the editor specifications presented in Chapters 4 and 7), it may be preferable to suppress the display of errors until the user wishes to see them.

The ability to vary an object's display representation can be provided to the user by furnishing more than one unparsing declaration for the productions of the language. For each production up to two unparsing declarations are permitted. The first one specifies the production's *principal unparsing scheme*; the second one specifies its *alternate unparsing scheme*. The principal unparsing scheme is used by default when the production is instantiated. Thereafter, the user may manually toggle between the principal and alternate schemes, either selectively at an individual node of the tree or globally throughout the current buffer.

Example. To illustrate the idea of using the alternate unparsing schemes so that errors are reported only when the user requests them, we modify the programming-language editor from Chapter 4 so that error messages are displayed only in the alternate unparsing schemes.

```
decl    :    Declaration    [^ : @ " : " @ @]
                            [^ : @ error " : " @ @]

        ;
stmt    :    Assign          [^ ::= @ " := " @]
                            [^ ::= @ error " := " @ assignError]
        |    IfThenElse      [^ : "if " @ " then" "%t%n"
                                    @ "%b%n"
                             "else%t%n"
                                    @ "%b"]
                            [^ : "if " @ typeError " then" "%t%n"
                                    @ "%b%n"
                             "else%t%n"
                                    @ "%b"]
        |    While           [^ : "while " @ " do" "%t%n"
                                    @   "%b"]
                            [^ : "while " @ typeError " do" "%t%n"
                                    @   "%b"]

        ;
```

exp : Id   [ˆ ::= ˆ]
                              [ˆ ::= ˆ error]
       | Equal   [ˆ ::= "(" @ " = " @ ")"]
                              [ˆ ::= "(" @ " = " error @ ")"]
       | NotEqual   [ˆ ::= "(" @ " <> " @ ")"]
                              [ˆ ::= "(" @ " <> " error @ ")"]
       | Add   [ˆ ::= "(" @ " + " @ ")"]
                              [ˆ ::= "(" @ leftError " + " rightError @ ")"]
       ;

Thus, although the program shown below contains a number of errors, none are
reported because the messages about them are suppressed by the principal
unparsing scheme.

```
| main                                                                    |
|-------------------------------------------------------------------------|
| COMMAND: alternate-unparsing-on                                         |
|-------------------------------------------------------------------------|
| program <identifier> ;                                                  |
| var                                                                     |
|     a : integer;                                                        |
|     a : boolean;                                                        |
|     c : integer;                                                        |
| begin                                                                   |
|     b := c;                                                             |
|     while a do                                                          |
|         <statement>                                                     |
| end.                                                                    |
|-------------------------------------------------------------------------|
| Positioned at identifier                                                |
```

After the command **alternate-unparsing-on** is used to switch to the alternate
unparsing schemes, error messages appear at the locations of the program's
errors:

```
┌────────────────────────────────────────────────────────┐
│ ┌─────────────────────────────────────────────────────┐│
│ │main                                                  ││
│ └─────────────────────────────────────────────────────┘│
│ ┌─────────────────────────────────────────────────────┐│
│ │                                                      ││
│ │                                                      ││
│ │ program ⌜<identifier>⌟;                              ││
│ │ var                                                  ││
│ │     a { MULTIPLY DECLARED } : integer;               ││
│ │     a { MULTIPLY DECLARED } : boolean;               ││
│ │     c : integer;                                     ││
│ │ begin                                                ││
│ │     b { NOT DECLARED } := c;                         ││
│ │     while a { BOOLEAN EXPRESSION NEEDED } do         ││
│ │         <statement>                                  ││
│ │ end.                                                 ││
│ │                                                      ││
│ └─────────────────────────────────────────────────────┘│
│ ┌─────────────────────────────────────────────────────┐│
│ │ Positioned at identifier                             ││
│ └─────────────────────────────────────────────────────┘│
└────────────────────────────────────────────────────────┘
```

Error messages and textual input

Some problems arise with generated messages in connection with textual reedit-ing. In particular, if a generated message can appear in a selection that is edit-able as text, it is desirable that the user not have to explicitly delete the message text for the modified text to (re-)parse correctly. One possibility is to anticipate in the parsing grammar all possible messages that may occur in various loca-tions throughout the program.

A much simpler approach is to choose a pair of special delimiters that enclose all message text and treat all character sequences enclosed in these delimiters as whitespace. What makes this approach possible is the fact that message values (*i.e.* attribute values) are derived from the underlying abstract-syntax tree. Mes-sage values reflect the state of the tree before the user's input causes the tree to be modified; messages consistent with the state of the altered tree will be gen-erated after change propagation of attribute values quiesces. Consequently, we do not care about the old value of any message and are free to discard from the user's input all the characters of the message's old display representation.

For example, suppose we choose the convention that error messages be enclosed in the strings {-- and } so that they would appear as in the following example:

```
┌────────────────────────────────────────────────────────────────┐
│ main                                                             │
├────────────────────────────────────────────────────────────────┤
│                                                                  │
│ program <identifier>;                                            │
│ var                                                              │
│     a {-- MULTIPLY DECLARED } : integer;                         │
│     a {-- MULTIPLY DECLARED } : boolean;                         │
│     c : integer;                                                 │
│ begin                                                            │
│     b {-- NOT DECLARED } := c;                                   │
│     while a {-- BOOLEAN EXPRESSION NEEDED } do                   │
│         <statement>                                              │
│ end.                                                             │
├────────────────────────────────────────────────────────────────┤
│ Positioned at identifier                                         │
└────────────────────────────────────────────────────────────────┘
```

We would then change the declaration of phylum WHITESPACE so as to cause all error-message text to be discarded. For example, the following declaration filters out all strings enclosed in {-- and }:

WHITESPACE: < [\ \t\n]|([\{][\-][\-][^\}]*[\}]) >;

Error phyla

In the examples given above, the error messages are string constants (*i.e.* members of phylum STR). However, there are several good reasons for defining a phylum of error values whose members unparse as the error messages. For example, the programming-language editor from Chapter 4 would use phylum Error defined as follows:

```
Error
  : NoError( )
  | MultiplyDeclared( )     ["^" : " {-- MULTIPLY DECLARED }"]
  | NotDeclared( )          ["^" : " {-- NOT DECLARED }"]
  | BooleanNeeded( )        ["^" : " {-- BOOLEAN EXPRESSION NEEDED "]
  | IntNeeded( )            ["^" : " {-- INT EXPRESSION NEEDED }"]
  | IncompatibleTypes( )    ["^" : " {-- INCOMPATIBLE TYPES }"]
  | IncompatibleAssign( )   ["^" : " {-- INCOMPATIBLE TYPES IN := }"]
  ;
```

The attribute equations that establish error messages would be changed to use these values, as in the following equation:

```
stmt    :       IfThenElse, While {
                    local Error typeError;
                    typeError = (exp.type == IntTypeExp)
                                    ? BooleanNeeded : NoError;
                }

        ;
```

Working with error values instead of error strings allows error messages to be formatted better. By defining a phylum of error values whose members unparse as the error messages, the editor-designer can use formatting commands in the messages' unparsing declarations to control how error messages are formatted. With STR-valued error messages, the editor-designer would (usually) not have such control; ordinarily, when a term t is displayed, any percent signs in STR subterms of t and in STR-valued attributes of t are *not* interpreted as formatting commands. (Although it is possible to change this behavior using an SSL directive – see *The Synthesizer Generator Reference Manual* – this is not generally done.)

Example. The following unparsing declaration uses the %{, %o, and %} directives to specify that if it necessary to break the line in the middle of the error message, preference is given to breaking it between the two words:

```
Error   :       MultiplyDeclared
                    [^ : " %{{-- MULTIPLY %oDECLARED }%}"];
```

Creating a phylum of error values also allows one to define error values that have substructure, which is useful for defining parameterized error messages. For example, we could parameterize the NotDeclared operator with an IDEN-TIFIER whose value is displayed as part of the error message.

```
Error   :       NotDeclared(IDENTIFIER)
                    [^ : " {-- ID " ^ " NOT DECLARED }"];
```

In the following attribute equations, this operator is used to incorporate the undeclared variable in the message itself:

```
exp      :   Id {
                local Error error;
                error = with(identifier) (
                            IdentifierNull: NoError,
                            Identifier(i):
                                    IsDeclared(identifier, {Prog.env})
                                        ? NoError
                                        : NotDeclared(i)
                        );
             }
         ;
```

CHAPTER 9

Generating Code Using Attributes

In a system to support interactive program development, testing, and debugging, it is desirable to provide the ability to initiate execution at any time and have the program begin executing immediately, with no delay for compilation. Such a system should maintain the program in executable form at all times and update the program's object code in accordance with changes to the program's source code. The task of an *incremental compiler* in such a system would be to update the target code after a modification to the program, re-using as much old code as possible.

In practice, for the sake of efficiency, the system may have to support two kinds of executable representations. Some procedures of a program would be executed in native mode, using native code generated by a conventional compiler; selected procedures of the program (ones of particular interest to the programmer) would be executed interpretively, using target code maintained by the incremental compiler.

Incremental recompilation is an obvious application for an incremental attribute-updating mechanism, such as the one found in the Synthesizer Generator. By incrementally updating attributes whose defining equations express the generation of executable code, a language-based editor can produce and maintain target code as programs are created and modified [Reppy84, Mughal85].

Coupling an incremental compiler with a language-based editor has other benefits as well. Because a language-based editor has knowledge available to it about which portions of a program are incomplete, it can compile **halt** instructions for those locations. This makes it is possible to execute incomplete programs – until a **halt** instruction is encountered.

In this chapter, we demonstrate how the Synthesizer Generator can be used to generate a programming-language editor that maintains an executable representation of a program. Section 9.1 describes previous work on incremental compilation. Section 9.2 discusses how incremental attribute updating can be exploited to create and maintain interpretable target code as programs are modified.

9.1. Approaches to Incremental Recompilation

Previous systems have used several different approaches to the problem of maintaining an executable representation and incrementally updating it when the program is modified. These approaches are described and briefly compared below.

In the Cornell Program Synthesizer [Teitelbaum81], which supported a small subset of PL/I, the interior nodes of the program's derivation tree corresponded to instances of control constructs. Each interior node contained a code template for that construct. The leaves corresponded to simpler constructs such as assignment-statements and expression lists. Each leaf contained postfix stack code for executing the construct. When interior nodes were modified (by structural editing operations), an appropriate code template was substituted. After a leaf was modified (by editing the leaf's text), the modified text would be parsed and new stack code generated. Modifications to a program's declarations triggered more extensive reanalysis of the program. First the local declarations would be reexamined to determine new activation-record offsets, then the program would be traversed in preorder and new code generated for each of the leaves.

In the IPE incremental programming environment developed under GANDALF [Medina-Mora81], which supported a variant of C, non-context-free processing was invoked on a per-procedure basis: static-semantic checking was invoked whenever the programmer completed modifications to a procedure; code generation and link/loading were then invoked if the procedure was static-semantically correct. All global references were resolvable at code-generation/link time; all referenced global objects were required to have been previously declared, so space would have already been allocated for them. For example, procedure calls were made indirectly through entry points that were assigned when the procedures were created. The code generator generated native machine code in which all global references were absolute and all local references were relative to the program counter. Thus, because all references were independent of the physical location of the code, it was unnecessary to have a relinking step when blocks of code were relocated.

The DICE system [Fritzson84, Fritzson84a] was designed to support the development of programs for embedded systems, where it is convenient and often necessary for the programming environment to reside on a host computer and the program to be run on a target computer connected to the host. As in IPE, DICE generated position-independent code and used an extra level of indirection for procedure calls. One way that it differed was that it supported incremental compilation at the level of individual statements. Fritzson reported that this was usually an order of magnitude faster than recompiling the entire procedure. (The information needed for statement-level incremental compilation was needed anyway to support source-level debugging.)

The incremental compiler of the Magpie system [Schwartz84] and [Delisle84] translated Pascal source into machine code on a per-procedure basis as done in IPE. The feature that set Magpie apart from other work was that compilations took place under the control of a process that ran concurrently with the editing process. The compilation process had lower priority, so much of the compilation was performed when the user was idle. A procedure was queued for translation after the syntax and static semantics had been checked; the actual translation was postponed until the user was not making requests that required an immediate response. (The issue of structuring a programming environment as concurrent editing and code generation processes is also discussed in [Ford85].)

In discussing incremental compilation strategies, it is useful to make a distinction between the *granularity of recompilation* and the *extent of recompilation*: the term "granularity of recompilation" refers to the size of program fragments over which editing can take place before a recompilation occurs; the term "extent of recompilation" refers to the amount of code that is actually recompiled after a program is modified.

For example, the Cornell Program Synthesizer's granularity of recompilation was a single assignment-statement or expression, while the granularity of recompilation coincided with the extent of recompilation, unless the fragment modified was a declaration, in which case the extent of recompilation was the entire procedure. In both IPE and Magpie, recompilation was invoked only when the user had finished editing an entire procedure and the procedure was always recompiled in its entirety; thus, the granularity of recompilation always coincided with the extent of recompilation.

Although the granularity of recompilation and the extent of recompilation are separate aspects of the recompilation problem, they are related issues. In order to achieve good response time, a system that performs fine-granularity recompilations needs to confine the extent of recompilation as much as possible.

9.2. Incremental Recompilation Using Attributes

The Synthesizer Generator's incremental attribute-evaluation mechanism can be harnessed for incremental recompilation by defining attributes whose values represent the program's code. After a program is modified, the attribute-updating mechanism that is employed by generated editors to reestablish consistent attribute values causes the code attributes to be revised appropriately. With this scheme, the extent of recompilation depends on the number of code-related attributes that need new values after a program is modified.

One way to write a code-generation specification is to define a particular attribute of the tree's root so that it contains the code for the entire program. The attribute equations that specify how this attribute gets its value would combine the values of other attributes in the tree – ones that represent code fragments associated with subcomponents of the program. This approach has been used for code generation in compilers [Milos84], but there is a significant drawback to using it in an editor, where attributes are reevaluated. The chief drawback is that a change to any component of the tree will cause new attribute values to propagate all the way to the root of the program tree. To reduce the number of attributes that receive new values after a program is modified, a different approach is needed.

One alternative would be to have a number of individual code fragments in the tree and to coalesce them just prior to execution. The drawback of this approach is that the step of coalescing code introduces a delay before execution can begin.

9.2.1. Generating code graphs using SSL

The chief issue in using the Synthesizer Generator's attribution mechanism to generate and update code is how to limit the extent of recompilation. For example, one would like to have the property that when a single expression or assignment-statement is modified, updates are limited to just a few of the tree's code fragments. Rather than use either of the two schemes outlined above, we use the technique described in [Mughal85] to generate code represented as a graph of fragments. In this approach, individual fragments are located in attributes distributed throughout the program tree; however, they are linked together into a code graph for the entire program. Components of each fragment provide links to other fragments. The interpreter executes the fragments directly: initially, the interpreter is passed a link to the first fragment of the program; other fragments are accessed, as necessary, by following the appropriate links.

In this section, we present a sample SSL specification for generating such code. The example discussed is an extension to the editor specification that was presented in Chapter 4. Discussion of the extent-of-recompilation issue is postponed until Section 9.2.3.

The individual code fragments could contain any of a number of code representations: instructions in a machine's native code, code for an abstract stack machine (such as P-code), lambda expressions, or even source code in another high-level language. For expository purposes, we use here a simple stack code whose syntax is defined by the following SSL specification of the phylum CODE:

```
CODE : Halt( )                          [^ : "Halt"]
     | Quit( )                          [^ : "Quit"]
     | PushVar(identifier LINK)         [^ : "PushVar " ^ ..]
     | Store(identifier LINK)           [^ : "Store " ^ ..]
     | PushInt(INT LINK)                [^ : "PushInt " ^ ..]
     | TestEqualInt(LINK)               [^ : "TestEqualInt" ..]
     | TestNotEqualInt(LINK)            [^ : "TestNotEqualInt" ..]
     | AddInt(LINK)                     [^ : "AddInt" ..]
     | PushBool(BOOL LINK)              [^ : "PushBool" ^ ..]
     | TestEqualBool(LINK)              [^ : "TestEqualBool" ..]
     | TestNotEqualBool(LINK)           [^ : "TestNotEqualBool" ..]
     | BranchOnCondition(LINK LINK)     [^ : "BranchOnCondition" .. ..]
     ;
```

The construction of the code graph is specified with two sets of attributes named entry and next, which carry information used to link the fragmented code together. The entry attribute at the root of a given program segment is a link to the first instruction to be executed for that segment. The next attribute at the root of a given program segment is a link to the first instruction to be executed after the code for the given segment has been completed.

For the moment, assume that the type of the entry and next attributes is LINK:

```
stmt, stmtList, exp {
        synthesized LINK entry;
        inherited LINK next;
        };
```

We also assume that an operation LINK MakeLink(CODE c) creates a LINK from a CODE-valued attribute. The definitions of LINK and MakeLink are discussed further in Section 9.2.2.

The values of the entry and next attributes are incorporated into instructions to establish the code graph. Each stmt incorporates the LINK stmt.next into its code fragment, and passes up a LINK to the first instruction of this fragment in the attribute stmt.entry. Intermediate nodes in the abstract-syntax tree, such as each StmtListPair node in a statement list, merely pass on linking information in their entry and next attributes and do not contribute additional instructions to the code.

Example. Recall that phylum stmtList is defined by the following abstract syntax rules:

```
list stmtList;
stmtList:        StmtListNil( )
        |        StmtListPair(stmt stmtList)
        ;
```

Attributes entry and next are passed through the operators of phylum stmtList as follows:

```
stmtList:        StmtListNil  { stmtList.entry = stmtList.next; }
        |        StmtListPair  {
                        stmtList$1.entry = stmt.entry;
                        stmt.next = stmtList$2.entry;
                        stmtList$2.next = stmtList$1.next;
                        }
        ;
```

The equation that defines the entry point of the conditional-statement also illustrates how intermediate nodes in the abstract-syntax tree merely pass on linking information:

```
stmt    :        IfThenElse  { stmt$1.entry = exp.entry; };
```

This equation defines the entry point of the statement to be the entry point of the expression; whatever statement precedes the IfThenElse will receive a link to the expression, allowing the interpreter to jump to the expression directly rather than making a jump to the conditional-statement and then another jump to the expression.

The semantics of the individual control constructs of the source language are expressed in terms of CODE values as follows. Each construct has an associated code fragment, which is defined as the value of a local CODE-valued attribute. The LINK constructed from this fragment is passed to other (appropriate) components of the program using the entry and next attributes.

Example. The Prog operator has one code fragment represented by the local attribute named code. The code fragment consists of a single Quit instruction, which would cause the CODE interpreter to terminate execution. The LINK formed from attribute code is passed down the abstract-syntax tree, providing access to the final instruction to be executed when the program's body has completed:

```
program:     Prog {
                   local CODE code;
                   code = Quit;
                   stmtList.next = MakeLink(code);
                   }
         ;
```

Halt instructions are generated at all places where the CODE interpreter should abort execution, such as at unexpanded placeholders or at locations of type errors.

Example. Consider the attribute equations that define the code for the EmptyStmt and Assign operators. EmptyStmt represents an unexpanded statement, and its code is defined to contain a Halt instruction.

```
stmt    :     EmptyStmt {
                    local CODE code;
                    code = Halt;
                    stmt.entry = MakeLink(code);
                    }
        ;
```

An alternative way of defining EmptyStmt is to treat it as a skip statement, namely with the equation

```
stmt    :     EmptyStmt { stmt.entry = stmt.next; };
```

The abstract-syntax tree contains error attributes that indicate the presence or absence of errors in the program. Thus, the Assign operator's code is a Halt if either of two error conditions holds, indicated by particular values of the attributes named assignError and identifier.type:

```
stmt : Assign {
     local CODE code;
     code = (assignError != "" || identifier.type == EmptyTypeExp)
        ? Halt : Store(identifier, stmt.next);
     stmt.entry = exp.entry;
     exp.next = MakeLink(code);
     }
  ;
```

In a similar fashion, information about operand types available in the tree's type attributes can be used to choose a CODE operator of the appropriate type. For example, the equation for attribute code of operator Equal uses type information to choose between operators TestEqualInt and TestEqualBool:

```
exp : Equal {
     local CODE code;
     code = (error != "") ? Halt
        : exp$2.type == IntTypeExp ? TestEqualInt(exp$1.next)
        : TestEqualBool(exp$1.next);
     exp$1.entry = exp$2.entry;
     exp$2.next = exp$3.entry;
     exp$3.next = MakeLink(code);
     }
  ;
```

The complete sets of code-generation equations for the source language's statements and expressions are given in Figures 9.1 and 9.2, respectively.

To illustrate the code produced by these equations, consider the program used in Chapter 4:

```
program <identifier>;
var
    i : integer;
begin
    i := 1;
    while (i <> 100) do
        i := (i + 1)
end.
```

The code for this program is distributed among eleven local code fragments, which are displayed in the table given below. (In the table, the symbol . . . is used wherever the instruction's LINK field is the instruction on the next line.

```
stmt : EmptyStmt {
          local CODE code;
          code = Halt;
          stmt.entry = MakeLink(code);
          }
     | Assign {
          local CODE code;
          code = (assignError != "" || identifier.type == EmptyTypeExp)
                    ? Halt : Store(identifier, stmt.next);
          stmt.entry = exp.entry;
          exp.next = MakeLink(code);
          }
     | IfThenElse {
          local CODE code;
          code = (typeError != "") ? Halt
                    : BranchOnCondition(stmt$2.entry, stmt$3.entry);
          stmt$1.entry = exp.entry;
          exp.next = MakeLink(code);
          stmt$2.next = stmt$1.next;
          stmt$3.next = stmt$1.next;
          }
     | While {
          local CODE code;
          code = (typeError != "") ? Halt
                    : BranchOnCondition(stmt$2.entry, stmt$1.next);
          stmt$1.entry = exp.entry;
          exp.next = MakeLink(code);
          stmt$2.next = exp.entry;
          }
     | Compound {
          stmt.entry = stmtList.entry;
          stmtList.next = stmt.next;
          }
     ;
```

Figure 9.1. Code-generation equations for the five kinds of statements of the source language.

```
exp : EmptyExp { local CODE code;
                 code = Halt;
                 exp.entry = MakeLink(code);
                 }
    | IntConst {  local CODE code;
                  code = PushInt(STRtoINT(INTEGER), exp.next);
                  exp.entry = MakeLink(code);
                  }
    | True {      local CODE code;
                  code = PushBool(true, exp.next);
                  exp.entry = MakeLink(code);
                  }
    | False {     local CODE code;
                  code = PushBool(false, exp.next);
                  exp.entry = MakeLink(code);
                  }
    | Id {        local CODE code;
                  code = (identifier.type == EmptyTypeExp) ? Halt
                     : PushVar(identifier, exp.next);
                  exp.entry = MakeLink(code);
                  }
    | Equal {     local CODE code;
                  code = (error != "") ? Halt
                     : (exp$2.type == IntTypeExp) ?
                           TestEqualInt(exp$1.next)
                     : TestEqualBool(exp$1.next);
                  exp$1.entry = exp$2.entry;
                  exp$2.next = exp$3.entry;
                  exp$3.next = MakeLink(code);
                  }
    | NotEqual {  local CODE code;
                  code = (error != "") ? Halt
                     : (exp$2.type == IntTypeExp) ?
                           TestNotEqualInt(exp$1.next)
                     : TestNotEqualBool(exp$1.next);
                  exp$1.entry = exp$2.entry;
                  exp$2.next = exp$3.entry;
                  exp$3.next = MakeLink(code);
                  }
    | Add {       local CODE code;
                  code = (leftError != "" || rightError != "") ? Halt
                                             : AddInt(exp$1.next);
                  exp$1.entry = exp$2.entry;
                  exp$2.next = exp$3.entry;
                  exp$3.next = MakeLink(code);
                  }
    ;
```

Figure 9.2. Code-generation equations for the expressions of the source language.

For the two cases where the LINK field is not the next instruction in the table the
LINK field is indicated by a symbolic label.)

Label	Operator	Argument	LINK
	PushInt	1	. . .
	Store	i	. . .
a:	PushVar	i	. . .
	PushInt	100	. . .
	TestNotEqualInt		. . .
	BranchOnCondition		. . ., b
	PushVar	i	. . .
	PushInt	1	. . .
	AddInt		. . .
	Store	i	a
b:	Quit		. . .

For the moment, assume that function CodeForLink "coerces" a LINK to a
piece of CODE. An interpreter for CODE values can then be implemented as
function Interp of Figure 9.4. Auxiliary phyla and operations used by Interp
are defined in Figure 9.3.

9.2.2. Links and circularities

In using an attribute grammar to specify the generation of a code graph the
question of *circularities* naturally arises. In particular, in creating the code for
loops, we have to be careful to avoid circular dependences in the specification.

Obviously, linked code for loop constructs has to be circular at some level;
however, we must be careful not to confuse two different kinds of circularities.
The kind of circularity that causes problems in SSL is a circular dependence in a
specification's *attribute equations*; the circularity that is inherent in code for
loops is a circularity in the representation for the code, *i.e.* a circularity within
attribute *values*.

The code-generation equations defined above do, in fact, define a circular
attribute grammar, as one can see by examining the dependences of the While
operator:

$$\text{While.code} \rightarrow \text{exp.next} \rightarrow^+ \text{exp.entry}$$
$$\rightarrow \text{stmt\$2.next} \rightarrow^+ \text{stmt\$2.entry} \rightarrow \text{While.code}$$

To break the circularity, we introduce one level of indirection into the generated
code by making use of the built-in, primitive phylum ATTR to implement

```
list pushDownList;
pushDownList:    Empty( )
           |       Cons(val pushDownList)
                ;
val        :       Uninitialized( )                        [^ : "UNINITIALIZED"]
           |       IntVal(INT)
           |       BoolVal(BOOL)
                ;
list environ;
environ  :         EnvironNil( )
           |       EnvironPair(binding environ)            [^ : ^ ["%n"] ^]
                ;
binding  :         Binding(identifier val)                [^ : "<" ^ ":" ^ ">"];
environ Bind(identifier id, val v, environ s) {
        with(s) (
                EnvironNil: Binding(id, v) :: s,
                EnvironPair(Binding(i, vv), tail):
                        id == i ? Binding(id, v) :: tail
                              : Binding(i, vv) :: Bind(id, v, tail)
                )
        };
val ValOfId(identifier id, environ s) {
        with(s) (
                EnvironNil: Uninitialized,
                EnvironPair(Binding(i, v), tail): id == i ? v : ValOfId(id, tail)
                )
        };
exitStatus:        TerminatedNormally(environ)
                        [^ : "Terminated normally.%nFinal state:%n" ^]
           |       ExecutionAborted( )
                        [^ : "Execution aborted"]
                ;
```

Figure 9.3. Definitions for auxiliary phyla and operations used in the interpreter.

```
exitStatus Interp(LINK progCounter, environ s, pushDownList stack) {
  with(CodeForLink(progCounter)) (
    Halt: ExecutionAborted,
    Quit: TerminatedNormally(s),
    PushVar(id, next): Interp(next, s, ValOfId(id, s) :: stack),
    Store(id, next):
      with(stack) (
        Empty( ): ExecutionAborted,
        Cons(v, tail): Interp(next, Bind(id, v, s), tail)
        ),
    PushInt(i, next): Interp(next, s, Cons(IntVal(i), stack)),
    TestEqualInt(next):
      with(stack) (
        Cons(IntVal(v), Cons(IntVal(w), rest)):
          Interp(next, s, BoolVal(v == w) :: rest),
        default: ExecutionAborted
        ),
    TestNotEqualInt(next):
      with(stack) (
        Cons(IntVal(v), Cons(IntVal(w), rest)):
          Interp(next, s, BoolVal(v != w) :: rest),
        default: ExecutionAborted
        ),
    AddInt(next):
      with(stack) (
        Cons(IntVal(v), Cons(IntVal(w), rest)): Interp(next, s, IntVal(v + w) :: rest),
        default: ExecutionAborted
        ),
    PushBool(b, next): Interp(next, s, Cons(BoolVal(b), stack)),
    TestEqualBool(next):
      with(stack) (
        Cons(BoolVal(v), Cons(BoolVal(w), rest)):
          Interp(next, s, BoolVal(v == w) :: rest),
        default: ExecutionAborted
        ),
    TestNotEqualBool(next):
      with(stack) (
        Cons(BoolVal(v), Cons(BoolVal(w), rest)):
          Interp(next, s, BoolVal(v != w) :: rest),
        default: ExecutionAborted
        ),
    BranchOnCondition(comp1, comp2):
      with(stack) (
        Cons(BoolVal(true), rest): Interp(comp1, s, rest),
        Cons(BoolVal(false), rest): Interp(comp2, s, rest),
        default: ExecutionAborted
        )
    )
  };
```

Figure 9.4. Definition of an interpreter for phylum CODE.

LINKs. For example, we could add the following pre-processor definition to the above editor specification:

```
# define  LINK  ATTR
```

Phylum **ATTR** is a phylum of *attribute references*: if a is an attribute occurrence, then **&&**a is an ATTR-valued expression whose value is a reference to a. Operation MakeLink used in the code-generation equations given above could be implemented by introducing the following pre-processor macro:

```
# define  MakeLink(x)  (&&x)
```

In essence, these definitions break the circularity because some of the edges of the dependence cycle are replaced by attribute references. Ordinarily, every attribute occurrence a that appears on the right-hand side of a defining equation for attribute occurrence b introduces a dependence from a to b; however, an attribute equation that defines attribute occurrence b in terms of **&&**a does *not* introduce a dependence from a to b. It is this property that makes attribute references useful for representing links. For example, in the (revised) equations of the While operator, there is no dependence:

```
While.code → exp.next
```

Each **ATTR**-valued component of a code fragment represents a link to another code fragment. The links are only dereferenced during execution by the interpreter. Given an **ATTR** (LINK) from the current fragment, operation CodeForLink performs the indirection that is required to access the next code fragment.[1]

---

[1]The Synthesizer Generator does not provide a dereferencing operation on ATTR values, so the operation CodeForLink cannot be written directly in SSL; however the Synthesizer Generator does provide a mechanism for calling functions written in C (see *The Synthesizer Generator Reference Manual*). To implement CodeForLink it is necessary to declare its type with a foreign-function declaration:

```
CODE foreign CodeForLink(LINK a);
```

The actual definition of CodeForLink is written (in C) as follows:

```
FOREIGN CodeForLink(a)      /* SSL type: CODE */
    PROD_INSTANCE a;        /* SSL type: ATTR */
    {
    return(demand_value(AttrValue(a)));
    }
```

For illustrative purposes, we have implemented the data type CODE as a user-defined phylum, with the interpreter written as an SSL function. In practice, such an implementation will probably not be fast enough. A more efficient alternative is to implement CODE as a new primitive phylum and implement its interpreter in C. See *The Synthesizer Generator Reference Manual* for an indication as to how this may be done.

9.2.3. Extent of recompilation

Because code updating is performed by the attribute-updating mechanism employed in generated editors, the extent of recompilation after a program is modified corresponds to the number of code-related attributes that are given new values in the course of updating the program's attributes.

The code-generation declarations given above limit the extent of recompilation that a program modification triggers. The use of phylum ATTR to represent links serves to reduce the number of code-related attributes that receive new values after an editing transaction. The reason for this is that if a is an attribute instance that changes value, the value of &&a does not change. Consequently, even if the value of the next attribute passed in to a production has changed, the value of the entry attribute passed out will not change.

Because of this property, change propagation on the code attributes quiesces rapidly. For example, suppose we insert a new statement S_{n+1} at the end of a statement list $S_1 \cdots S_n$. Attribute code for S_n is reevaluated because it must incorporate a new LINK – the LINK received from S_{n+1}. However, no updates to code attributes are performed for any of the statements that precede S_n because the values of the respective next attributes they receive remain unchanged. In essence, we have acquired greater incrementality during program editing at the cost of an additional level of indirection during execution.

CHAPTER 10

Interactive Program Verification

One school holds that a program should be developed hand-in-hand with a proof that the program satisfies its specification [Dijkstra76, Gries81]. Support for this programming methodology can be provided in the form of a proof editor that permits a programmer to create and modify program proofs. The editor provides the programmer with feedback about errors that exist in a proof as it is developed, using knowledge embedded within the editor of the programming logic's inference rules [Reps84].

The subject of this chapter is the design of an editor for creating and modifying proofs of programs; in particular, we discuss how the Synthesizer Generator can be used to build such an editor. The chapter is organized into four sections. Section 10.1 presents an example of a program and proof being manipulated. This example motivates the formulation of interactive proof checking described in Section 10.2; following a brief introduction to a few basic concepts from logic, Section 10.2 describes how the generation of a program's verification conditions can be expressed with an attribute grammar. Section 10.3 discusses how the checking of predicate-logic proofs can be expressed with an attribute grammar. Section 10.4 describes some enhancements to the basic approach aimed at making the user's task less tedious when proofs are created and modified.

10.1. An Introductory Example

To illustrate the proof editor, we present a sample editing session where the goal is to create a program for computing the product of two integers using repeated addition. More precisely, the goal is to create a fragment of code such that, whenever variable b is greater than 0, variable z is assigned the product of a and b. Thus, the pre- and post-conditions of the desired fragment are b >= 0 and z = a*b, respectively.

A program and a proof of correctness can be presented as a *proof outline*. In a proof outline, the program is annotated with a pre-condition and a post-condition, and invariant assertions are provided for each loop. These annotations provide a formal specification of the program's intended behavior.

Let us suppose that our initial attempt to create the multiplication program resulted in the following proof outline:

```
┌─────────────────────────────────────────────────────────────┐
│ main                                                          │
├─────────────────────────────────────────────────────────────┤
│                                                               │
│ {b >= 0}                                                      │
│ y := b                                                        │
│ z := 0                                                        │
│ while y >= 0 with invariant y >= -1 & a*y+z = a*b do          │
│     y := y - 1                                                │
│     z := z + a                                                │
│ od  /* Exit obligation not established */                     │
│ {|z = a*b|}                                                   │
│                                                               │
├─────────────────────────────────────────────────────────────┤
│ Positioned at form                                            │
└─────────────────────────────────────────────────────────────┘
```

The correctness of a program is established if certain *proof obligations* of the proof outline demonstrate the consistency of the proof outline's statements and its assertions.

Proof obligations concern disjoint sections of straight-line code. For the example shown above there are three of them, which we refer to as the *initialization obligation*, the *invariance obligation*, and the *exit obligation*, respectively.

Initialization obligation:

{b >= 0}
y := b
z := 0
{y >= −1 & a*y+z = a*b}

Invariance obligation:

{y >= 0 & y >= −1 & a*y+z = a*b}
y := y − 1
z := z + a
{y >= −1 & a*y+z = a*b}

Exit obligation:

{~(y >= 0) & y >= −1 & a*y+z = a*b}
{z = a*b}

The initialization obligation expresses the requirement that the (claimed) invariant of the loop be established when execution of the loop is begun. The role of the invariance obligation is to show that the predicate given as the loop-invariant actually is an invariant for the loop: execution of the loop-body starting in a state that satisfies the conjunction of the condition and the invariant reestablishes the invariant. The role of the exit obligation is to show that the conjunction of the invariant and the negation of the loop-condition implies the post-condition of the loop.

In a conventional program-verification system, a verification-condition generator reduces the question of consistency between the proof outline's statements and assertions to that of the validity of formulae in the underlying logic. One drawback of conventional verification tools is that the formulae generated in this process are divorced from the program context in which they arise. By contrast, a language-based proof editor can provide information about mistakes in a proof outline by determining which proof obligations are not satisfied and displaying warning messages to indicate the location of unsatisfied obligations. For example, the comment /* Exit obligation not established */ is a warning supplied by the editor, indicating that the while-loop's exit obligation fails to be satisfied.

Now suppose that, in an attempt to correct the proof outline, the first clause of the invariant assertion is changed to y >= 0.

```
┌─────────────────────────────────────────────────────────────┐
│ ┌───────────────────────────────────────────────────────┐   │
│ │ main                                                    │   │
│ └───────────────────────────────────────────────────────┘   │
│ ┌───────────────────────────────────────────────────────┐   │
│ │                                                         │   │
│ │ {b >= 0}                                                │   │
│ │ y := b                                                  │   │
│ │ z := 0                                                  │   │
│ │ while y >= 0 with invariant │y >= 0│ & a*y+z = a*b do   │   │
│ │         /* Invariance obligation not established */     │   │
│ │     y := y – 1                                          │   │
│ │     z := z + a                                          │   │
│ │ od                                                      │   │
│ │ {z = a*b}                                               │   │
│ │                                                         │   │
│ └───────────────────────────────────────────────────────┘   │
│   Positioned at prop                                          │
└─────────────────────────────────────────────────────────────┘
```

With the change, the message about the failure to establish the exit condition disappears. However, the loop now carries a new message, /* Invariance obligation not established */, indicating that the loop-body fails to re-establish the invariant on each iteration of the loop.

The modification of the proof outline changed the proof obligations from the previous ones to the following ones:

Initialization obligation:
{b >= 0}
y := b
z := 0
{y >= 0 & a*y+z = a*b}

Invariance obligation:
{y >= 0 & y >= 0 & a*y+z = a*b}
y := y – 1
z := z + a
{y >= 0 & a*y+z = a*b}

Exit obligation:
{~(y >= 0) & y >= 0 & a*y+z = a*b}
{z = a*b}

In operational terms, the error in the program is that the loop-condition permits the loop to execute one too many times. The problem can be corrected by changing the loop-condition to be y > 0. With this change, the program's statements are now consistent with the assertions that annotate it, and all warnings in the program disappear:

```
┌─────────────────────────────────────────────────────────────┐
│ main                                                          │
├───────────────────────────────────────────────────────────────┤
│                                                               │
│ {b >= 0}                                                      │
│ y := b                                                        │
│ z := 0                                                        │
│ while ┌─────┐ with invariant y >= 0 & a*y+z = a*b do          │
│       │y > 0│                                                 │
│       └─────┘                                                 │
│     y := y − 1                                                │
│     z := z + a                                                │
│ od                                                            │
│ {z = a*b}                                                     │
│                                                               │
├───────────────────────────────────────────────────────────────┤
│ Positioned at cond                                            │
└─────────────────────────────────────────────────────────────┘
```

10.2. Generating Verification Conditions

The logic embedded in the proof editor is based on an elementary logic of programs described in [Hoare69] and a first-order predicate logic described in [Gentzen69, Kleene52]. After reviewing a few elementary concepts of logic, we discuss how to encode a logic in an editor specification's attribute equations.

10.2.1. Background

A logic consists of *sentences* together with rules that permit one to demonstrate that certain sentences are *theorems*. The logic's *axioms* specify a collection of sentences that are theorems without further demonstration. The logic's *inference rules* specify how one sentence (the conclusion) may be deduced from other sentences (the premises).

A sentence is a theorem if and only if it can be deduced from the axioms by successive applications of inference rules. A *proof* is a demonstration of theoremhood; it is a systematic listing of sentences, inference rules, and axioms that indicate how the given sentence is deduced from the axioms.

The axioms and inference rules of a logic can be presented using a notation due to Gentzen in which the premises and conclusion are listed above and below a horizontal bar:

Inference rule: $\dfrac{premise_1 \quad premise_2 \quad \ldots \quad premise_k}{conclusion}$

An axiom is an inference rule that has no premises:

Axiom: $\dfrac{\quad\quad}{\textit{formula}}$

Axioms and inference rules may be parameterized by *meta-variables*, which can be instantiated by objects of the appropriate kind. For example, the reflexive property of equality might be specified by the axiom:

Reflexivity: $\dfrac{\quad\quad}{I = I}$

For example, in a logic for integer arithmetic, the meta-variable I stands for any arithmetic expression.

It is convenient to consider a proof as an upward-branching tree, where the root is the sentence to be proven and the leaves are invocations of axioms. For example, suppose a logic contains the following axioms and inference rules:

$$\dfrac{\quad\quad}{\text{true}} \qquad \dfrac{A}{(A \mid B)} \qquad \dfrac{A \quad B}{(A\ \&\ B)}$$

Then a proof of the sentence (true & (true I false)) would be represented by the following tree of deductions:

$$\dfrac{\quad\quad}{\text{true}} \quad \dfrac{\dfrac{\quad\quad}{\text{true}}}{(\text{true} \mid \text{false})}$$
$$\overline{(\text{true}\ \&\ (\text{true} \mid \text{false}))}$$

In a Hoare-style logic for reasoning about programs, the sentences are triples of the form $\{P\}S\{Q\}$, where P and Q are logical formulae and S is a program fragment (*i.e.* a list of statements). A triple is an assertion that a terminating execution of S begun in a state that satisfies P terminates in a state satisfying Q.

The axioms and inference rules of the logic are rules for manipulating triples; they permit inferring new triples from old triples. For example, straight-line code can be verified using the *axiom of assignment* and the *rule of composition* [Hoare69]:

$$\dfrac{\quad\quad\quad\quad\quad\quad}{\{P_{exp}^{id}\}\ id := exp\ \{P\}} \qquad\qquad \dfrac{\{P\}\ S_1\ \{Q\} \quad \{Q\}\ S_2\ \{R\}}{\{P\}\ S_1; S_2\ \{R\}}$$

(The notation P_{exp}^{id} denotes the result of substituting *exp* for all occurrences of *id* in P.)

In addition to the rules for manipulating triples, there are also rules for reasoning about pre- and post-conditions; it is possible to strengthen a pre-condition and weaken a post-condition:

$$\frac{P \Rightarrow Q \quad \{Q\} \ S \ \{R\}}{\{P\} \ S \ \{R\}} \qquad\qquad \frac{\{P\} \ S \ \{Q\} \quad Q \Rightarrow R}{\{P\} \ S \ \{R\}}$$

10.2.2. Using SSL to generate verification conditions

The proof editor treats (purported) proofs as objects with constraints on them; modifying one part of a proof may introduce an inconsistency in some other part of the proof, yet simultaneously correct an inconsistency in a third part of the proof. Providing feedback to the user involves checking a collection of constraints on the components of the proof. The editor keeps the user informed of errors and inconsistencies in a proof by reexamining the proof's constraints after each modification and annotating the proof with warning messages to indicate locations where constraints are violated.

Because SSL permits expressing constraints on a language, it is a suitable formalism for creating the proof-checking editor illustrated in Section 10.1. The axioms and inference rules of the programming logic are expressed as productions and attribute equations of the editor's defining attribute grammar. Dependences among attributes, as defined in the attribute equations of such a grammar, express dependences among parts of a proof.

(The programming language discussed in this chapter has a slightly different abstract syntax from the language used in earlier chapters; the phylum definitions for the language's abstract syntax are presented in Figure 10.1.)

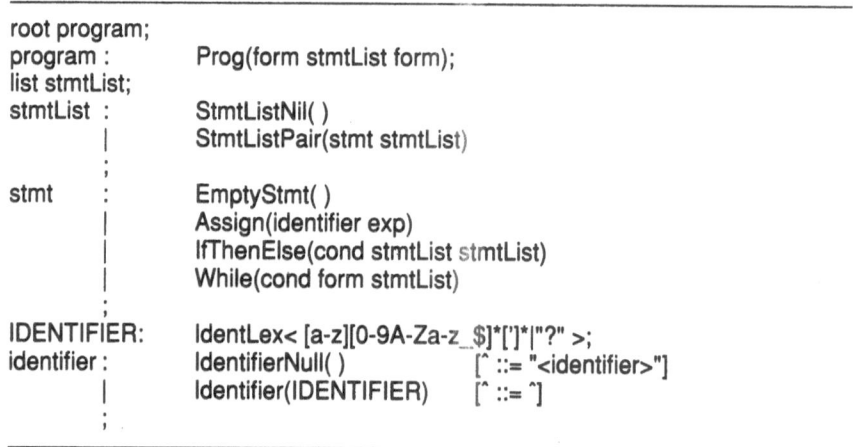

```
root program;
program :          Prog(form stmtList form);
list stmtList;
stmtList :         StmtListNil( )
        |          StmtListPair(stmt stmtList)
        ;
stmt    :          EmptyStmt( )
        |          Assign(identifier exp)
        |          IfThenElse(cond stmtList stmtList)
        |          While(cond form stmtList)
        ;
IDENTIFIER:        IdentLex< [a-z][0-9A-Za-z_$]*[']*|"?" >;
identifier :       IdentifierNull( )         [^ ::= "<identifier>"]
        |          Identifier(IDENTIFIER)    [^ ::= ^]
        ;
```

Figure 10.1. Phylum definitions for the abstract syntax of programs and statements.

The phyla exp, prop, cond, and form represent arithmetic expressions, arithmetic propositions, boolean formulae for statement conditions, and logical formulae, respectively; their definitions are given in Figures 10.2 and 10.3.

Generation of verification conditions for a program in this language can be expressed with an attribute grammar using two attributes pre and post. Attribute pre is a synthesized attribute of nonterminals stmt and stmtList whose value is a formula in the language of assertions (*i.e.* an element of phylum form); attribute post is an inherited attribute of stmt and stmtList whose value is also a formula in the language of assertions. The relationships among these attributes that express partial correctness of programs are given by the attribution equations presented in Figure 10.4 and Figure 10.5, which are adapted from an attribute grammar given in [Gerhart75].

The attribute equations of the grammar treat statements as backward predicate transformers [Dijkstra76]. For example, in an assignment-statement the relationship between attributes pre and post is that attribute pre is defined as attribute post with the expression on the right-hand side of the assignment substituted for all occurrences of the left-hand-side identifier. For while-loops, the post-condition of the loop-body and the pre-condition of the parent statement are both defined in terms of the loop-invariant.

Inconsistencies between a proof outline's statements and its assertions are detected according to the values of the local attributes proof_oblig, invar_oblig, and exit_oblig, defined by the equations given in Figure 10.5. In these attribute equations, function IsTheorem is a decision procedure – a procedure that

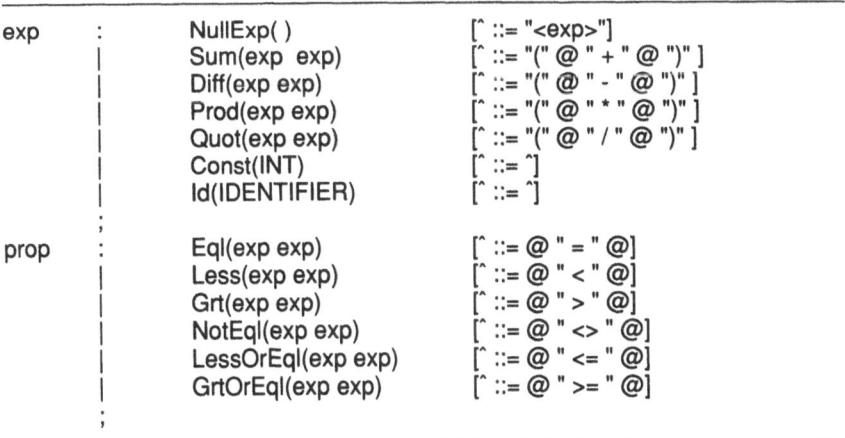

Figure 10.2. Phylum definitions for arithmetic expressions and propositions.

```
cond    :       NullCond( )                 [^ ::= "<condition>"]
        |       TrueCond( )                 [^ ::= "true"]
        |       FalseCond( )                [^ ::= "false"]
        |       PropCond(prop)              [^ ::= ^]
        |       NotCond(cond)               [^ ::= "¬" @]
        |       AndCond(cond cond)          [^ ::= "(" @ " & " @ ")"]
        |       OrCond(cond cond)           [^ ::= "(" @ " | " @ ")"]
        |       ImpliesCond(cond cond)      [^ ::= "(" @ " => " @ ")"]
        ;

form    :       NullForm( )                 [^ ::= "<formula>"]
        |       True( )                     [^ ::= "true"]
        |       False( )                    [^ ::= "false"]
        |       PropForm(prop)              [^ ::= ^]
        |       Not(form)                   [^ ::= "¬" @]
        |       And(form form)              [^ ::= "(" @ " & " @ ")"]
        |       Or(form form)               [^ ::= "(" @ " | " @ ")"]
        |       Implies(form form)          [^ ::= "(" @ " => " @ ")"]
        |       Exists(identifier form)     [^ ::= "(some " @ "." @ ")"]
        |       All(identifier form)        [^ ::= "(all " @ "." @ ")"]
        ;

form CondToForm(cond c) {
        with (c) (
                NullCond: NullForm,
                TrueCond: True,
                FalseCond: False,
                PropCond(p): PropForm(p),
                NotCond(a): Not(CondToForm(a)),
                AndCond(a, b): And(CondToForm(a), CondToForm(b)),
                OrCond(a, b): Or(CondToForm(a), CondToForm(b)),
                ImpliesCond(a, b): Implies(CondToForm(a), CondToForm(b)),
                )
        };
```

Figure 10.3. Phylum definitions for statement conditions and logical formulae. Function CondToForm converts between phylum cond and phylum form.

```
stmt, stmtList {
        synthesized form pre;
        inherited form post;
        };
program : Prog { stmtList.post = form$2; };
stmtList : StmtListNil { stmtList.pre = stmtList.post; }
        | StmtListPair {
            stmtList$1.pre = stmt.pre;
            stmtList$2.post = stmtList$1.post;
            stmt.post = stmtList$2.pre;
            }
        ;
stmt    : EmptyStmt { stmt.pre = stmt.post; }
        | Assign { stmt.pre = Subst(stmt.post, identifier.id, exp); }
        | IfThenElse {
            stmt.pre = And(Implies(CondToForm(cond), stmtList$1.pre),
                            Implies(Not(CondToForm(cond)), stmtList$2.pre));
            stmtList$1.post = stmt.post;
            stmtList$2.post = stmt.post;
            }
        | While {
            stmt.pre = form;
            stmtList.post = form;
            }
        ;
```

Figure 10.4. Attribute equations to generate pre- and post-conditions for the statements of the language.

```
ERROR: NoError( )
       | InvarErr( )
            [@ : "%t%t%n/* Invariance obligation not established */%b%b"]
       | ExitErr( )
            [@ : " /* Exit obligation not established */"]
       | AssertErr( )
            [@ : " /* Assertion not established */"]
       ;
program: Prog {
            local ERROR proof_oblig;
            proof_oblig = IsTheorem(Implies(form$1, stmtList.pre))
                                    ? NoError : AssertErr;
         }
       ;
stmt    : While {
            local ERROR invar_oblig;
            invar_oblig = IsTheorem(Implies(And(form, CondToForm(cond)),
                                    stmtList.pre)) ? NoError : InvarErr;
            local ERROR exit_oblig;
            exit_oblig = IsTheorem(Implies(And(form, Not(CondToForm(cond))),
                                    stmt.post)) ? NoError : ExitErr;
         }
       ;
```

Figure 10.5. Attribute equations to check verification conditions.

returns true if the sentence supplied as its argument is a theorem in the assertion-language logic.

At this point, we encounter one of the stumbling blocks of automatic verification systems: the sentences produced to check a proof outline's proof obligations are ordinarily in an undecidable theory. For instance, the assertion language used to express the verification conditions constructed by the rules given above is undecidable; no decision procedure exists for first-order predicate logic [Turing37].

10.3. Checking Proofs of Verification Conditions

The problem of the undecidability of the assertion language can be side-stepped by having the user create and manipulate the required proofs, instead of having the system try to establish theorems automatically. We make the user responsible for proving theorems that an automatic theorem prover might be incapable of proving. (From a practical standpoint, this approach is unsatisfactory because the user is forced to prove theorems that automatic techniques *are* capable of establishing. To provide an adequate tool, it is necessary to include automatic deductive capabilities in the editor so that the user does not have to supply complete (and repetitive) details of a proof; this is discussed further in Section 10.4.)

Providing the user the opportunity to create proofs necessitates certain changes to the underlying abstract syntax; the operators whose attribute equations invoke IsTheorem in Figure 10.4 are changed to include proof nonterminals for the proof obligations of the production. For instance, the While operator is changed to

stmt   : While(cond form proof stmtList proof);

At the first proof nonterminal, the user must create a proof of

Implies(And(form, CondToForm(cond)), stmtList.pre)

At the second, the user must create a proof of

Implies(And(form, Not(CondToForm(cond))), stmt.post)

A first-order predicate logic can be formalized as a *sequent calculus* [Gentzen69, Kleene52]. A sentence of a sequent calculus, or *sequent*, consists of two sets of formulae, separated by an arrow, such as:

$$\{A_1, A_2, \ldots, A_m\} \rightarrow \{B_1, B_2, \ldots, B_n\} \tag{10.1}$$

The set $\{A_1, A_2, \ldots, A_m\}$, on the left, is called the *antecedent*, the set $\{B_1, B_2, \ldots, B_n\}$, on the right, the *succedent*. A sequent is a theorem in the sequent calculus if it can be derived from the system's axioms and rules of inference.

It can be shown that a sequent is a theorem in the sequent calculus if and only if, in one of the more familiar forms of the predicate calculus, such as a natural-deduction calculus or a Hilbert-style calculus, a formula in the succedent can be demonstrated taking the formulae in the antecedent as assumptions [Gentzen69]. Informally then, one can think of the formulae of the antecedent as known facts and the formulae of the succedent as goals, one of which is to be demonstrated; thus, the informal meaning of the sequent (10.1) is no different from asserting the formula

$$A_1 \wedge A_2 \wedge \cdots \wedge A_m \Rightarrow B_1 \vee B_2 \vee \cdots \vee B_n$$

The inference rules of sequent calculus allow us to infer new sequents from old sequents. For each logical operator there are two inference rules: an *analysis* rule and a *synthesis* rule. The analysis rule for a (logical) operator $\oplus$ expresses how a formula of the form $A \oplus B$ may be introduced into an antecedent; the synthesis rule for $\oplus$ expresses how $A \oplus B$ may be introduced into a succedent.

For example, using the meta-variables A and B to represent single formulae and the meta-variables Γ and Δ to represent finite sets of formulae, the rules for the implication operator $\Rightarrow$ are expressed as:

Implication analysis: $\dfrac{\Gamma \to \Delta \cup \{A\} \quad \Gamma \cup \{B\} \to \Delta}{\Gamma \cup \{A \Rightarrow B\} \to \Delta}$ (10.2a)

Implication synthesis: $\dfrac{\Gamma \cup \{A\} \to \Delta \cup \{B\}}{\Gamma \to \Delta \cup \{A \Rightarrow B\}}$ (10.2b)

The implication analysis rule (10.2a) says (roughly) that to prove a goal under the assumption $A \Rightarrow B$, we must demonstrate A, and we must demonstrate our goal assuming B. The implication synthesis rule (10.2b) says (again roughly) that to demonstrate $A \Rightarrow B$, we must show that by assuming A we can demonstrate B.

An attribute grammar can be used to express the rules of sequent calculus as follows. A sequent is represented by an instance of the nonterminal proof together with its two inherited attributes: ant (for antecedent) and suc (for succedent). Each of the operators for proof represents a rule of inference or an axiom scheme (see below). The operators that correspond to inference rules contain additional proof nonterminals whose ant and suc attributes are defined in terms of attributes ant and suc of the parent proof nonterminal. The context in which the inference rule is invoked is checked to ensure that it represents an appropriate deductive step.

For example, the productions corresponding to the implication inference rules are shown in Figure 10.6. In each production in Figure 10.6, there are two form nonterminals on the right-hand side that determine how an inference rule is instantiated. The formulae derived from them determine the components of the formula being analyzed or synthesized, as well as the antecedents and succedents of the right-hand-side proof nonterminals. The equations for the error attribute ensure that the formula being analyzed (synthesized) really is in the left-hand-side proof nonterminal's ant (suc) attribute.

The axioms of the sequent calculus are expressed in three schemes:

$$\overline{\Gamma \cup \{\text{false}\} \to \Delta}$$ (10.3a)

$$\overline{\Gamma \cup \{A\} \to \Delta \cup \{A\}}$$ (10.3b)

$$\overline{\Gamma \to \Delta \cup \{\text{true}\}}$$ (10.3c)

```
ERROR: AnErr( )           [@ : " <-- inappropriate analysis"]
       | SynErr( )         [@ : " <-- inappropriate synthesis"]
       ;
proof {
   inherited condList ant;
   inherited condList suc;
   synthesized ERROR error;
   };
proof : ImpAnalysis (form form proof proof)
       [@ :"analyze (" @ " => " @ ") by implication-analysis" proof$1.error
          "%nshow " form$1 "%t%n"
        @ "%b%n"
          "assume " form$2 "%t%n"
        @ "%b%l"]
   {  proof$1.error = InList(Implies(form$1, form$2), proof$1.ant)
                                    ? NoError : AnErr;

      proof$2.ant = proof$1.ant;
      proof$2.suc = form$1 :: proof$1.suc;
      proof$3.ant = form$2 :: proof$1.ant;
      proof$3.suc = proof$1.suc;
   }
   | ImpSynthesis (form form proof)
     [@ :"synthesize (" @ " => " @ ") by implication-synthesis" proof$1.error
        "%nassume " form$1 "%n"
        "show " form$2 "%t%n"
      @ "%b%l"]
   {  proof$1.error = InList(Implies(form$1, form$2), proof$1.suc)
                                    ? NoError : SynErr;
      proof$2.ant = form$1 :: proof$1.ant;
      proof$2.suc = form$2 :: proof$1.suc;
   }
   ;
BOOL InList(form f, condList l) {
        with(l) (
               NullList: false,
               Cons(g, m): f == g || InList(f, m)
               )
        };
```

Figure 10.6. Grammar rules corresponding to the implication inference rules.

Axiom scheme (10.3a) says that if false is assumed, then any formula can be demonstrated; (10.3b) says that if formula A is assumed, then A is demonstrated; (10.3c) says that true is demonstrated, no matter what the assumptions are. These three axiom schemes can be combined into a single production whose local attribute error indicates whether an application of the production completes a branch of the proof. The SSL specification for this production is shown in Figure 10.7.

```
proof : Immediate( )        [@ ::= "immediate" proof.error] {
            proof.error = IsImmediate(proof.ant, proof.suc) ? NoError : NotSo;
            }
        ;
BOOL IsImmediate(condList ant, condList suc) {
    InList(False, ant) || Overlap(ant, suc) || InList(True, suc)
    };
BOOL Overlap(condList ant, condList suc) {
    with(ant) (
        NullList: false,
        Cons(f, l):
            with(suc) (
                NullList: false,
                Cons(g, m): InList(g, ant) || InList(f, suc) || Overlap(l, m)
                )
        )
    };
```

Figure 10.7. Definitions for the operator corresponding to axiom schema (10.3a) – (10.3c). The attribute equation of the rule checks whether an application of the production completes a branch of the proof.

The axioms and inferences rules of a sequent calculus for first-order predicate logic are listed in Figure 10.8.

We also need to provide inference rules for terms of phyla prop and exp. For example, rules for equality must be incorporated in our logical system. The rules for equality can be expressed as follows, using the meta-variables J, K, and L to represent expressions (*e.g.* arithmetic expressions):

$$\frac{\Gamma \cup \{J{=}J\} \to \Delta}{\Gamma \to \Delta} \tag{10.4a}$$

$$\frac{\Gamma \to \Delta \cup \{J{=}K\} \quad \Gamma \cup \{K{=}J\} \to \Delta}{\Gamma \to \Delta} \tag{10.4b}$$

$$\frac{\Gamma \to \Delta \cup \{J{=}K\} \quad \Gamma \to \Delta \cup \{K{=}L\} \quad \Gamma \cup \{J{=}L\} \to \Delta}{\Gamma \to \Delta} \tag{10.4c}$$

Each such inference rule corresponds to an additional operator of phylum proof. For instance, the productions corresponding to rules (10.4a)–(10.4c) are given in Figure 10.9.

Axiom schema.

$$\overline{\Gamma \cup \{\text{false}\} \to \Delta} \qquad \overline{\Gamma \cup \{A\} \to \Delta \cup \{A\}} \qquad \overline{\Gamma \to \Delta \cup \{\text{true}\}}$$

Rules of inference for propositional logic.

$\wedge$ analysis: $\dfrac{\Gamma \cup \{A, B\} \to \Delta}{\Gamma \cup \{A \wedge B\} \to \Delta}$

$\wedge$ synthesis: $\dfrac{\Gamma \to \Delta \cup \{A\} \quad \Gamma \to \Delta \cup \{B\}}{\Gamma \to \Delta \cup \{A \wedge B\}}$

$\vee$ analysis: $\dfrac{\Gamma \cup \{A\} \to \Delta \quad \Gamma \cup \{B\} \to \Delta}{\Gamma \cup \{A \vee B\} \to \Delta}$

$\vee$ synthesis: $\dfrac{\Gamma \to \Delta \cup \{A, B\}}{\Gamma \to \Delta \cup \{A \vee B\}}$

$\neg$ analysis: $\dfrac{\Gamma \to \Delta \cup \{A\}}{\Gamma \cup \{\neg A\} \to \Delta}$

$\neg$ synthesis: $\dfrac{\Gamma \cup \{A\} \to \Delta}{\Gamma \to \Delta \cup \{\neg A\}}$

$\Rightarrow$ analysis: $\dfrac{\Gamma \to \Delta \cup \{A\} \quad \Gamma \cup \{B\} \to \Delta}{\Gamma \cup \{A \Rightarrow B\} \to \Delta}$

$\Rightarrow$ synthesis: $\dfrac{\Gamma \cup \{A\} \to \Delta \cup \{B\}}{\Gamma \to \Delta \cup \{A \Rightarrow B\}}$

Additional rules of inference for predicate logic.

$\exists$ analysis: $\dfrac{\Gamma \cup \{A(b)\} \to \Delta}{\Gamma \cup \{\exists x.A(x)\} \to \Delta}$
where b is a variable not occurring free in $A(x)$

$\exists$ synthesis: $\dfrac{\Gamma \to \Delta \cup \{A(t)\}}{\Gamma \to \Delta \cup \{\exists x.A(x)\}}$
where t is a term free for x in $A(x)$

$\forall$ analysis: $\dfrac{\Gamma \cup \{A(t)\} \cup \{\forall x.A(x)\} \to \Delta}{\Gamma \cup \{\forall x.A(x)\} \to \Delta}$
where t is a term free for x in $A(x)$

$\forall$ synthesis: $\dfrac{\Gamma \to \Delta \cup \{A(b)\}}{\Gamma \to \Delta \cup \{\forall x.A(x)\}}$
where b is a variable not occurring free in $A(x)$

Figure 10.8. Axioms and inference rules of a sequent calculus for first-order predicate logic.

```
proof    :  Reflexivity(exp proof)
            [@ : "by reflexivity on " @ "%n"
                    "assume " exp " = " exp "%t%n"
                        @  "%b%|"]
            {        proof$1.error = NoError;
                     proof$2.ant = PropForm(Eql(exp, exp)) :: proof$1.ant;
                     proof$2.suc = proof$1.suc;
                     }
         |  Symmetry(exp exp proof proof)
            [@ : "by symmetry on " @ ", " @ "%n"
                    "show " exp$1 " = " exp$2 "%t%n"
                        @  "%b%n"
                    "assume " exp$2 " = " exp$1 "%t%n"
                        @  "%b%|"]
            {        proof$1.error = NoError;
                     proof$2.ant = proof$1.ant;
                     proof$2.suc = PropForm(Eql(exp$1, exp$2)) :: proof$1.suc;
                     proof$3.ant = PropForm(Eql(exp$2, exp$1)) :: proof$1.ant;
                     proof$3.suc = proof$1.suc;
                     }
         |  Transitivity(exp exp proof exp proof proof)
            [@ : "by transitivity on " @ ", " @ ", " @ "%n"
                    "show " exp$1 " = " exp$2 "%t%n"
                        @  "%b%n"
                    "show " exp$2 " = " exp$3 "%t%n"
                        @  "%b%n"
                    "assume " exp$1 " = " exp$3 "%t%n"
                        @  "%b%|"]
            {        proof$1.error = NoError;
                     proof$2.ant = proof$1.ant;
                     proof$2.suc = PropForm(Eql(exp$1, exp$2)) :: proof$1.suc;
                     proof$3.ant = proof$1.ant;
                     proof$3.suc = PropForm(Eql(exp$2, exp$3)) :: proof$1.suc;
                     proof$4.ant = PropForm(Eql(exp$1, exp$3)) :: proof$1.ant;
                     proof$4.suc = proof$1.suc;
                     }
         ;
```

Figure 10.9. Grammar rules corresponding to the inference rules for equality.

10.4. Automatic Deductive Capabilities

In Section 10.3, we side-stepped the undecidability of predicate logic by having the user write proofs, instead of having the editor try to establish theorems automatically. In practice, this approach is untenable; the editor described in the previous section would be maddeningly tedious to use because it forces the user to provide complete (and repetitive) details for every proof.

To provide an adequate tool, it is necessary to include automatic deductive capabilities in the editor. Two methods are possible: the editor can be extended with *decision procedures* – algorithms for deciding simple theories – and *proof tactics* – procedures that attempt to construct a proof tree but may leave some nodes unexpanded for the user to fill in later [Gordon79].

10.4.1. Decision procedures

The editor can be extended with decision procedures by making use of known algorithms for deciding simple theories. For example, an algorithm for deciding the theory of equality with uninterpreted function symbols can be used as the basis of a procedure for propositional inference [Nelson81, Johnson82]. Such algorithms can be incorporated into the editor using the production

```
proof : Automatic( ) [@ ::= "automatic" proof.error] {
         proof.error = IsAutomatic(proof.ant, proof.suc)
                            ? NoError : NotSo;

    }
  ;
```

where IsAutomatic is a propositional-inference procedure that returns true if it can establish the second argument from the first argument.

Any decision procedure for a subtheory of the assertion language has certain inherent limitations. For example, the production given above will generate warning messages when the sentence to be established requires the use of an inference rule that the automatic procedure never attempts to apply.

Example. Proving the sequent

$$\{a, b, d\} \rightarrow \{a \wedge (b \wedge (c \Rightarrow d))\} \tag{10.5}$$

requires the use of the implication synthesis rule to establish the formula $c \Rightarrow d$, as in the starred branch of the following proof tree:

$$\cfrac{\{a,b,d\}\rightarrow\{a\}\quad \cfrac{\{a,b,d\}\rightarrow\{b\}\quad \cfrac{\cfrac{}{\{a,b,c,d\}\rightarrow\{d\}}}{\{a,b,d\}\rightarrow\{c\Rightarrow d\}}(*)}{\{a, b, d\} \rightarrow \{b \wedge (c \Rightarrow d)\}}}{\{a, b, d\} \rightarrow \{a \wedge (b \wedge (c \Rightarrow d))\}}$$

Thus, a decision procedure that never applies implication synthesis cannot establish (10.5).

When the automatic-inference procedure is not immediately applicable, there are other ways to reduce the amount of detail that the user must supply. It is possible to devise a mechanism for the user to isolate the terms that prevent the automatic-inference procedure from succeeding so that the user can apply

appropriate inference rules to those terms explicitly. The mechanism is based
on an additional inference rule termed the *cut rule*, which is expressed as follows:

$$\text{Cut rule:} \quad \frac{\Gamma \rightarrow \{A\} \quad \Gamma \cup \{A\} \rightarrow \Delta}{\Gamma \rightarrow \Delta} \tag{10.6}$$

Cut rule (10.6) says that to prove some goal, if we can demonstrate some formula A, then A can be used as an assumption in the proof of the goal. The cut
rule permits a user to isolate a formula rather easily by using automatic inferences to skip over the easy intermediate steps.

  Example. Returning to the example above, if we choose $c \Rightarrow d$ as the cut formula A, the proof branches into two subproofs whose sequents are

$$\{a, b, d\} \rightarrow \{c \Rightarrow d\} \tag{10.7a}$$

and

$$\{a, b, d, c \Rightarrow d\} \rightarrow \{a \wedge (b \wedge (c \Rightarrow d))\}. \tag{10.7b}$$

We are then able to apply implication synthesis directly to (10.7a), and the
automatic inference rule can be used to establish (10.7b) because a proof can be
found that makes no use of implication synthesis:

$$\frac{\{a,b,d,c \Rightarrow d\} \rightarrow \{a\} \quad \dfrac{\dfrac{}{\{a,b,d,c \Rightarrow d\} \rightarrow \{b\}} \quad \dfrac{}{\{a,b,d,c \Rightarrow d\} \rightarrow \{c \Rightarrow d\}}}{\{a, b, d, c \Rightarrow d\} \rightarrow \{b \wedge (c \Rightarrow d)\}}}{\{a, b, d, c \Rightarrow d\} \rightarrow \{a \wedge (b \wedge (c \Rightarrow d))\}}$$

10.4.2. Proof tactics

A proof tactic is a method for applying inference rules repeatedly and recursively until none is applicable [Gordon79]. In proof editors, a proof tactic may
be employed to automatically construct a proof fragment; the tactic may sometimes construct a complete a proof tree, but in general it will leave some unexpanded proof nodes for the user to fill in later [Bates85].

  Example. Given an unexpanded proof nonterminal representing the sequent
given above as equation (10.5), a proof tactic could apply the and-synthesis rule
twice to produce the attributed derivation tree that corresponds to the inference:

$$\frac{\{a,b,d\} \rightarrow \{a\} \quad \dfrac{\{a,b,d\} \rightarrow \{b\} \quad \{a,b,d\} \rightarrow \{c \Rightarrow d\}}{\{a, b, d\} \rightarrow \{b \wedge (c \Rightarrow d)\}}}{\{a, b, d\} \rightarrow \{a \wedge (b \wedge (c \Rightarrow d))\}}$$

leaving an unexpanded proof nonterminal with sequent $\{a, b, d\} \rightarrow \{c \Rightarrow d\}$.

The specification of two proof tactics, both much simpler than the one illustrated above, is presented in Figure 10.10. The rules given there cause input of the form !A (respectively !S) to be interpreted as a command to invoke a tactic that inserts, at the current proof nonterminal, an analysis production (synthesis

```
ANALYZE:        AnalyzeLex< "!A" >;
SYNTHESIZE:     SynthesizeLex< "!S" >;
ProofCommand { synthesized proof abs; };
proof ˜ ProofCommand.abs;
ProofCommand ::= (ANALYZE) {
        ProofCommand.abs =
            with({proof.ant}) (
                NullList: [proof],
                Cons(hd, *): with (hd) (
                    Not(a): NotAnalysis(a,[proof]),
                    And(a,b): AndAnalysis(a,b,[proof]),
                    Or(a,b): OrAnalysis(a,b,[proof],[proof]),
                    Implies(a,b): ImpAnalysis(a,b,[proof],[proof]),
                    Exists(i,a): ExistsAnalysis(i,a,[proof]),
                    All(i,a): AllAnalysis(i,a,NullExp,[proof]),
                    default: [proof]
                    )
                );
        }
    | (SYNTHESIZE) {
        ProofCommand.abs =
            with({proof.suc}) (
                NullList: [proof],
                Cons(hd, *): with (hd) (
                    Not(a): NotSynthesis(a,[proof]),
                    And(a,b): AndSynthesis(a,b,[proof],[proof]),
                    Or(a,b): OrSynthesis(a,b,[proof]),
                    Implies(a,b): ImpSynthesis(a,b,[proof]),
                    Exists(i,a): ExistsSynthesis(i,a,NullExp,[proof]),
                    All(i,a): AllSynthesis(i,a,[proof]),
                    default: [proof]
                    )
                );
        }
    ;
```

Figure 10.10. Specification of a proof tactic. Input of the form !A (respectively !S) is interpreted as a command to insert, at the current proof nonterminal, an analysis production (synthesis production) that is appropriate for the outermost operator of the first formula listed in the current proof nonterminal's ant (suc) attribute.

production) that is appropriate for the outermost operator of the first formula listed in the current proof nonterminal's ant (suc) attribute.

CHAPTER 11

The Implementation

This chapter provides a brief introduction to several aspects of the Synthesizer Generator's implementation. The chapter is organized into four sections: Section 11.1 outlines the basic organization of the implementation; Sections 11.2, 11.3, and 11.4 describe algorithms used in the system.

The material discussed in this chapter is related to the material that appears in Chapter 12. As indicated by its title – "Incremental Attribute Evaluation for Ordered Attribute Grammars" – Chapter 12 concerns an algorithm for incremental attribute evaluation, one of several such algorithms that are incorporated in the Synthesizer Generator. The material of Chapter 12 should properly be part of the present chapter, but it has been placed in a separate chapter due to its length. Chapter 12 is self-contained and can be understood without having first read Chapter 11.

11.1. Basic Organization of the Implementation

The central components of every generated editor are the *attributed-tree module*, the *SSL-expression interpreter*, the *editor module*, the *display module*, the editor's *grammar tables*, the *scanner*, the *parser*, and the sequences of *byte-codes* that are the internal representation of SSL expressions. The first four of these components are common to all generated editors. The last four components – the grammar tables, the scanner, the parser, and the byte-code sequences – vary among editors for different languages.

It is convenient to think of the Synthesizer Generator as being divided into two major components:

- The editing kernel, consisting of the four subcomponents that are the back-bone of all generated editors. Although each different SSL specification generates an editor with distinct characteristics, all share the common operations and user interface of the editing kernel.

- The generator proper, which is the part of the system that generates editors from editor specifications. This is split into two parts: the *SSL translator*, the part that actually processes the SSL source, and a shell program, named sgen, that coordinates the activity of the SSL translator with that of several other UNIX utilities employed in the task of creating an editor.

11.1.1. The organization of generated editors

Grammar tables

An editor's grammar tables contain information about the editor's defining attribute grammar. Among them are six tables that contain properties of phyla, phylum occurrences, operators, operator occurrences (productions), attributes, and attribute occurrences. The general rule followed in these tables is that properties are contained in the most general structure that applies. For example, properties of phylum occurrences (respectively, operator occurrences and attribute occurrences) that are common to all occurrences of the given phylum (respectively, operator and attribute) are factored out and stored in the phylum's (operator's, attribute's) entry in the table of phylum (operator, attribute) properties.

The attributed-tree module

The attributed-tree module implements a set of operations for manipulating attributed trees. One of the operations of the attributed-tree module is the incremental algorithm used for updating a tree's attribute values after the tree is modified. This algorithm is applied each time an attributed tree is modified; it alters as many of the tree's attribute values as is necessary to ensure that the values of *all* of the tree's attributes are mutually consistent. In generated editors, incremental attribute evaluation can be carried out by one of several algorithms. One of the algorithms is described in [Reps82], [Reps83], and Chapter 5 of [Reps84]; a second algorithm is described in detail in Chapter 12; additional algorithms described in [Hoover87] are under development.

The SSL-expression interpreter

In SSL, expressions appear on the right-hand sides of attribute equations, in function bodies, and on the right-hand sides of transformation declarations. All such expressions are evaluated by the SSL-expression interpreter using a sequence of byte codes that are generated by the SSL translator.

The SSL interpreter is invoked by the attributed-tree module in two different situations. One of these occurs when the change-propagation algorithm requires that a new value be computed for one of the tree's attribute instances; the interpreter is invoked to reevaluate the expression that appears on the right-hand side of the attribute's defining equation. The second situation in which the interpreter is invoked occurs when a transformation is applied to an attributed tree; after the transformation's left-hand-side pattern has been matched to the attributed tree, which creates a binding for the pattern's variables, the right-hand-side expression is evaluated to generate the replacement component.

The SSL-expression interpreter implements a straightforward stack-machine. There is an op-code for each basic SSL operation; its associated action changes one or more of the elements at the top of the stack.

SSL values are represented as elements of type PROD_INSTANCE. A PROD_INSTANCE is a pointer to a block of storage that contains the value's subcomponents. There is an op-code for constructing values of each of the predefined primitive phyla. In addition, there is also an op-code for constructing values of user-defined phyla; when it is encountered by the interpreter, a new PROD_INSTANCE is created to represent the given operator, with an appropriate number of values taken off the top of the stack as the operator's arguments. The storage that is used for representing PROD_INSTANCEs is allocated out of the heap. The method of *deferred reference-counting* [Deutsch76, Rovner84] is used to reclaim these blocks of storage; this reclamation method is described in Section 11.4, "Deferred Reference Counting."

As illustrated in Chapter 4, Chapter 7, and elsewhere, precisely the same sort of declarations are used in editor specifications to define new attribute types as are used to define the abstract syntax of editable objects. Conceptually, the abstract-syntax tree being edited and the attributes attached to its nodes are all just (typed) objects in a single universe of (typed) terms. The uniform treatment of syntactic values and attribute values carries over to the implementation as well; *both* kinds of values are implemented as PROD_INSTANCEs.[1] One

---

[1]In fact, there are some slight differences between a PROD_INSTANCE that represents a syntactic value and one that represents (a component of) an attribute value; however, both are subsumed under the type PROD_INSTANCE.

benefit of this implementation is that tree storage is reclaimed by the same mechanism that reclaims attribute values.

The editor module

The objects manipulated in an editor are contained in a collection of named *buffers*. Typically, each file being edited is read into a distinct buffer. The buffer is then associated with the given file until either a different file is read into that buffer or the given buffer is written to a different file. Each buffer has an associated syntactic mode, which corresponds to one of the phyla declared in the editor specification. Typically, this is the root phylum of the specification, but a buffer with arbitrary syntactic mode may be created using the **new-buffer** command.

When a buffer's selection is editable as text, the text representation of the selection is captured into a *text buffer* that is displayed in the object pane in place of the original selection. During such text editing, prior to parsing and translation of the text buffer back into structural form, the selection exists as text, not as structure. During text editing, the selection contains a *character selection*, designated on the screen by an unhighlighted character or I-beam within the highlighted selection. Operations within the selection are defined textually, not structurally; insertions and deletions of characters take place at the position of the character selection.

After each editing operation, the image of the buffer that is displayed on the screen must be updated to reflect any changes that have occurred. To reduce the amount of time spent creating the new display image, generated editors incorporate an incremental display algorithm.

The display module

The terminal's screen is divided into *windows*, with each window divided into three regions, named (from top to bottom) the *command line*, the *object pane*, and the *help pane*. Any command names or transformation names that the user types are echoed on the command line. The command line is also used to display system messages. The window's buffer is displayed in the object pane. The collection of transformations that are enabled for the buffer's current selection are displayed in the help pane.

In editors generated for ordinary video-display terminals, windows are tiled on the screen, arranged in horizontal slabs. In editors generated for high-resolution, bitmapped workstations, resizable and overlapping windows are supported. For machines with a mouse, the object pane is equipped with a horizontal scroll bar along its bottom edge and a vertical scroll bar along its right edge.

11.1.2. The organization of the editor-generation component

The SSL translator takes an SSL specification as input and produces the editor's grammar tables, the byte-code sequences to be used by the interpreter for evaluating the specification's SSL expressions, and several files that define the editor's scanner and parser. The translator creates the grammar tables as an intermediate file of C source code consisting of a number of initialized arrays. It generates a second intermediate file consisting of the stack code for evaluating the specification's expressions. It also generates lex source for producing the editor's scanner and yacc source for producing the parser.

These files are processed further by other tools to create the final executable image. Most of the tools involved are standard UNIX tools, including lex [Lesk75], yacc [Johnson78], the C preprocessor, and the C compiler. The activities of the different tools that participate in creating an editor are coordinated by the sgen shell program.

The SSL translator performs several tests and normalizations on the declarations that appear in an editor specification. For example, the specification's phylum/operator definitions are tested to see if any phylum's completing term is defined circularly. In addition, copy rules are generated for uses of upward remote attribute sets. These normalizations are described in Section 11.2 and Section 11.3, respectively.

To detect errors in editor specifications, the SSL translator checks for type errors in the specification's expressions, which appear in attribute equations, function declarations, transformation declarations, and entry declarations. Our experience has been that the SSL type checker detects a high percentage of errors in editor specifications.

The SSL translator also performs other analyses aimed at improving the performance of the incremental attribute evaluation algorithm. In particular, the translator applies a test that determines whether the specification's attribute equations define an ordered attribute grammar [Kastens80]; if the grammar passes the test, the translator generates evaluation plans for a visit-sequence evaluator. The orderedness test is described in Chapter 12, "Incremental Attribute Evaluation for Ordered Attribute Grammars."

A second analysis involves examining each expression that appears on the right-hand side of an attribute equation to determine whether the expression computes a one-to-one function in each of its arguments. The motivation for this analysis is discussed in Section 12.6.

The SSL translator also applies some conventional code-optimization techniques to improve the code generated for the expressions that appear in editor specifications. The optimizations performed include the following:

- The translator discovers occurrences of constant expressions and performs constant folding so that a constant expression does not have to be evaluated repeatedly. At the beginning of each editing session, each constant expression is evaluated, and the value computed is saved in a table. The code executed for the individual occurrences of a constant expression consists of a single op-code that fetches the value from the appropriate entry of the constant table.

- The translator generates code so that the evaluation of a boolean expression is short-circuited when enough of the expression has been evaluated to determine the value of the entire expression.

- The translator discovers tail-recursive function calls and generates a special "tail-call" op-code in place of the op-code for an ordinary call. Because a tail-recursive function call re-uses the active function's existing activation record, the SSL evaluation stack remains the same depth no matter how many levels of recursive invocation arise during execution. This technique removes the upper bound on the depth of tail-recursive calls that would otherwise exist due to overflow of the execution stack.

A simple debugger available in generated editors can be used to examine the actions of the SSL-expression interpreter. A user of the debugger must, to a certain extent, be aware of the optimizations that are performed on the code. First, because of constant folding, the code executed to push an occurrence of a constant expression onto the stack consists of just a single op-code. Second, because of the optimization to short-circuit boolean expressions, part of each boolean expression may not be evaluated. The evaluation of the expression terminates when enough of the expression has been evaluated to determine the value of the entire expression. Third, because a tail-recursive function call on a function re-uses the function's activation record, only one instance of the function call appears on the stack, and there is only one exit point for a tail-recursive function, rather than one for each recursive invocation.

11.2. Finiteness of Completing Terms

This section describes how a specification's phylum/operator definitions are tested to see if each phylum's completing term is finite.

The first operator declared for each phylum in an editor specification is the phylum's completing operator. The completing operator is used to construct a default representative of the phylum, called the completing term. (As explained in Chapter 5, the definition of the completing term is slightly different for list phyla and optional phyla.) An instance of a phylum's completing term is used at each unexpanded occurrence of the phylum in a program's derivation tree.

The finiteness test is performed by procedure TestFinitenessOfCompletingTerms of Figure 11.1. In TestFinitenessOfCompletingTerms, graph G represents inter-phylum dependences. Each node in G corresponds to a phylum. An edge from the node for phylum p to the node for phylum q indicates that the completing term of q is a component of the completing operator of p.

```
procedure TestFinitenessOfCompletingTerms(Syntax)
declare
    Syntax : a set of phylum/operator declarations
    p , q : phyla of Syntax
    G : a directed graph <vertex set, edge set>
    i : an integer
    Op : an operator of Syntax
    Phy_Op,i : the phylum of Op 's i^th argument
begin
    G := <{ the phyla in Syntax }, ∅>
    for each phylum p in Syntax do
        if p is a non-optional list phylum then
            q := the phylum of the first argument of p 's binary operator
            Insert edge (p , q ) into the edge set of G
        else if p is an optional phylum then skip
        else
            Op := the completing operator of phylum p
            for i := 1 to NumberOfArguments(Op ) do
                Insert edge (p , Phy_Op,i ) into the edge set of G
            od
        fi
    od
    if G contains a directed cycle then
        error: "The completing terms of Syntax are not finite" fi
end
```

Figure 11.1. An algorithm to test whether the completing terms of an editor specification are finite.

G is built up by examining the completing operator of each phylum; an edge is inserted in G for each component of the phylum's completing operator depending on whether the phylum is an ordinary phylum, an optional phylum, or a list phylum, as follows:

- The completing term of a non-optional list phylum p is the singleton list constructed by applying the binary operator of the list to the completing term of its left-argument phylum q and to the list's nullary operator. Accordingly, an edge from p to q is inserted in G.

- The completing term of an optional list phylum is the term constructed from the phylum's nullary production; the completing term of an optional non-list phylum is the term constructed from the first nullary production that appears in the phylum's operator declarations. Consequently, optional phyla introduce no edges into the graph.

- For all other phyla, the completing term is created by applying the completing operator to the completing terms of its argument phyla. Consequently, for an ordinary phylum p, an edge is introduced in G from p to each argument phylum.

A cycle in G indicates that at least one phylum of the editor specification has a non-finite completing term.

11.3. Generating Copy Rules for Upward Remote Attribute Sets

This section describes how copy rules are generated by the SSL translator for uses of upward remote attribute sets.

A weakness of some parser-generator languages that are based on attribute grammars is the need to provide explicit copy rules whose sole purpose is to propagate common information throughout a derivation tree. Such rules do no more than pass information from where it is defined to where it is used. When the pattern of information flow is regular, a shorthand notation can obviate the need for such rules, thereby eliminating much of the tedium of writing attribute-grammar specifications.

SSL provides one such shorthand with its notation for *upward remote attribute sets*, a concept adopted from the GAG system [Kastens82]. An upward remote attribute set, written as

$$\{id_1.attr_1, id_2.attr_2, \ldots, id_n.attr_n\}$$

may be used on the right-hand side of an attribute equation to denote the value of an attribute instance that occurs higher up in the derivation tree. Each id_i is either a phylum name or an operator name. If id_i is a phylum name, then $attr_i$ must be a synthesized or inherited attribute of that phylum; if id_i is an operator name, then $attr_i$ must be a local attribute of a production with that operator as its right-hand side.

Within the attribute equations of a production p, an upward remote attribute set refers to an attribute that is not local to p; it refers to an attribute of a different production, one that necessarily occurs above any instance of production p. By "above," we mean "between any instance of the production p and the root of the tree." The value of an upward remote attribute set in a given instance of production p is the value of the $id_i.attr_i$ that occurs first on the path from the given production instance to the root of the tree, not including the given production instance or its left-hand-side phylum.

For an upward remote attribute set to be well formed, at least one of the $id_i.attr_i$ must be guaranteed to occur in every conceivable tree that can contain the given production. In different instances of p, the upward remote attribute set can be resolved to different $id_i.attr_i$ of the set. Note that each id_i must be unique in a given upward remote attribute set. If id_i is a phylum and id_j is an operator of phylum id_i, then $id_j.attr_j$ takes precedence over $id_i.attr_i$.

More specifically, suppose an upward remote attribute set

$$\{id_1.attr_1, id_2.attr_2, \ldots, id_n.attr_n\}$$

occurs in an equation associated with production p, of the form

$$X_0 \; : \; Op(X_1 X_2 \ldots X_m);$$

Now consider a particular instance of p in some derivation tree. Let Op, Op_1, Op_2, $\cdots$, Op_k be the sequence of operator instances on the path from the given instance of p to the root of the tree. Let j be the least integer $1 \leq j \leq k$ such that either some id_i is Op_j (where $1 \leq i \leq n$), or else some id_i is the left-hand-side phylum occurrence of Op_j. Then, in this instance of p, $\{id_1.attr_1, id_2.attr_2, \ldots ,id_n.attr_n\}$ denotes the value of $id_i.attr_i$ in Op_j. An occurrence of an upward remote attribute set is improper if there exists a derivation tree such that none of the id_i appear on the path to the root.

Example. Consider the upward remote attribute set that appears on the right-hand side of the attribute equation in the following declarations:

$$B \; : \; Op(C,D) \; \{ C.c = \{A.a, B.b, D.d\}; \};$$

In each instance p of $B : Op(C,D)$, the instance of $C.c$ receives the value of the instance of $A.a$, $B.b$, or $D.d$ that occurs closest to p on the path from p's left-hand-side phylum instance to the root of the derivation tree. Note that SSL does allow $B.b$ and $D.d$ to occur in the upward remote attribute set, as illustrated above; they refer to the closest instance of these attributes *not including the attributes of the current production instance*.

To accommodate upward remote attribute sets, the SSL translator applies an algorithm to translate an editor specification that contains upward remote attribute sets to one without such abbreviations. In the process, it introduces new inherited attributes and defining equations that propagate appropriate attribute values, as necessary, to each instance of an upward remote attribute set in the derivation tree. The algorithm also detects improper uses of the notation.

The basic idea underlying the algorithm is as follows: for each occurrence of an upward remote attribute set, a search of the grammar is initiated to determine the set of productions deriving the phyla on the left-hand sides of the productions whose equations refer to upward remote attribute sets. Any production thus found whose left-hand-side phylum is not among those to which a remote reference has been made constitutes a potential "conduit" through which the value of one of the attributes can flow. Under the assumption that a "source" production defining the value of one of the attributes in an upward remote attribute set will eventually be found, we add to each production encountered a new attribute and equation that will cause the value of one of the remote attributes sought, if found, to be propagated.

A branch of the search for a given upward remote attribute set S may terminate in one of three ways:

1) A production is encountered that contains one of the members of S. In this case, an attribute equation is generated to pass the value down the tree.

2) A production is encountered whose left-hand-side phylum already has an attribute that passes the set S down the tree. In this case, a previous branch of the search has already encountered the production, and there is no need to repeat the search.

3) A production is encountered whose left-hand-side phylum symbol is the start symbol, but the start symbol is not among the phyla of S. This indicates that the notation has been used improperly, because otherwise this branch of the search would have terminated at a production that defines one of S's attributes.

The fact that productions are effectively "marked" by the addition of attribute equations to pass a specific upward remote attribute set ensures that the algorithm terminates, since there are only a finite number of productions in an editor specification.

A unique attribute identifier must be provided for each *set* of attributes to which a remote reference is made. This identifier is used to label the newly introduced attributes of any production through which a value among those in the corresponding attribute set must be propagated. Note that even if the attribute sets in several different upward remote attribute sets overlap, we must, in general, provide a separate attribute to propagate a value in each set because the values being passed down are not always the same.

We use the following notation for newly introduced attribute identifiers: for upward remote attribute set S, we denote the corresponding attribute identifier as $[S]$. For example, $[id_1.attr_1, \ldots, id_n.attr_n]$ represents the (inherited) attribute that is used to pass down the value of one of the attributes in the set $\{id_1.attr_1, id_2.attr_2, \ldots, id_n.attr_n\}$.

To distinguish among multiple occurrences of the same phylum on the right-hand side of some production, we make the following definitions.

- A phylum X has *context* $<P,j>$ if X occurs on the right-hand side of production P as the jth occurrence of an X phylum in P.
- For a given grammar, each phylum Z occurs in some bounded number of contexts. NumContexts(Z) denotes the number of contexts in which Z occurs.
- Each phylum's contexts can be assigned a position in the range $1..$NumContexts(Z). The notation Context(Z,i) denotes the ith context in which Z occurs, for $1 \leq i \leq$ NumContexts(Z).

Using this notation, procedure GenerateCopyRules for generating copy rules to resolve uses of upward remote attribute sets is given in Figure 11.2.

The procedure of Figure 11.2 can be improved by detecting cases in which the value that will be propagated by attributes corresponding to *different* upward remote attribute sets are guaranteed to be the *same*. This will be the case in regions of the grammar where all the attributes that occur in the (set) difference of two upward remote attribute sets cannot exist on any path from the root to the given production. The algorithm of Figure 11.2 will generate separate new attributes for the two upward remote attribute sets. This can be avoided by using attribute-identifier labels that correspond to the subset of the upward remote attribute set's elements whose phylum or operator component can occur on some derivation path to the given production.

Assuming the sets of phylum names and operator names are disjoint, for each phylum X in grammar G, we define CanDerive(X) to be the following set:

CanDerive(X) =
$\quad \{ Y \mid \exists$ derivations in G such that ROOT $\rightarrow^* \alpha Y \beta$ and $Y \rightarrow^+ \gamma X \delta \}$
$\quad \cup \{ Op \mid \exists$ derivations in G such that ROOT $\rightarrow^* \alpha Y \beta$,
$\qquad\qquad Y : Op (\gamma Z \delta)$ is a production, and $Z \rightarrow^* \rho X \pi \}$.

For phylum Z and attribute set $S = \{id_1.attr_1, \ldots, id_n.attr_n\}$, define

---

procedure GenerateCopyRules
declare
   worklist: a set of attributes
   S : a set of attributes
   X, W, Z: phylum names
   P : a production
   i, j: integers
begin
   worklist $:= \varnothing$
   for each occurrence of $\{id_1.attr_1, \ldots, id_n.attr_n\}$ in any production $W \rightarrow \alpha$ **do**
      $S := \{id_1.attr_1, \ldots, id_n.attr_n\}$
      Replace $\{id_1.attr_1, \ldots, id_n.attr_n\}$ with a new attribute $W.[S]$
      Insert $W.[S]$ into worklist
   od
   while worklist $\neq \varnothing$ **do**
      $Z.[S] :=$ RemoveElement(worklist)
      for $i := 1$ **to** NumContexts(Z)**do**
         $<P, j> :=$ Context(Z, i)
         $X :=$ the left-hand-side phylum of P
         if for any local attribute x of P, $P.x \in S$ **then**
            Add the equation "$Z\$j.[S] := x$" to the equations of P
         else if for any attribute x of X, $X.x \in S$ **then**
            Add the equation "$Z\$j.[S] := X.x$" to the equations of P
         else if X is the grammar's start symbol **then**
            error: "improper upward remote reference"
         else if X has attribute $[S]$ **then**
            Add the equation "$Z\$j.[S] := X.[S]$" to the equations of P
         else
            Attach a new inherited attribute $[S]$ to X
            Insert $X.[S]$ into worklist
            Add the equation "$Z\$j.[S] := X.[S]$" to the equations of P
         fi
      od
   od
end

Figure 11.2. An algorithm for generating copy rules to resolve uses of upward remote attribute sets.

Project(S, Z) to be the subset of S consisting of elements whose phylum or operator component is an element of CanDerive(Z):

Project(S, Z) = $\{id_i.attr_i \mid id_i.attr_i \in S$ and $id_i \in$ CanDerive(Z)$\}$.

The version of GenerateCopyRules given in Figure 11.3 contains the improvement described above. (This improvement is not incorporated in the algorithm used in the Synthesizer Generator.)

```
procedure GenerateCopyRules
declare
    worklist: a set of attributes
    S, T: a set of attributes
    X, W, Z: phylum names
    P: a production
    i, j: integers
begin
    worklist := ∅
    for each occurrence of {id₁.attr₁, . . . , idₙ.attrₙ} in any production W → α do
        S := {id₁.attr₁, . . . , idₙ.attrₙ}
        T := Project(S, W)
        Replace {id₁.attr₁, . . . , idₙ.attrₙ} with a new attribute W.[T]
        Insert W.[T] into worklist
    od
    while worklist ≠ ∅ do
        Z.[S] := RemoveElement(worklist)
        for i := 1 to NumContexts(Z)do
            <P, j> := Context(Z, i)
            X := the left-hand-side phylum of P
            if for any local attribute x of P, P.x ∈ S then
                Add the equation "Z$j.[S] := x" to the equations of P
            else if for any attribute x of X, X.x ∈ S then
                Add the equation "Z$j.[S] := X.x" to the equations of P
            else if X is the grammar's start symbol then
                error: "improper upward remote reference"
            else if X has attribute [T] such that T = Project(S, X) then
                Add the equation "Z$j.[S] := X.[T]" to the equations of P
            else
                T := Project(S, X)
                Attach a new inherited attribute [T] to X
                Insert X.[T] into worklist
                Add the equation "Z$j.[S] := X.[T]" to the equations of P
            fi
        od
    od
end
```

Figure 11.3. An improved algorithm for generating copy rules to resolve uses of upward remote attribute sets.

11.4. Deferred Reference Counting

It is occasionally necessary to interface generated editors to C to make use of existing packages written in C, to express computations that would be awkward to express in SSL, or for the sake of efficiency. When this is necessary, it is important to understand the storage-reclamation method used in the implementation and the operations that implement it.

Storage reclamation in editors generated with the Synthesizer Generator is handled with a greatly simplified version of the deferred reference-counting scheme first proposed in [Deutsch76]. The simplified method used in the Synthesizer Generator is similar to the one described in [Rovner84].

In a deferred reference-counting scheme, each reference falls into one of two categories: *actual references* and *shadow references*. Actual references are similar to the ordinary references that arise in a conventional reference-counting scheme, in that actual references to a node are reflected in the node's reference-count field. At any given moment, the reference-count field of a node contains the number of actual references to the node. By contrast, shadow references to a node are not reflected in the node's reference-count field.

The penalty of the conventional reference-counting method is that every operation that introduces or removes a reference to a node must adjust the node's reference count accordingly. The key observation behind the deferred reference-counting method is that the great majority of all operations performed only manipulate the stack. In deferred reference counting, all references to nodes that emanate from the stack are treated as shadow references. Although stack-manipulation operations do change the total number of references that exist, for most operations the net effect is to change only the total number of shadow references. The deferred reference-counting method holds an advantage over the conventional reference-counting method because it allows most stack-manipulation operations to avoid the usual overhead for adjusting reference counts. For SSL, the only stack-manipulation operation that affects the number of actual references is the operation for constructing a value of a user-defined phylum.

Operations that introduce or remove actual references perform the appropriate operation to increment or decrement the node's (actual) reference count. For example, whenever the SSL interpreter creates a new actual reference to n by a construction operation, operation rc_incr(n) is performed. The actual reference count of n is decremented by an rc_decr(n) operation; if rc_decr(n) drops n's reference count to zero then n is a candidate for reclaiming. However, it is not possible to reclaim n *immediately* because there may be shadow references to the node. Instead, n is placed in the zero-count set (zc_set) and reclaiming is deferred until the moment when zc_set reaches its capacity (zc_max_set_size).

When invoked, reclaiming is performed in three stages:

Stage 1:

In the first stage, all shadow references are converted into actual references. The SSL stack is traversed, and the (actual) reference count is incremented for every shadow reference to a node. At the end of Stage 1, each node's reference-count field reflects the *total* number of references to the node.

Stage 2:

The second stage empties the zero-count set; every node in zc_set whose reference count is still zero is immediately reclaimed, together with all attributes and descendants whose reference count drops to zero as a result. By virtue of Stage 1, no value referenced from the SSL stack will be reclaimed.

Stage 3:

The third stage re-establishes the invariant condition: "All references emanating from the stack are shadow references." The actual reference count of every node referred to from the SSL stack is decremented; that is, all references from the stack are converted back into shadow references. If, in the process, a node's reference count drops back to zero, the node is again inserted into the zc_set.

Operation rc_alloc(n) performed on a newly-created node n merely sets the actual reference count of the node to zero. For a node created by the SSL interpreter, the node is immediately pushed onto the expression stack, thereby creating a shadow reference. At the same time, the newly created node is inserted into the zero-count set so that, in the event that it is popped off the stack without ever being referenced, it may eventually be reclaimed.

CHAPTER 12

Incremental Attribute Evaluation for Ordered Attribute Grammars

By far the most involved of the algorithms employed in the Synthesizer Generator are its algorithms for incremental attribute updating. In generated editors, incremental attribute updating is carried out by one of several change-propagation algorithms. One of the algorithms used is described in [Reps82], [Reps83], and Chapter 5 of [Reps84], which works for arbitrary noncircular attribute grammars. Alternatively, when the grammar falls into the class of *ordered attribute grammars* [Kastens80], a much more efficient algorithm specialized to that class can be used.

The ordered attribute grammars are a subclass of the noncircular grammars, and almost all grammars arising in practice are ordered. However, if a specification fails the orderedness test, an editor can still be generated that uses the more general change-propagation algorithm. Any grammar that is circular will fail to be ordered. In this case, the generated editor may loop endlessly as it follows a cycle of attribute dependences in the abstract-syntax tree. To detect this possibility in advance, Release 3 will incorporate a general test of circularity.

Editors generated from ordered specifications are far more efficient than editors generated from unordered specifications. First, the change-propagation algorithm runs far more quickly; second, the version of the attributed-tree module tailored for ordered grammars uses a much more compact representation of tree nodes in which certain extra information needed for the more general change-propagation algorithm is eliminated.

Ordered attribute grammars were introduced in [Kastens80] to simplify the construction of a *distributed-control evaluator* – an evaluator that uses a collection of finite-state machines to control the evaluation process. This chapter discusses the application of this idea to incremental attribute evaluation and describes a change-propagation algorithm for ordered attribute grammars. The algorithm presented uses exactly the same machines produced by Kastens's construction for change propagation, but gives an alternative interpretation to the instructions in the machines' finite-state control.

The chapter is organized into seven sections, as follows. Sections 12.1 and 12.2 motivate the idea of a distributed-control evaluator. Sections 12.3 and 12.4 discuss Kastens's work on visit-sequence evaluators for ordered attribute grammars. Section 12.5 describes how to adapt the Kastens evaluator for performing change propagation. Section 12.6 discusses an optimization to the change-propagation technique described in Section 12.5; the improvement is based on being able to analyze a specification's attribute-definition functions to determine which attributes are defined by one-to-one functions. Section 12.7 addresses what to do if the Synthesizer Generator reports that Kastens's construction fails.

12.1. Greedy Evaluation

Distributed-control evaluation can be viewed as an improvement on a nondeterministic *greedy evaluation* method that is described in this section.

Because attributes are defined strictly in terms of other attributes in a single production, when one attribute instance is evaluated, other attribute instances in the same production instance are also apt to be ready for evaluation; consequently, an evaluator can reduce the number of times it has to switch to a new evaluation context by updating as many attributes as possible at one production instance before moving to the next. The greedy evaluation method attempts to cluster attribute evaluations in this way. The method is asymptotically neither better nor worse than methods that do not cluster evaluations, but in practice it can be better if switching to a new evaluation context is expensive.

To further characterize partially attributed derivation trees, we introduce the notion of deficiency: a production instance p is *deficient* if any of its attribute instances are ready for evaluation. Operation Update(p) evaluates all attribute instances of p that are ready for evaluation.

Because attributes are defined solely in terms of attributes of a single production, the only production instances that can become deficient when production instance $p: t_0 \rightarrow t_1 \cdots t_n$ is updated are the *neighbors of p*, that is, the production instance that derives t_0 and the production instances derived from t_k, for $k = 1 \cdots n$. Consequently, a greedy evaluation algorithm can keep track of all deficient production instances in a work-list, as is done by procedure Evaluate of Figure 12.1.

The greedy evaluation method of Figure 12.1 has the drawback that the attributes of a production instance p are repeatedly searched to discover which of them are ready for evaluation; in the statement of the algorithm as given, the searches are concealed in the operations to test whether p is deficient and to update p. These searches are carried out whenever the evaluator switches to a new context, so a production instance will be searched each time it or one of its neighbors is updated by the evaluator.

12.2. Distributed-Control Evaluation

A distributed-control evaluator eliminates the need for a run-time search to determine which attributes of a production instance are ready for evaluation. In place of the search, the evaluator makes use of an evaluation schedule that is generated by analyzing attribute dependences in the grammar; this analysis is performed once and for all at editor-generation time.

The scheduling information takes the form of a collection of *plans*, one for each production in the grammar. The plans can be thought of as the transition tables of a collection of finite-state machines, where there is a different kind of machine for each production in the grammar. Each state in the machine associated with production p corresponds to a run-time situation in which a particular

---

```
procedure Evaluate(T)
declare
    T: an unattributed derivation tree
    S: a set of production instances
    p, p': production instances
begin
    S := the set of deficient production instances of T
    while S ≠ ∅ do
        Select and remove a production instance p from S
        Update(p)
        for each production instance p' that is a neighbor of p do
            if p' is deficient then Insert p' into S fi
        od
    od
end
```

Figure 12.1. A greedy attribute-evaluation method. Evaluations are clustered by updating as many attributes as possible at one production instance before moving on to the next.

set of p's attributes are available. A transition of the machine represents either an instruction to evaluate an attribute or an instruction to transfer control to a neighboring machine.

To make it easier to discuss distributed-control evaluation, we introduce the following terminology: if production instance $t_0 \rightarrow t_1 \cdots t_n$ is an instance of production p, we say that p *applies at node* t_0; the machine for the production that applies at node t_0 will be referred to as the *machine that applies at* t_0.

Conceptually, a distributed-control evaluator is made up of instances of the machines that apply at each node of the tree. At a given stage of evaluation, a single machine of the distributed-control evaluator is active. Initially, the active machine is the machine that applies at the root of the tree. During the course of evaluation, control passes from machine to machine; an important feature of the evaluation pattern of a distributed-control evaluator is that such transfers of control are exclusively transfers from neighbor to neighbor. Evaluation continues until all machines reach their final state, at which point the tree is fully attributed.

During evaluation, the distributed-control evaluation technique is time-efficient because, instead of determining the evaluation order at run-time, the evaluator uses an evaluation sequence that has been pre-computed by statically analyzing the grammar at construction-time. An additional advantage is that to keep track of the run-time situation at a production instance t, it is only necessary to know the state of the machine that applies at t. The distributed-control evaluation technique is space-efficient because at run-time it is not necessary to provide an actual copy of the machine for each production instance. The label on each node n that indicates what production applies at n, denoted by n.ruleIndicator, completely determines which machine description applies.

The use of the term "distributed-control evaluator" is not meant to convey the impression that the attributes of a tree are evaluated in parallel by separate processors; on the contrary, a tree's attributes are evaluated by a single procedure that interprets descriptions of the machines that make up the distributed-control evaluator for the tree.

Four varieties of distributed-control evaluators have been discussed in the literature: *tree-walk evaluators* [Warren75, Kennedy76], *coroutine evaluators* [Warren76], *local-control automata* [Cohen79], and *visit-sequence evaluators* [Kastens80]. The feature that distinguishes the visit-sequence evaluator from the others is its simplicity. The transition diagram of each machine of a visit-sequence evaluator is a single sequence of instructions, with no branching. For the other three kinds of distributed-control evaluators, a machine's transition diagram is, in general, a directed acyclic graph.

Tree-walk evaluators, coroutine evaluators, and local-control automata have the virtue that they handle, or can be adapted to handle, *arbitrary* noncircular attribute grammars. However, for a distributed-control evaluator to work in linear-time for an arbitrary noncircular grammar, each tree node must be labeled with information about attribute dependences in the subtree derived from the node; this information is then used as an additional argument to the machines' transition function [Warren75, Cohen79]. This requirement increases the space overhead for using these methods. For a description of an attribute-updating algorithm based on the tree-walk evaluation method, see Chapter 9 of [Reps84].

In practice, it seems as if the additional power of the more general machines is not warranted. A visit-sequence evaluator can be constructed for essentially all attribute grammars that arise in practice. Consequently, in the Synthesizer Generator, the algorithm for attribute updating based on distributed-control evaluation is an adaptation of the visit-sequence method. The algorithm used in the Synthesizer Generator is described below; a description of essentially the same method can also be found in [Yeh83].

12.3. Evaluation of Ordered Attribute Grammars by Visit-Sequence Evaluators

A visit-sequence evaluator has a particularly simple structure that allows the evaluation method to be viewed as a collection of non-branching coroutines. When control is transferred to node x, the machine that applies at x resumes execution, and the instructions in its plan control the evaluation process until there is a transfer of control to the machine that applies at a child of x or at the parent of x. During the course of evaluation, each node may receive control several times, successive visits bringing additional inherited attributes and causing new attribute evaluations and visits to the node's children.

The activities of every pair of adjacent machines must be coordinated. For example, suppose that node x is an interior node of the tree, that x is an instance of nonterminal X, and that the two production instances in which x occurs are instances of the productions $p : X \rightarrow \alpha$ and $q : Y \rightarrow \beta X \gamma$. The synthesized attributes of x are evaluated by the plan for p, and the inherited attributes of x are evaluated by the plan for q. In general, the interaction between the machine that applies at x (a p machine) and the machine that applies at x.parent (a q machine) takes the following form: the q machine computes a subset of x's inherited attributes and transfers control down to the p machine; the p machine computes a subset of x's synthesized attributes and transfers control back up to the q machine. (In both cases, other evaluations and transfers of control may be interspersed with the ones that affect x; here we are concerned solely with actions that affect x directly.) Thus, the attributes of x get evaluated in alternating groups of inherited attributes and synthesized attributes.

The interaction pattern described above holds for any pair of adjacent machines. Therefore, in deriving a grammar's plans, we must take into account the interactions between every possible pair of adjacent machines. For example, different instances of the production $p:X \rightarrow \alpha$ may be adjacent to production $q:Y \rightarrow \beta X \gamma$ and to production $r:Z \rightarrow \beta' X \gamma'$. Moreover, the plan for p cannot vary depending on whether it is adjacent to q or to r; in the plan for p, the interface through X must be compatible with both.

The interface between any two plans must reflect the dependences that hold among X's attributes. Visit-sequence evaluators apply to the class of *partitionable attribute grammars*,[1] which are characterized by the following property of the dependences among the nonterminals' attributes:

> ... for each symbol a partial order over the associated attributes can be given, such that in any context of the symbol the attributes are evaluable in an order which includes that partial order.
>
> [Kastens80]

The *ordered attribute grammars* are a subclass of the partitionable grammars for which there is a particularly efficient way to determine the plans for a visit-sequence evaluator.

The adjective "partitionable" refers to the use that is made of the above-mentioned partial order in the construction of the evaluator's plans. The partial order is used to partition each nonterminal's attribute set into a sequence of disjoint subsets that alternate between one that consists entirely of inherited attributes and one that consists entirely of synthesized attributes. In addition, the partitions respect the evaluation requirements of each nonterminal's attributes; that is, the partitions $A_k(X)$ associated with nonterminal X's attributes are defined so that for each tree node x, if $x.a \in A_i(X)$, $x.b \in A_j(X)$, and $i > j$, then $x.a$ can be evaluated before $x.b$.

These partitions define the interface between adjacent machines. The plan for each production is created using the production's local attribute dependences and the partitions for each of the production's nonterminals. For ordered attribute grammars, this construction is described in more detail in Section 12.4, "Construction of a Visit-Sequence Evaluator." The reader may also wish to consult [Kastens80] or [Waite83].

---

[1]The term is used in [Kastens82] and [Waite83]; in [Kastens80], the class is called the *arranged orderly grammars*.

The characteristics of a visit-sequence evaluator may be summarized as follows:

- With each production $X_0 \rightarrow X_1 \cdots X_n$, there is a fixed sequence of instructions $I_1, I_2, \cdots, I_j$.
- Each instruction either calls for the evaluation of a synthesized attribute of X_0, the evaluation of an inherited attribute of X_i, for $1 \leq i \leq n$, a transfer of control to the machine that applies at X_i, for $1 \leq i \leq n$, or a transfer of control to the machine that applies at the parent of X_0. There are three types of instructions:

  1) An EVAL(i, a) instruction causes attribute instance $X_i.a$ to be evaluated. Note that for $i = 0$, a must be a synthesized attribute, but for $i = 1, \cdots, n$, a must be an inherited attribute.
  2) A VISIT(i, r) instruction for $i = 1, \cdots, n$ causes control to be transferred down to the machine that applies at X_i for the rth time.
  3) A SUSPEND(r) instruction causes the machine to return control to the parent of X_0 for the rth time. Each plan P has one distinguished SUSPEND instruction, the final instruction of the plan.

- For any given derivation tree T, the instances of the plans associated with T's production instances act as cooperating coroutines.
- Evaluation starts at the beginning of the plan that applies at the root of T; it finishes when the root's plan executes a SUSPEND instruction.

When a VISIT instruction is executed, control is transferred across one of the right-hand-side nonterminal occurrences of the production; when a SUSPEND instruction is executed it is transferred across the left-hand-side nonterminal occurrence. For both types of instructions, the parameter denoted above by r indicates the number of times control has been transferred across the given nonterminal occurrence. This quantity, called the *visit number*, is used as a parameter for establishing the state of the neighbor machine that receives control.

The visit-sequence evaluation procedure, called VSEvaluate, is given in Figure 12.2. A tree T is evaluated by calling VSEvaluate(T).

To record the execution state of the tree, VSEvaluate makes use of two variables, currentNode and planIndex. Variable currentNode records the node whose machine is currently active. Variable planIndex is an offset into currentNode's plan; it indicates what instruction of the plan is to be executed next. Each time control is transferred to some node x, the value of planIndex is determined and the machine that applies at x is re-awakened in that state. The machine then executes the next sequence of instructions in the plan for x, up until the next instruction that transfers control to a neighboring machine.

```
procedure VSEvaluate(T)
declare
    T: an unattributed derivation tree
    currentNode: the node of T whose machine is currently active
    planIndex, r, i: integers
    a: an attribute name
    currentNode_i: the i^th node of the production instance at currentNode
begin
    currentNode := root(T)
    planIndex := 1
    forever do
        if Plan[currentNode.ruleIndicator][planIndex] has the form EVAL(i, a) then
            Execute the attribute-definition function to evaluate currentNode_i.a
            planIndex := planIndex + 1
        else if Plan[currentNode.ruleIndicator][planIndex] has the form VISIT(i, r) then
            planIndex := MapVisitToPlanIndex(currentNode_i.ruleIndicator, 0, r)
            currentNode := currentNode_i
        else if Plan[currentNode.ruleIndicator][planIndex] has the form SUSPEND(r) then
            if currentNode = root(T) then return fi
            planIndex := MapVisitToPlanIndex(currentNode.parent.ruleIndicator,
                                             currentNode.sonNumber,
                                             r)
            currentNode := currentNode.parent
        fi
    od
end
```

Figure 12.2. An attribute-evaluation method for ordered attribute grammars (Kastens).

A visit-sequence evaluation strategy is encoded in two tables, named Plan and MapVisitToPlanIndex. Table Plan is a table of plans indexed by production. The current plan is retrieved from this table by the expression:

Plan[currentNode.ruleIndicator].

The current instruction of the plan is determined by:

Plan[currentNode.ruleIndicator][planIndex].

Table MapVisitToPlanIndex is used to determine the resumption state of the machine that receives control after VSEvaluate executes a VISIT or SUSPEND instruction. The value retrieved from MapVisitToPlanIndex is an index into table Plan; it is assigned to variable planIndex. The value is determined on the basis of three pieces of information: a production, a nonterminal-occurrence number in the production, and a visit number. More precisely, when machine m receives control after a transfer through the interface at node x, the state of m is determined as a function of three parameters:

1) the production that applies at m (denoted by m.ruleIndicator),
2) the nonterminal-occurrence number of x in the production corresponding to m (0 for a VISIT instruction, the quantity x.sonNumber for a SUSPEND instruction), and
3) the visit number, recorded in the VISIT or SUSPEND instruction, which indicates the number of times m has been activated because of a transfer through x.

Table MapVisitToPlanIndex maps these three quantities to an offset within m's plan. When control is transferred using a VISIT(i, r) instruction, the new state is selected by

planIndex := MapVisitToPlanIndex(currentNode$_i$.ruleIndicator, 0, r).

When control is transferred using a SUSPEND(r) instruction, the new state is selected by

planIndex := MapVisitToPlanIndex(currentNode.parent.ruleIndicator,
                                 currentNode.sonNumber,
                                 r).

In either case, after currentNode is assigned the node that is receiving control, the new machine resumes execution at the instruction given by

Plan[currentNode.ruleIndicator][planIndex].

When a machine is re-awakened, its resumption state is established by consulting MapVisitToPlanIndex to determine the proper value for planIndex, using the visit-number as one of the three parameters. Because the visit-number parameter is a component of each VISIT and SUSPEND instruction, VSEvaluate does not require any information about machine states to be stored with individual nodes of the tree; this property is one reason why VSEvaluate is so storage-efficient compared to other attribute-evaluation algorithms.

12.4. Construction of a Visit-Sequence Evaluator

In determining the next action to take at evaluation time, a visit-sequence evaluator does not need to examine directly any of the dependences that exist among attributes or attribute instances; this work has been done once and for all at construction time and compiled into the evaluator's plans. Constructing a visit-sequence evaluator involves finding all situations that can possibly occur during attribute evaluation and making an appropriate plan for each production of the grammar. In this section, we describe Kastens's algorithm for creating these plans; further information about the construction can be found in [Kastens80] and in [Waite83].

Kastens's method of constructing a visit-sequence evaluator is based on an analysis of attribute dependences. The information gathered from this analysis is used to simulate possible run-time evaluation situations implicitly and to build an evaluation plan that works correctly for all situations that can arise. In particular, the construction method ensures that whenever an EVAL instruction is executed to evaluate some attribute instance, all the attribute's arguments will already have been given values.

The Kastens construction consists of five distinct steps. Our description of the construction basically follows that given in [Kastens80], although Step 3 and Step 5 are stated somewhat differently.

12.4.1. Steps 1 and 2: Determining transitive dependences

The detail that most complicates the plan-construction algorithm is that the evaluation context of a given production may be different for different instances of the production in an abstract-syntax tree. By a production instance's *evaluation context*, we mean the transitive dependences that exist among the production instance's attribute instances due to chains of dependences that run throughout the tree.

Kastens's construction side-steps the problem of a production having different evaluation contexts by making what is essentially a worst-case assumption. The dependences that exist among a nonterminal's attributes must obey the following restriction: for each nonterminal X, there must exist an acyclic relation among the attributes of X that covers the actual dependence relation in every tree. The attributes of each of the grammar's nonterminals are required to have such a covering dependence relation. We use the notation $TDS(X)$ (standing for "Transitive Dependences among a Symbol's attributes") to denote the covering dependence relation for nonterminal X.

Using covering dependence relations in place of a tree's actual dependence relations is a key part of the construction. The advantage of using the TDS relations is that they are a precomputed approximation to the actual dependence relations. By using $TDS(X)$ in place of the actual dependence relation that holds at X, we are being pessimistic because the edges that occur in $TDS(X)$ may correspond to combinations of dependences that never actually appear together in any one tree. In fact, an individual edge in $TDS(X)$ may represent a dependence that never actually exists in *any* tree. However, as long as this does not lead to the introduction of any cycles, using an approximate dependence relation in place of the actual dependence relation merely places additional restrictions on the evaluation order, without actually making it impossible to choose an order.

To express the covering restrictions more precisely, we introduce the following terminology and notation:

- The notation $A(X)$ denotes the attribute instances of tree-node X.
- As in Chapter 3, functional dependences among attribute occurrences in a production p (or attribute instances in a tree T) are represented by a directed graph, called, in both cases, an attribute-dependence graph. The graph is denoted by $D(p)$ (respectively, $D(T)$) and defined as follows:

  1) For each attribute occurrence (instance) b, the graph contains a vertex b'.

  2) If attribute occurrence (instance) b appears on the right-hand side of the attribute equation that defines attribute occurrence (instance) c, the graph contains an edge (b', c'), directed from b' to c'. (An edge from b' to c' indicates that b' is used to define the value of c'.)

- Given directed graphs $A = (V_A, E_A)$ and $B = (V_B, E_B)$, which may or may not be disjoint, the *union* of A and B, denoted by $A \cup B$, is defined as follows:

$$A \cup B = (V_A \cup V_B, E_A \cup E_B).$$

- Given a directed graph $A = (V, E)$, a *path* from vertex a to vertex b is a sequence of vertices $[v_1, v_2, ..., v_k]$ such that $a = v_1$, $b = v_k$, and $\{(v_i, v_{i+1}) \mid i = 1, ..., k-1\} \subseteq E$.

- Given a directed graph $A = (V, E)$ and a set of vertices $V' \subseteq V$, the *projection* of A onto V', denoted by A/V', is defined as $A/V' = (V', E')$, where $E' = \{(v, w) \mid v, w \in V'$ and there exists a path $[v = v_1, v_2, ..., v_k = w]$ such that $v_2, ..., v_{k-1} \notin V'\}$. (That is, A/V' has an edge from $v \in V'$ to $w \in V'$ when there exists a path from v to w in A that does not pass through any other elements of V'.)

With this notation, the salient property of the covering restriction can be characterized as follows: for all trees T and nodes $\hat{X}$ in T, the graph $D(T)/A(\hat{X})$ must be a subgraph of $TDS(X)$, where the attribute instances of nonterminal instance $\hat{X}$ are identified with the corresponding attributes of nonterminal X.

Although a nonterminal's attributes may have different dependence relations in different trees, the use of the TDS relation to represent a nonterminal's evaluation context side-steps this problem by making a worst-case assumption: *all the different dependence relations for a nonterminal's attributes are assumed to exist simultaneously at each of the nonterminal's instances.*

One consequence of representing a nonterminal's evaluation context by the *TDS* relation is that the actions of the visit-sequence evaluation machines are independent of the context actually provided by the rest of the tree.

A second consequence of representing a nonterminal's evaluation context by the *TDS* relation is that it causes Kastens's construction to fail to build an evaluator for some grammars. For example, Kastens's construction fails on attribute grammars for which, for some production $p : X_0 \rightarrow X_1 \cdots X_k$, the graph

$$D(p) \cup TDS(X_0) \cup TDS(X_1) \cup \cdots \cup TDS(X_k)$$

is cyclic. The restrictions of the algorithm are not usually a handicap because most grammars that arise in practice meet the requirements. Those grammars that fail the condition can usually be adjusted to meet the requirements (see Section 12.7).

In Steps 1 and 2 of Kastens's construction of visit-sequences for ordered attribute grammars, the goal is to determine the transitive dependences among a nonterminal's attributes. This information is recorded in the relation $TDS(X)$. Initially, all the *TDS* relations are empty. The construction that builds them up involves the auxiliary relation $TDP(p)$ (standing for "Transitive Dependences in a Production"), which expresses dependences among the attributes of a production's nonterminal occurrences.

The basic operation used in Steps 1 and 2 is procedure AddEdgeAndInduce($TDP(p), (a, b)$) whose arguments are the *TDP* graph of some production p and a pair of attribute occurrences in p. AddEdgeAndInduce carries out three actions:

1) Edge (a, b) is inserted into graph $TDP(p)$.
2) Any additional edges needed to transitively close $TDP(p)$ are inserted into $TDP(p)$.
3) In addition, for each edge added to $TDP(p)$ by either action 1 or 2, (*i.e.* either the edge (a, b) itself or some other edge (c, d) added to reclose $TDP(p)$), AddEdgeAndInduce may add an edge to one of the *TDS* graphs. In particular, for each edge added to $TDP(p)$ of the form $(X_i.m, X_i.n)$, where X_i is an occurrence of nonterminal X and $(X.m, X.n) \notin TDS(X)$, an edge $(X.m, X.n)$ is added to $TDS(X)$.

Each edge of a $TDS(X)$ graph can be *marked* or *unmarked*; the edges that AddEdgeAndInduce adds to the $TDS(X)$ graphs are unmarked.

The *TDS* graphs are generated by the first two steps of Kastens's algorithm. The first step, an initialization step, is carried out by procedure Step1, given in Figure 12.3. Step1 initializes the grammar's *TDP* graphs with edges represent-

```
procedure Step1
declare
    p : a production
    X_i, X_j : nonterminal occurrences
    a, b : attributes
begin
    for each production p do
        for each attribute occurrence X_j.b of p do
            for each argument X_i.a of X_j.b do
                if (X_i.a, X_j.b) ∉ TDP(p) then
                    AddEdgeAndInduce(TDP(p), (X_i.a, X_j.b)) fi
            od
        od
    od
end
```

Figure 12.3. Initialization of the *TDP* and *TDS* graphs.

ing all direct dependences that exist between the grammar's attribute occurrences. Because the edges of the *TDP* graphs are entered by calls to AddEdgeAndInduce, Step1 also serves to initialize the *TDS* graphs. Through the side effects of the calls on AddEdgeAndInduce, Step1 creates unmarked edges in the *TDS* graphs due to all direct dependences occurring in the grammar.

Procedure Step2, given in Figure 12.4, determines a set of induced transitive dependences by performing a closure operation on the *TDP* and *TDS* relations. In Step2, the invariant for the **while**-loop is

```
procedure Step2
declare
    X : a nonterminal
    X̂ : a nonterminal occurrence
    p : a production
begin
    while there is an unmarked edge (X.a, X.b) in one of the TDS relations do
        mark (X.a, X.b)
        for each occurrence X̂ of X in any production p do
            if (X̂.a, X̂.b) ∉ TDP(p) then AddEdgeAndInduce(TDP(p), (X̂.a, X̂.b)) fi
        od
    od
end
```

Figure 12.4. Computation of the dependence relations *TDP* and *TDS*.

If a relation $TDP(p)$ contains an edge e' that corresponds to a marked edge e in one of the TDS relations, then e has been induced in all the other relations $TDP(q)$.

When all edges in TDS are marked, the effects of all direct dependences have been induced in the TDP and TDS relations. Thus, the $TDS(X)$ graphs computed by Step2 are guaranteed to cover the actual transitive dependences among the attributes of X that exist at any occurrence of X in any derivation tree.

If any of the TDP relations is circular after Step1 or Step2, then the construction halts with failure. Failure after Step1 indicates a circularity in the equations of an individual production; failure after Step2 can indicate that the grammar is circular, but Step2 can also fail for some noncircular grammars.

12.4.2. Step 3: Partitioning

In Section 12.3, we described how the activities of adjacent machines joined at an instance of nonterminal X cause the attributes of the node to be evaluated in alternating groups of inherited attributes and synthesized attributes. The third step of Kastens's construction uses the TDS relations computed in Steps 1 and 2 to partition each nonterminal's attributes into these evaluation groups. Each set in the partition of nonterminal X's attributes consists either entirely of synthesized attributes or entirely of inherited attributes. Each partition set is assigned a number in Step 3 that corresponds to a reversal of the order in which partitions are evaluated by machines that adjoin at an X node; that is, partition set $A_1(X)$ is evaluated last.

The partition sets $A_1(X)$, $A_2(X)$, $\cdots$, $A_k(X)$ are defined by the following recursive definition (where $n \geq 1$):

$$A_{2n-1}(X) = \{X.a \in \text{synthesized attributes of } X \mid \text{if } (X.a, X.b) \in TDS(X),$$
$$\text{then } X.b \in A_m(X), \text{ for some } m, 1 \leq m \leq 2n-1\}$$

$$A_{2n}(X) = \{X.a \in \text{inherited attributes of } X \mid \text{if } (X.a, X.b) \in TDS(X),$$
$$\text{then } X.b \in A_m(X), \text{ for some } m, 1 \leq m \leq 2n\}.$$

The partitioning of a grammar's nonterminals is carried out by procedure Step3, given in Figure 12.5.

The body of Step3's outermost loop is a variation on topological sorting that uses two worklists, SynWorklist and InhWorklist, rather than one. SynWorklist contains only synthesized attributes, InhWorklist only inherited attributes. The body of the outer loop is executed once for each nonterminal X in the grammar. At each iteration, graph G, a copy of $TDS(X)$, is sorted as if all its edges had

procedure Step3
declare
   G : a directed graph
   SynWorklist, InhWorklist: sets of attributes
   k : an integer
   b , c : attributes
begin
   for each nonterminal X **do**
      $G := TDS(X)$
      SynWorklist := { $b \in$ synthesized attributes of X | out-degree$_G$ $(b) = 0$ }
      InhWorklist := { $b \in$ inherited attributes of X | out-degree$_G$ $(b) = 0$ }
      $k := 1$
      while SynWorklist $\neq \emptyset \lor$ InhWorklist $\neq \emptyset$ **do**
         if k is odd **then**
            while SynWorklist $\neq \emptyset$ **do**
               Select and remove an attribute b from SynWorklist
               Partition[$X.b$] := k
               for each c that is a predecessor of b in G **do**
                  Remove edge (c, b) from G
                  if out-degree$_G$ $(c) = 0$ **then**
                     if c is a synthesized attribute of X **then** Insert c into SynWorklist
                     else Insert c into InhWorklist
                     fi
                  fi
               od
            od
         else
            while InhWorklist $\neq \emptyset$ **do**
               Select and remove an attribute b from InhWorklist
               Partition[$X.b$] := k
               for each c that is a predecessor of b in G **do**
                  Remove edge (c, b) from G
                  if out-degree$_G$ $(c) = 0$ **then**
                     if c is a synthesized attribute of X **then** Insert c into SynWorklist
                     else Insert c into InhWorklist
                     fi
                  fi
               od
            od
         fi
         $k := k + 1$
      od
      numberOfVisitsNeeded(X) := max(1, $k/2$)
   od
end

Figure 12.5. Computation of disjoint partitions for the attributes of each nonterminal X according to the dependences in $TDS(X)$.

been reversed in direction. Thus, SynWorklist and InhWorklist are initialized with the vertices of G that have out-degree 0.

Variable k contains the current partition number. Variable Partition is a table, indexed by attribute occurrence, that records an attribute occurrence's partition number; the partition set of attribute occurrence $X.b$ is set by the assignment

Partition[$X.b$] := k

The two worklists contain the sets of attributes that are ready to be assigned to partitions k and $k + 1$. The parity of k determines whether the active worklist is SynWorklist or InhWorklist.

G changes as attributes are considered to reflect only the dependences among attributes that have not yet been assigned to a partition set. The out-degree of each vertex reflects the number of unassigned attributes that depend on the vertex. An edge (b, c) in G indicates that attributes b and c are unassigned and that c depends on b. This means that after consideration of attribute c, all its incoming edges (b, c) are deleted from G, and if this action causes b to have out-degree 0, b is inserted in the appropriate worklist because all successors have already been assigned to a partition set.

Step3 also computes the quantity numberOfVisitsNeeded(X) for each nonterminal X. This indicates the number of VISIT/SUSPEND transfer pairs that must take place across each occurrence of nonterminal X. Note that to ensure that the visit-sequence evaluator has a chance to evaluate every attribute of the tree, at a minimum one pair of transfers must take place across each nonterminal occurrence so that every machine of the tree gets activated at least once.

12.4.3. Steps 4 and 5: Converting partitions into plans

The final two steps of Kastens's construction convert the partition information into evaluation plans. The step that actually emits the plans (the fifth and final step) is carried out by what is essentially a topological sort of each of the grammar's *TDP* graphs. One problem that arises is that when a graph is topologically sorted there is considerable choice at each step as to what should be considered next; if we were to sort the *TDP* graphs computed by Step 2, there is no guarantee that compatible plans would be created for machines that can be adjacent in a derivation tree.

The purpose of the fourth step of Kastens's construction is to ensure that the plans that are created for machines that can be adjacent in a tree are compatible with the partitions found in Step 3. The role of Step 4 can be stated succinctly as follows:

> When we choose a partition, this choice fixes the order in which certain attributes may be computed. In this respect the partition acts like a set of

dependencies, and its effect may be taken into account by adding these dependencies to the ones arising from the attribution rules.

[Waite83]

Thus, the fourth step of Kastens's construction adds additional edges between attribute occurrences in the grammar's *TDP* graphs that are in different partitions. This step ensures that compatible plans are generated for machines that can be adjacent in some derivation tree. This step is carried out by procedure Step4, given in Figure 12.6.

If all the *TDP* (*p*) graphs are acyclic after Step 4, then the grammar is *ordered*. One of the problems with Kastens's construction is that Step 4 may introduce cycles into the *TDP* graphs. If any cycles are introduced by Step 4, the construction halts with failure. (This failure is reported by the SSL translator as a *type 3 circularity*.) For a discussion of what can be done when this kind of failure occurs, see Section 12.7, "What to Do When a Grammar Fails the Orderedness Test."

The final step of Kastens's construction makes use of the *TDP* graphs (as amended by Step 4) to create the actual plan for each production. In this step, a topological sort of each *TDP* graph is carried out. At each stage of the topological sort of *TDP* (*p*), a certain set *S* of the vertices of *TDP* (*p*) have been considered. Such a state corresponds to a (run-time) evaluation state at a node where *p* applies in which the elements of *S* are available. The plan-creation step is carried out by procedure Step5, of Figure 12.7.

---

procedure Step4
declare
    X_i : a nonterminal occurrence
    p : a production
    a , b : attributes
begin
    for each production p **do**
        for each nonterminal occurrence X_i in p **do**
            for each pair $<X_i.a , X_i.b>$ of X_i 's attribute occurrences **do**
                if Partition[$X_i.a$] > Partition[$X_i.b$] **then**
                    Insert edge $(X_i.a , X_i.b)$ into *TDP* (*p*) **fi**
        od
        od
    od
end

Figure 12.6. Completion of *TDP* graphs with edges from higher-numbered partition-set elements to lower-numbered elements.

---

procedure Step5
declare
  p : a production
  i, j, k : integers
  X_i, X_j : nonterminal occurrences
  a : an attribute
  numberOfVisitsScheduled(X_i): an integer associated with nonterminal occurrence X_i
  worklist, S : sets of vertices of $TDP(p)$
  v, w : individual vertices of $TDP(p)$
  $V_{k,j}$: a condensation vertex of $TDP(p)$
begin
  for each production $p : X_0 \rightarrow X_1 \cdots X_k$ **do**
[1] **for** $j := 0$ to k **do**
    for each partition set S of attributes of X_j that are input attributes of p **do**
      Condense $TDP(p)$ with respect to S, replacing S with a vertex $V_{\text{Partition}[S], j}$
    od
    numberOfVisitsScheduled(X_j) := 0
  od
  maxPartition := the maximum value of Partition for any partition set of X_0
[2] **if** maxPartition is even **then**
    Remove vertex $V_{\text{maxPartition}, 0}$ from $TDP(p)$ together with all edges emanating from it
  fi
  MapVisitToPlanIndex[$p, 0, 1$] := 1
  workList := the set of $TDP(p)$'s vertices with in-degree 0
  while workList $\neq \varnothing$ **do**
    Select and remove a vertex v from worklist
    if v is a condensation vertex of the form $V_{k,0}$ **then**
      numberOfVisitsScheduled(X_0) := numberOfVisitsScheduled(X_0) + 1
      Append SUSPEND(numberOfVisitsScheduled(X_0)) to Plan[p]
      MapVisitToPlanIndex[$p, 0$, numberOfVisitsScheduled(X_0) + 1] := length(Plan[p]) + 1
    else if v is a condensation vertex of the form $V_{k,i}$, where $i > 0$ **then**
      numberOfVisitsScheduled(X_i) := numberOfVisitsScheduled(X_i) + 1
      Append VISIT(i, numberOfVisitsScheduled(X_i)) to Plan[p]
      MapVisitToPlanIndex[p, i, numberOfVisitsScheduled(X_i)] := length(Plan[p]) + 1
    else /* v corresponds to an output attribute occurrence $X_i.a$ */
      Append EVAL(i, a) to Plan[p]
    fi
    for each vertex w that is a successor of v in $TDP(p)$ **do**
      Remove edge (v, w) from $TDP(p)$
      if in-degree(w) = 0 **then** Insert w into workList **fi**
    od
  od
[3] **for** $i := 1$ to k **do**
    if numberOfVisitsNeeded(X_i) $\neq$ numberOfVisitsScheduled(X_i) **then**
      numberOfVisitsScheduled(X_i) := numberOfVisitsScheduled(X_i) + 1
      Append VISIT(i, numberOfVisitsScheduled(X_i)) to Plan[p]
      MapVisitToPlanIndex[p, i, numberOfVisitsScheduled(X_i)] := length(Plan[p]) + 1
    fi
  od
[4] Append SUSPEND(numberOfVisitsScheduled(X_0) + 1) to Plan[p]
  od
end

Figure 12.7. The algorithm to create tables Plan and MapVisitToPlanIndex from the grammar's *TDP* graphs.

Several aspects of Step5 may need clarification. A plan is constructed by repeatedly selecting an instruction whose action is permitted under the known dependence constraints, scheduling it as the next instruction in the plan, and then determining what the evaluation state would be after the instruction is executed. In general, EVAL instructions correspond to what are called the *output attributes* of the production – the synthesized attributes of the left-hand-side nonterminal and the inherited attributes of the right-hand-side nonterminals. An EVAL instruction is scheduled for an output attribute of the production if in the given evaluation state all of its arguments are available; this corresponds to the attribute having in-degree 0 in $TDP(p)$.

VISIT and SUSPEND instructions correspond to the production's *input attributes* – the inherited attributes of the left-hand-side nonterminal and the synthesized attributes of the right-hand-side nonterminals. Synthesized attributes of the right-hand-side nonterminals correspond to VISIT instructions, inherited attributes of the left-hand-side nonterminal to SUSPEND instructions. More precisely, a VISIT instruction corresponds to a partition set of synthesized attributes of a right-hand-side nonterminal; a SUSPEND instruction corresponds to a partition set of inherited attributes of the left-hand-side nonterminal.

Because it is a partition set as a whole that corresponds to a VISIT or SUSPEND instruction, rather than an individual input attribute on its own, each input partition set S is condensed in line [1] to a representative element, denoted by $V_{\text{Partition}[S], j}$. (By *condensing* a graph G with respect to vertex set S, we mean the operation of replacing S in G with a representative element v, where v becomes the source for all edges that formerly emanated from members of S as well as the target for all edges that were formerly directed to members of S.) A VISIT instruction to a child X_i is scheduled when Step5 considers a condensation vertex that represents a partition set consisting of X_i's synthesized attributes. A SUSPEND instruction is scheduled when Step5 considers a condensation vertex that represents a partition set consisting of the left-hand-side nonterminal's inherited attributes.

One exception to the rule given above concerns the initial transfer of control to the production, which is not preceded by a SUSPEND instruction. Accordingly, if the maximum value of Partition for X_0 is even (*i.e.* it corresponds to a set of X_0's inherited attributes), the condensation vertex that corresponds to this set is removed from the TDP graph along with all its outgoing edges, without generating a SUSPEND instruction; this is handled by the conditional-statement in line [2].

A second aspect of Step5 that may need clarification concerns the loop at line [3], which may generate an additional VISIT instruction for each right-hand-side nonterminal. One situation in which the extra VISIT is necessary arises when the lowest numbered nonempty partition of a right-hand-side nonterminal occurrence of X is a partition set of inherited attributes – that is, when $A_1(X)$ is empty and $A_2(X)$ is nonempty. In this case, it is necessary to generate an additional VISIT instruction so that the visit-sequence evaluator has a chance to evaluate attributes that depend on the attributes of $A_2(X)$.

Another situation in which it is necessary to generate an additional VISIT to a right-hand-side nonterminal occurrence X_i is when X_i has no attributes at all. In this case, the VISIT is needed to ensure that the visit-sequence evaluator has a chance to evaluate the attributes in the subtree rooted at X_i.

A third aspect of Step5 that may need clarification concerns the plan's final SUSPEND instruction. Because there is no (inherited) partition set of nonterminal occurrence X_0 that corresponds to the final suspension of control, the final instruction of the plan must be generated explicitly; this is the purpose of line [4].

In addition to constructing the plan for each production, Step5 also constructs the other component of the visit-sequence evaluator – table MapVisitToPlanIndex. Whenever a VISIT or SUSPEND instruction is emitted, Step5 makes a record of the current length of the plan (+ 1); this length represents the index of the appropriate instruction at which the plan is to resume execution after control is transferred back.

12.5. Incremental Updating by Visit-Sequence-Driven Change Propagation

Recall from Chapter 3 that an *incremental attribute evaluator* is an algorithm that is applied after each operation that restructures a derivation tree to make the tree's attributes consistent again. Although any non-incremental attribute evaluator can be applied to completely reevaluate the tree, the goal is to minimize work by confining the scope of reevaluation that is required. After each modification to a derivation tree, only a subset of the tree's attributes requires new values; this subset is referred to as AFFECTED.

To be more precise, let T' denote the inconsistent tree resulting from a subtree replacement and T'' denote T' after its attributes have been updated. We define AFFECTED to be the set of attribute instances that have different values in the two trees. It is important to bear in mind that when updating begins, it is not known which attributes are members of AFFECTED; AFFECTED can only be determined during the updating process itself.

Because, by definition, the work required to update T' must be $O(|\text{AFFECTED}|)$, we say that an incremental evaluator is *asymptotically optimal* if its cost is $O(|\text{AFFECTED}|)$. It should be pointed out that in determining the cost, we neglect the true cost of evaluating attribute-definition functions and count them as unit steps when, in fact, they may be a great deal more expensive. Our analysis of the algorithm's cost is based on the number of attribute reevaluations performed, plus any additional bookkeeping costs associated with determining the reevaluation order.

In this section, we describe how the visit-sequence evaluation method can be used for incremental attribute evaluation. We demonstrate how the tables of a visit-sequence evaluator can be used to determine an optimal reevaluation order for a change-propagation algorithm. The algorithm described updates a tree in $O(|\text{AFFECTED}|)$ steps after a subtree replacement and is thus asymptotically optimal.

One way for an incremental attribute evaluator to achieve optimal behavior is based on the following observations:

> If, in the course of propagating new values, an attribute is ever (temporarily) reassigned a value other than its correct final value, spurious changes are apt to propagate arbitrarily far beyond the boundaries of AFFECTED, leading to suboptimal running time. To avoid this possibility, a change propagator should schedule attribute reevaluations such that any new value computed is necessarily the correct final value. That is, an attribute should not be reevaluated until all of its arguments are known to have their correct final values.
>
> [Reps83]

This last observation describes a sufficient condition on the order in which attributes are reevaluated that will ensure asymptotically optimal behavior of a change-propagation algorithm.

A reevaluation order that never assigns an attribute a value that is not its correct final value can only be determined by taking into account both direct and transitive dependences among attributes. In the optimal updating algorithm for arbitrary noncircular grammars, called PROPAGATE in [Reps82], [Reps83], and Chapter 5 of [Reps84], such dependences are represented explicitly by edges in a scheduling graph. PROPAGATE can be understood as a generalization of Knuth's topological-sorting algorithm. As in the topological-sorting algorithm, PROPAGATE keeps a work-list of attributes that are ready for reevaluation. (In topological sorting, the work-list consists of nodes ready for enumeration.) An attribute is placed on the work-list when its in-degree is reduced to zero in a scheduling graph whose edges reflect dependences among attributes that have not yet been reevaluated (enumerated).

Whereas in topological sorting the vertices of the scheduling graph are known *a priori*, in PROPAGATE the set of vertices of the scheduling graph is generated *dynamically*, at the same time as its vertices are being enumerated. Some of the edges of the scheduling graph represent transitive dependences among attributes; during change propagation these edges play a particularly important role in determining an optimal evaluation order. The presence of such edges ensures that an attribute is never updated until all its ancestors have been considered – and thus have their correct, final values. On the other hand, removing such an edge allows PROPAGATE to dispense in unit time with areas of the tree in which attribute values cannot possibly change value.

The incremental attribute evaluation method outlined above has the advantage of being applicable to arbitrary noncircular attribute grammars; unfortunately, its generality is achieved at the expense of storage economy. Not only are attribute reevaluations scheduled according to an attribute's position in a graph that is constructed during the updating process, but each node in the derivation tree must also be labeled with an additional graph structure to record transitive attribute dependences in the tree. In practice, the storage used for these graphs dominates the storage for the attribute values.

The visit-sequence-driven method for change propagation eliminates the need for these graphs, yet retains the ability to update a tree's attributes in an optimal manner. Although the method is restricted to a subclass of the noncircular grammars, it allows us to dispense with much of the space overhead that plagues the more general method. The visit-sequence-driven method is also much more efficient in time than the other method because the reevaluation order is determined by the machine's plans rather than dynamically by interpreting a scheduling graph.

The salient property of the visit-sequence evaluation method is that a grammar's plans implicitly establish a total ordering on the attribute instances of each of the grammar's derivation trees. When an unattributed derivation tree T is (non-incrementally) evaluated by a visit-sequence evaluator, the order in which EVAL instructions are performed respects the partial order of the tree's attribute-dependence graph. The evaluation order dictated by the grammar's plans is a linearization of T's attribute-dependence graph: for each attribute instance b, the instruction to evaluate b is preceded by instructions to evaluate all of b's arguments. We call this the *visit-sequence evaluation order of T*.

The evaluation plan for each production p also represents an acceptable *reevaluation* order for the attribute instances of any instance of p. In addition, because a visit-sequence evaluator's plans implicitly define a total order on the attributes of T that respects the partial order of T's attribute-dependence graph, the plans implicitly take into account direct and transitive dependences among a tree's attributes. The implicit order given by the plans is used in place of the explicit representation of attribute dependences that the scheduling graph provides in the change-propagation algorithm that applies to arbitrary noncircular grammars.

The basic idea behind the visit-sequence-driven algorithm for change propagation is to make use of exactly the same plans that are used for non-incremental attribute evaluation, thereby having attribute reevaluations scheduled in an order that respects the visit-sequence evaluation order. Using the visit-sequence evaluator's plans for change propagation ensures that an attribute instance does not get considered until all its arguments have been considered, and consequently that an attribute can never be given a value that is not its correct final value.

The second key idea behind the visit-sequence-driven algorithm for change propagation is that it is possible to ignore VISIT and SUSPEND instructions under certain conditions. Doing so allows us to skip, in unit-time, having to reevaluate (or even having to examine) an arbitrarily large number of attributes that cannot possibly change value.

The key to avoiding wasted transfers of control is to keep track of which production instances contain attributes that depend on attributes that changed value. In VSEvaluate, the procedure for non-incremental evaluation of Figure 12.2, evaluation begins by activating the machine that applies at the root of the tree. In VSEvaluate, the state of the active machine is determined by the value of variables currentNode and planIndex. One of the ways that the visit-sequence-driven change-propagation algorithm extends VSEvaluate is that it makes use of an additional state variable, Reactivated, whose value is a set of "reactivated" machines. At all times during updating, the active machine is a member of Reactivated. Re-evaluations are scheduled according to the EVAL instructions of the active machine's plan, but any VISIT or SUSPEND instruction is ignored if it would transfer control to a machine that is not a member of Reactivated.

To summarize, VSPropagate, the visit-sequence-driven change-propagation algorithm, differs from VSEvaluate in the following ways:

- When change propagation is initiated, Reactivated consists of the production instances that lie on either side of the point of subtree replacement. Initially, the machine for the upper production is given control.
- Whenever an attribute b changes value, all neighbors that contain attributes that depend on b are "reactivated" by making them members of Reactivated.
- All VISIT and SUSPEND instructions that transfer control to neighbors that are not members of Reactivated are ignored.
- When a plan reaches its final SUSPEND instruction and the parent is not a member of Reactivated, the algorithm halts.

These ideas are incorporated into the statement of VSPropagate given in Figure 12.8.

Updating begins at node nodeOfSubtreeReplacement.parent – the parent of the node at which the subtree replacement was performed. To carry out reevaluations in an order that respects the visit-sequence evaluation order of T, the machine that applies at nodeOfSubtreeReplacement.parent must be reactivated in its initial state. As updating progresses, VISIT and SUSPEND instructions will call for control to be transferred to neighboring machines. Whereas during non-incremental visit-sequence evaluation, a VISIT(i, r) instruction always causes control to be transferred to the ith child and a SUSPEND instruction always causes control to be transferred to the parent, during change propagation the goal is to skip over as many unnecessary VISITs and SUSPENDs as possible. In particular, transfers of control are ignored in the following two situations:

- When the machine at node x reaches a VISIT(i, r) instruction, if the ith child of x is not a member of Reactivated, x retains control and proceeds to the next instruction in its plan.
- When the machine at x reaches a SUSPEND instruction, if the parent of x is not a member of Reactivated, x retains control and continues executing the plan for x.

Ignoring such instructions allows the algorithm to skip over, in unit-time, arbitrarily large sections of the tree in which attribute values cannot possibly change. When a machine does transfer control to a neighboring machine, Map-VisitToPlanIndex is used to establish the new machine's execution state whether or not evaluation activity at the node has previously been suppressed. Thus, when a machine receives control it performs the rest of its instructions in the same order as it would during non-incremental evaluation. Because the visit-sequence evaluation order is a total order on the attributes of T that respects the partial order given by $D(T)$, omitted VISIT and SUSPEND instructions preceding a subsequent "reactivation" are irrelevant.

When the machine that applies at node x executes an EVAL instruction that changes the value of attribute b, all attributes that use b as an argument may become inconsistent. These attributes belong to a production instance p' that is one of the neighbors of the production instance at x. If b is a synthesized attribute of x, p' is the production instance that derives x; if b is an inherited attribute of a child of x, p' is the production instance derived from the child. Attributes in p' will get reevaluated only if p' is a member of Reactivated; thus, because p' may contain inconsistent attributes, p' is made a member of

procedure VSPropagate(T, nodeOfSubtreeReplacement)
declare
    T: a fully attributed derivation tree
    nodeOfSubtreeReplacement, currentNode: nodes of T
    planIndex, r, i: integers
    a: an attribute name
    currentNode$_i$: the ith node of the production instance at currentNode
    Reactivated: the set of reactivated machines
    oldValue: an attribute value
begin
    currentNode := nodeOfSubtreeReplacement.parent
    planIndex := MapVisitToPlanIndex(currentNode.ruleIndicator, 0, 1)
    Reactivated := {currentNode, nodeOfSubtreeReplacement}
    forever do
      if Plan[currentNode.ruleIndicator][planIndex] has the form EVAL(i, a) **then**
        oldValue := the value of currentNode$_i$.a
        Execute the attribute-definition function to reevaluate currentNode$_i$.a
        if oldValue ≠ the value of currentNode$_i$.a **then**
          if i ≠ 0 **then** neighborNode := currentNode$_i$
          else if currentNode ≠ root(T) **then** neighborNode := currentNode.parent
          else neighborNode := **null**
          fi
          if neighborNode ≠ **null** **and** currentNode$_i$.a has successors in the
               production that applies at neighborNode **then**
            Insert neighborNode into Reactivated
          fi
        fi
        planIndex := planIndex + 1
      else if Plan[currentNode.ruleIndicator][planIndex] has the form VISIT(i, r) **then**
        if currentNode$_i$ ∈ Reactivated **then**
          planIndex := MapVisitToPlanIndex(currentNode$_i$.ruleIndicator, 0, r)
          currentNode := currentNode$_i$
        else planIndex := planIndex + 1
        fi
      else if Plan[currentNode.ruleIndicator][planIndex] has the form SUSPEND(r) **then**
        if currentNode = root(T) **then return fi**
        if currentNode.parent ∈ Reactivated **then**
          planIndex := MapVisitToPlanIndex(currentNode.parent.ruleIndicator,
                        currentNode.sonNumber, r)
          currentNode := currentNode.parent
        else if Plan[currentNode.ruleIndicator][planIndex] is the last instruction of
          Plan[currentNode.ruleIndicator] **then return**
        else planIndex := planIndex + 1
        fi
      fi
    od
end

Figure 12.8. An optimal change-propagation algorithm for ordered attribute grammars.

Reactivated. (Because Reactivated may be implemented by using one bit per tree node, insertions and membership tests are unit-cost operations.)

The secret to the optimal behavior of VSPropagate is that the size of Reactivated is kept proportional to the number of attributes that have received new values since updating began. The algorithm confines its activity to the region of the tree in which attributes have changed value; it expands this region only when it assigns a new value to an attribute that is at an extremity of the region. Initially, just after a subtree replacement at nodeOfSubtreeReplacement, Reactivated consists of the machines that apply at nodeOfSubtreeReplacement and nodeOfSubtreeReplacement.parent. Thereafter, a new machine is added to Reactivated only when a new member of AFFECTED is identified. VSPropagate achieves optimal behavior by ensuring that whenever an attribute is reevaluated, the value computed is the attribute's final value. Because a machine is reactivated only when a new member of AFFECTED is identified, the cost of VSPropagate is $O(|\text{AFFECTED}|)$ and thus is asymptotically optimal.

Allowing syntactic references within attribute equations complicates the problem of incremental attribute updating. The value of an attribute defined with a syntactic reference to node N may become inconsistent whenever a modification is made inside the subtree rooted at N; consequently, a modification at node M may introduce inconsistencies in attributes at nodes along the "spine" of the tree from M to the tree's root, rather than just in the immediate neighborhood of M. However, the updating algorithm can be applied as long as the region containing all inconsistent attributes is known [Reps83]. Note that the initially inconsistent region does not necessarily extend all the way to the tree's root, as only certain productions have equations with syntactic references. In the interest of brevity, a detailed discussion of the modification to VSPropagate needed for handling syntactic references is omitted.

12.6. Optimizations for One-to-One Functions

When change propagation is employed to update the attributes of an abstract-syntax tree, each new attribute value computed is compared to the old attribute value to see if changes need to be propagated further. Because testing equality of attribute values may be expensive, it is advantageous if we can avoid performing some of the equality tests.

Such an optimization is possible for attributes whose attribute-definition function is the identity function. (Such attribute equations are often called *copy rules*.) The basic idea is that because the identity function is one-to-one, if the function's argument has changed value, then the new value computed is guaranteed to be different from the old value; thus, it is wasteful to perform a test to see if the attribute has changed value. When the incremental attribute-evaluation algorithm reevaluates an attribute defined by an identity function, it should be possible to save the overhead of comparing the attribute's new value with its old value.

This is an important optimization, because in practice a large proportion of attribute-definition functions are identity functions [Wilner71]. Moreover, the principle holds for attributes defined by *any* one-to-one function, not just the identity function. Consequently, the SSL translator tests the specification's attribute equations to try to discover which attributes are defined by one-to-one functions.

If the first attribute instance in a chain of one-to-one functions changes value, then the rest of the elements in the chain must also change value. It is important to note, however, that this is only true when *all* the old values in the chain are consistent (*i.e.* identical). Change propagation can terminate without reaching the end of the chain if, initially, some of the old values are inconsistent with their predecessor's value.

However, the only possible inconsistent instances of attributes defined by one-to-one functions are attributes of nonterminals in the region of the tree that was modified. In the case of a subtree-replacement operation, these inconsistencies are confined to the attributes of two production instances – the one derived from the node of the subtree replacement and the one that derives the node of the subtree replacement. Thus, it is necessary to treat the attributes of nonterminals in the initially inconsistent region that are defined by copy rules as if they were not part of any chain; that is, for such an attribute it is still necessary to test its new and old values for equality whenever the attribute's value is recomputed.

To carry out the optimization of suppressing equality tests for attributes defined by one-to-one functions, the change-propagation method must have one additional property. It must be the case that the only attributes that are reevaluated are ones whose arguments have changed value. (If this property holds, then the information that an attribute is defined by a one-to-one function is sufficient to conclude that it changed value when evaluated.) This property does not hold for the version of VSPropagate presented in Figure 12.8: once a machine is reactivated in some state, it may actually carry out many "needless evaluations" because all the machine's subsequent EVAL instructions are carried out, regardless of whether any of the attribute's arguments changed value.

To achieve the property that the only attributes reevaluated are ones whose arguments change value, we introduce an additional set, named needToBeEvaluated, used as follows:

- Set needToBeEvaluated is initialized to contain all the attribute instances of the production instance derived from the node of the subtree replacement and the one that derives the node of the subtree replacement.
- When the value of an attribute instance b changes, every successor of b is inserted into needToBeEvaluated.
- When VSPropagate reaches the EVAL instruction for b, the attribute-definition function for b is executed only if $b \in$ needToBeEvaluated.

Because needToBeEvaluated may be implemented by using one bit per attribute instance, insertions, deletions, and membership tests are unit-cost operations. Note that the needToBeEvaluated set is a useful optimization in its own right (*i.e.* even in the absence of special treatment for one-to-one functions) because in general, it eliminates useless function evaluations.

These ideas are incorporated into the version of VSPropagate presented in Figure 12.9.

12.7. What to Do When a Grammar Fails the Orderedness Test

Kastens's algorithm for constructing a visit-sequence evaluator tests for a condition – "orderedness" – that is sufficient to guarantee that a grammar is noncircular. Although almost all attribute grammars arising in practice pass the orderedness test, an editor-designer will occasionally write a grammar that fails the test. Frequently, this indicates the existence of an error in the specification, but it can also mean that one has encountered one of the limitations of Kastens's construction.

A grammar can fail to be ordered in one of three ways, due to circularities that are detected after steps 1, 2, and 4 of Kastens's algorithm. These errors are reported as being circularities of type 1, 2, and 3, respectively.

- A type 1 circularity indicates a circularity in the dependences of an individual production.
- A type 2 circularity indicates a circularity in the approximation of the productions' transitive dependences that the algorithm computes.
- A type 3 circularity indicates a circularity induced by the dependences that are added between attribute partitions.

The orderedness test is pessimistic in the sense that a type 2 circularity does not necessarily indicate that a grammar is circular. All grammars that are circular will be reported as having either type 1 or type 2 circularities; however, some noncircular grammars will also be reported as having type 2 circularities.

```
procedure VSPropagate(T, nodeOfSubtreeReplacement)
declare
    T: a fully attributed derivation tree
    nodeOfSubtreeReplacement, currentNode: nodes of T
    planIndex, r, i: integers
    a: an attribute name
    currentNodeᵢ: the iᵗʰ node of the production instance at currentNode
    Reactivated: the set of reactivated machines
    oldValue: an attribute value
    needToBeEvaluated: a set of attribute instances
begin
    currentNode := nodeOfSubtreeReplacement.parent
    planIndex := MapVisitToPlanIndex(currentNode.ruleIndicator, 0, 1)
    Reactivated := {currentNode, nodeOfSubtreeReplacement}
    needToBeEvaluated := the set of all attribute instances in the productions that apply at
        currentNode and nodeOfSubtreeReplacement
    forever do
        if Plan[currentNode.ruleIndicator][planIndex] has the form EVAL(i, a) then
            if currentNodeᵢ.a ∈ needToBeEvaluated then
                remove currentNodeᵢ.a from needToBeEvaluated
                oldValue := the value of currentNodeᵢ.a
                Execute the attribute-definition function to reevaluate currentNodeᵢ.a
                if (currentNodeᵢ.a is defined by a one-to-one attribute-definition function
                        and currentNode ≠ nodeOfSubtreeReplacement
                        and currentNode ≠ nodeOfSubtreeReplacement.parent)
                        cor oldValue ≠ the value of currentNodeᵢ.a then
                    if i ≠ 0 then neighborNode := currentNodeᵢ
                    else if currentNode ≠ root(T) then neighborNode := currentNode.parent
                    else neighborNode := null
                    fi
                    if neighborNode ≠ null and currentNodeᵢ.a has successors in the
                            production that applies at neighborNode then
                        Insert neighborNode into Reactivated
                    fi
                    Insert all successors of currentNodeᵢ.a into needToBeEvaluated
                fi
            fi
            planIndex := planIndex + 1
        else if Plan[currentNode.ruleIndicator][planIndex] has the form VISIT(i, r) then
            <Same as in Figure 12.8>
        else if Plan[currentNode.ruleIndicator][planIndex] has the form SUSPEND(r) then
            <Same as in Figure 12.8>
        fi
    od
end
```

Figure 12.9. An improved change-propagation algorithm that suppresses equality tests for attributes whose attribute-definition functions are one-to-one.

A type 3 circularity indicates that the grammar is definitely not circular, but indicates a failure of Kastens's method for constructing a visit-sequence evaluator, due to the use of a representation that only approximates the actual dependences among the grammar's attributes. A common way a type 3 circularity arises is when a grammar has two disjoint threadings of attribute dependences through the same productions, one threaded left-to-right and the other threaded right-to-left. Such a grammar is noncircular but has a type 3 circularity.

Example. The grammar given in Figure 12.10 illustrates the type 3 circularity that arises in a specification that has both a left-to-right threading and a right-to-left threading. When sgen processes this specification, it produces the error message:

```
root Root;
Root    :        Top (X);
X       :        Null ( )
        |        Pair (X  X)
        ;
/* Left-to-right threading of attribute dependences*/
X {
                 inherited INT a;
                 synthesized INT b;
        };
Root    :        Top   { X.a = 0; };
X       :        Null  { X.b = X.a; }
        |        Pair  { X$2.a = X$1.a;
                         X$3.a = X$2.b;
                         X$1.b = X$3.b;
                       }
        ;
/* Right-to-left threading of attribute dependences */
X {
                 inherited INT c;
                 synthesized INT d;
        };
Root    :        Top   { X.c = 0; };
X       :        Null  { X.d = X.c; }
        |        Pair  { X$3.c = X$1.c;
                         X$2.c = X$3.d;
                         X$1.d = X$2.d;
                       }
        ;
```

Figure 12.10. A grammar with both a left-to-right threading and a right-to-left threading of attribute dependences. This grammar has a type 3 circularity.

In Pair, X<v_no=1>.b is circularly defined
In Pair, X<v_no=1>.c is circularly defined
In Pair, X<v_no=2>.a is circularly defined
In Pair, X<v_no=2>.d is circularly defined
Your grammar has what is officially known as a 'type 3 circularity'.
A type 3 circularity does not necessarily mean that
the grammar is circular. Usually there are too many
ways in which the attributes of a non-terminal might be ordered.
Try putting some extra dependencies into the grammar to
imply an order to the evaluation of independent attributes.[2]

Consider the origin of the type 3 circularity in this specification: after Step 2 of
the Kastens construction, graph *TDS* (X) has vertex set {X.a, X.b, X.c, X.d} and
edge set {(X.a, X.b), (X.c, X.d)}. In Step 3 of the construction, which partitions *TDS* (X), both of X's synthesized attributes, X.b and X.d, are placed in one
partition, and both inherited attributes, X.a and X.c, are placed in a second partition, as follows:

Partition[X.a] := 2
Partition[X.b] := 1
Partition[X.c] := 2
Partition[X.d] := 1

Using this partition, Step 4 augments TDP(X:Pair) with the edges
(X$1.a, X$1.d),   (X$1.c, X$1.b),   (X$2.a, X$2.d),   (X$2.c, X$2.b),
(X$3.a, X$3.d), and (X$3.c, X$3.b), which, in conjunction with the edges from
the production's direct dependences, results in the cycle X$2.c, X$2.b, X$3.a,
X$3.d, X$2.c . . .

When a type 3 circularity arises, it is possible to work around the approxima-
tions made during the orderedness test by adding additional dependences to the
specification that do not change its meaning. One way to accomplish this is by
using attribute equations that have a conditional expression whose condition is
always true; attributes that appear in the false branch of the conditional introduce attribute dependences but can never contribute to the attribute equation's
value.

Example. One way to eliminate the type 3 circularity from the previous
example is to change the second equation of operator Top to read

---

[2]In this error message, X<v_no=1> refers to X$2. The quantity "v_no" is the phylum-occurrence
number: the phylum-occurrence number of the left-hand-side phylum occurrence is 0; the right-
hand-side occurrences are numbered 1, 2, *etc.*

X.c = true ? 0 : X.b;

(in place of the original equation X.c = 0;). The new version introduces an artificial dependence from X.b to X.c. With this change, the edge set of *TDS* (X) after Step 2 is

{(X.a, X.b), (X.b, X.c), (X.c, X.d)}.

The partition of *TDS* (X) created by Step 3 then puts X.a and X.b in higher-numbered partition sets than they were in previously:

Partition[X.a] := 4
Partition[X.b] := 3
Partition[X.c] := 2
Partition[X.d] := 1

In effect, the modified equation causes the evaluation of the right-to-left thread to be delayed until after the left-to-right thread has been evaluated.

There are several other ways to eliminate the type 3 circularity from the example. For instance, there are two other ways to modify the grammar to force the right-to-left thread to be delayed until after the left-to-right thread has been evaluated. One way is to change the equation for X\$2.c to

X   :   Pair { X\$2.c = true ? X\$3.d : X\$2.b; };

The second way is to change the equation for X\$3.c to

X   :   Pair { X\$3.c = true ? X\$1.c : X\$3.b; };

Yet another way to eliminate the type 3 circularity is to force the left-to-right thread to be delayed until after the right-to-left thread has been evaluated. This can be accomplished by using any of the following three attribute equations in place of the corresponding equation in the original specification:

Root   :   Top { X.a = true ? 0 : X.d; };
X   :   Pair { X\$2.a = true ? X\$1.a : X\$2.d; };
X   :   Pair { X\$3.a = true ? X\$2.b : X\$3.d; };

APPENDIX A

Syntax of SSL

In the following grammar, nonterminals are printed in Times italic and terminals in Helvetica roman (*e.g. specification* and root). The alternatives of each nonterminal symbol appear indented below it on consecutive lines. The alternatives of *binary-infix-operator* and *unary-prefix-operator* are exceptions and appear on the same line, separated by spaces. The characters $\oplus$, $[\![$, $]\!]$, $]\!]^{*}$, and $]\!]^{+}$ have been adopted as meta-symbols. Their meanings are:

$\alpha \oplus \beta$	α or β
$[\![\alpha]\!]$	optional occurrence of α
$[\![\alpha]\!]^{*}$	zero or more occurrences of α
$[\![\alpha]\!]^{+}$	one or more occurrences of α
$[\![\alpha]\!]_{\beta}^{*}$	$[\![\alpha\ [\![\beta\alpha]\!]^{*}]\!]$
$[\![\alpha]\!]_{\beta}^{+}$	$\alpha[\![\beta\alpha]\!]^{*}$

The following nonterminals denote identifiers:

attribute-name, base-type-name, compile-time-option-name, C-type-name, external-computer-name, parameter-name, function-name, lexeme-name, local-attribute-name, op-name, operator-name, pattern-variable-name, phylum-name, state-name, store-name, style-name, view-name.

specification

    ⟦*declaration* ⟧⁺

declaration

    root *phylum* ;

    list ⟦*phylum* ⟧⁺ ;

    optional ⟦*phylum* ⟧⁺ ;

    optional list ⟦*phylum* ⟧⁺ ;

    ⟦*phylum* ⟧⁺ { ⟦*field* ⟧⁺ } ;

    phylum ⟦exported⟧ *function-name*(⟦*phylum parameter-name*⟧*)
        { *expression* } ;

    phylum ~ ⟦<*state-name*>⟧ *phylum.attribute-name* ⟦*attribution* ⟧ ;

    phylum-name : ⟦*alternative* ⟧⁺ ;

    phylum-name ::= ⟦*alternative* ⟧⁺ ;

    left ⟦*token* ⊕*phylum* ⟧⁺ ;

    right ⟦*token* ⊕*phylum* ⟧⁺ ;

    nonassoc ⟦*token* ⊕*phylum* ⟧⁺ ;

    transform *phylum* ⟦*transform-clause*⟧⁺ ;

    style ⟦*style-name*⟧⁺ ;

    ⟦sparse⟧ view ⟦*view-name*⟧⁺ ;

    phylum foreign *function-name*(⟦*phylum parameter-name*⟧*
        ⟦repeated⟧) ;

    typedef *C-type-name base-type-name* with (*op-name*, *op-name*, *op-name*,
        op-name, *op-name*, *op-name*, *op-name*, *op-name*, *op-name*) ;

    store ⟦*store-declaration*⟧⁺ ;

    ext_computers ⟦*external-computer-name*⟧⁺ ;

    let *compile-time-option-name* = *constant* ;

    forall ⟦⟦ list ⟧*phylum-name*⟧⁺ in ⟦*quantified-declaration*⟧⁺ end ;

quantified-declaration
> *phylum* : *operator-name* = *base-type-name* = ;
>
> *phylum* [[**exported**]] *function-name*([[*phylum parameter-name*]] *)
>   { *expression* } ;
>
> *phylum* **foreign** *function-name*([[*phylum parameter-name*]], *
>   [[**repeated**]]) ;

alternative
> *lexeme-name* < [[*<state-name>*]] *regular-expression* [[*<state-name>*]] >
>
> [[*operator-name*]], * [[*parameters*]] [[*attribution* ⊕ *unparsing*]] *
>
> *operator-name* = *base-type-name* =

parameters
> ([[*phylum*]] *)
>
> ([[*token* ⊕ *phylum*]] * [[**prec** *token* ⊕ *phylum*]])

token
> *character-constant*

attribution
> { [[*local-field* ⊕ *attribute-equation* ⊕ *view-predicate*]] * }

local-field
> [[**demand**]] [[*store-list*]] **local** *phylum attribute-name* ;

attribute-equation
> *output-attribute* = *expression* ;

view-predicate
> **in** [[*view-name*]] $_,^+$ **on** *expression* ;

output-attribute
> *phylum-occurrence.attribute-name*
>
> *local-attribute-name*

unparsing
> [[[[*view-name*]], * [[**@** ⊕ **^**]] [[**:** ⊕ **::=**]]
>   [[*resting-place-denoter* ⊕ *unparsing-item*]] *]

resting-place-denoter
    @ $\oplus$ ˆ $\oplus$ ..

unparsing-item
    string-constant

    phylum-occurrence

    phylum-occurrence.attribute-name

    local-attribute-name

    [[[*unparsing-item*]]*]

field
    [[demand]] [[*store-list*]] synthesized *phylum attribute-name* ;

    [[demand]] [[*store-list*]] inherited *phylum attribute-name* ;

transform-clause
    on *string-constant pattern* : *expression*

store-declaration
    store-name phylum with (*op-name* , *op-name* , *op-name* , *op-name*)

store-list
    store ([[*store-name*]]$^{+}_{,}$)

expression
    constant

    variable

    expression binary-infix-operator expression

    unary-prefix-operator expression

    function-name([[*expression*]]$^{*}_{,}$)

    operator-name([[*expression*]]$^{*}_{,}$)

    expression (*expression*)

    [*phylum* |–> *expression* [[, *expression*]]]

    expression [*expression* |–> *expression*]

    expression [*expression*]

    expression [*expression* : *expression*]

      expression [*expression* :]

      with (*expression*) ([[*pattern* : *expression*]]$_,^+$)

      unparse (*expression* [[, *view-name*]])

      parse (*expression* , *phylum* , *expression*)

      expression ? *expression* : *expression*

      let [[[[*pattern* = *expression*]]$_{and}^+$]]$_;^+$ in (*expression*)

      (*expression*)

      expression { } . *attribute-name*

pattern

      constant

      pattern-variable-name

      *

      default

      operator-name([[*pattern*]]$_,^*$)

      pattern-variable-name as *pattern*

constant

      [*phylum*]

      < *phylum* >

      false ⊕ true

      decimal-constant

      octal-constant

      real-constant

      character-constant

      string-constant

      nil

      nil_attr

variable

    phylum-occurrence

    phylum-occurrence.attribute-name

    local-attribute-name

    { ⟦*phylum .attribute-name* ⊕ *operator-name.local-attribute-name*⟧$_,^+$ }

    parameter-name

    pattern-variable-name

    pattern-variable-name.attribute-name

phylum-occurrence

    $$

    phylum

    phylum **$***decimal-constant*

phylum

    phylum-name

    phylum-name [⟦*phylum* ⟧$_,^+$]

binary-infix-operator

    # * / % + - :: @ < <= > >= == != & ˆ | && || !

unary-prefix-operator

    - ! ~ & * &&

regular-expression

    character

    string-constant

    character

    [⟦*character* ⊕*character* −*character* ⟧$^+$]

    [ˆ⟦*character* ⊕*character* −*character* ⟧$^+$]

    ˆ*regular-expression*

    *regular-expression***$**

    regular-expression?

regular-expression*

regular-expression+

regular-expression regular-expression

regular-expression | *regular-expression*

(*regular-expression*)

regular-expression / *regular-expression*

regular-expression { *decimal-constant* , *decimal-constant* }

decimal-constant
   $[\![1 \oplus 2 \oplus \cdots \oplus 9]\!] [\![digit]\!]^*$

octal-constant
   $0[\![digit]\!]^*$

real-constant
   $[\![digit]\!]^+.[\![digit]\!]^+[\![e[\![+\oplus-]\!] [\![digit]\!]^+]\!]$

   $[\![digit]\!]^+e[\![+\oplus-]\!] [\![digit]\!]^+$

character-constant
   '*character*'

string-constant
   "$[\![character]\!]^*$"

character
   $a \oplus b \oplus c \oplus \cdots$

   octal-constant

   $\backslash n \oplus \backslash r \oplus \backslash b \oplus \backslash t$

digit
   $0 \oplus 1 \oplus \cdots \oplus 9$

APPENDIX B

Invoking the Synthesizer Generator

NAME

    sgen – Synthesizer Generator

SYNOPSIS

    sgen [option] ... file ...

DESCRIPTION

Sgen is a system for generating a language-based editor from a language specification. Editor specifications are written in the Synthesizer Specification Language (SSL). Arguments to sgen whose names end with .ssl are taken to be SSL source files. Arguments to sgen whose names end with .c (.o) are taken to be C source (object) files. They are compiled and linked into the generated editor. In the absence of the −o flag, the generated editor is called syn.out.

To use sgen, the location of a directory containing the Synthesizer Generator must be specified. This can be done in one of two ways: either as the value of environment variable SYNLOC or as the contents of file /usr/local/lib/synloc. This location is referred to below as SYNLOC. The default system location is SYNLOC/sys.

Options to sgen include:

−a *alt_directory*

    Search for .ssl files in directory (directories) *alt_directory* if they are not found in the current directory.

−b

> Use the COLLECTIONS implementation of maps instead of the AVL-tree implementation. Available only with the ATO attribute-evaluation kernel. (See the −kernel flag.)

−d

> Make all attributes demand attributes.

−dbx

> Invoke dbx on the SSL language processor. So that dbx can run ssl with the proper arguments, an appropriate run command is placed in a file named .rundbx. This command may be invoked by giving the dbx command: source .rundbx.

−debug

> Use a version of the SSL interpreter that includes the SSL debugger.

−D *name*

> Define *name* for the macro preprocessor. The .ssl source files are processed by the C preprocessor, as are any .c files specified as arguments to sgen.

−G

> Force sgen to provide diagnostic output about attribute dependences.

−I *name*

> Append *name* to the macro preprocessor's search path.

−kernel *kernel*

> Use an alternative attribute-evaluation strategy. Allowable values are UNORDERED, ORDERED, and ATO. The default strategy is ATO.
>
> The UNORDERED kernel implements Reps's original algorithm for incremental attribute evaluation. It works for any noncircular attribute grammar but has a somewhat high time and space overhead.
>
> The ORDERED kernel incorporates an incremental version of Kastens's algorithm for attribute evaluation. It is more efficient than the UNORDERED kernel but works only for the ordered subclass of attribute grammars.
>
> The ATO kernel incorporates Hoover's attribute-updating algorithm based on approximate topological ordering. It works for any

noncircular attribute grammar and provides an optional implementation of MAP-valued attributes that is particularly efficient (see the
−b flag). Although the ATO evaluator works well in practice, it
does not have the optimal worst-case behavior of the other kernels.

−K

Test the grammar for circularity.

−l

Do not remove generated intermediate files.

−L *lexdecls*

When sgen invokes lex, prepend declarations from the file *lexdecls*.

−n

Provide warnings about attribute equations that are not in normal
form.

−o *output*

Name the generated editor *output* instead of syn.out.

−pg

Create editor that does profiling.

−r

If possible, avoid making unnecessary calls on yacc, lex, and cc.
Sgen compares the newly generated intermediate files with any
previously generated intermediate files in the directory. If certain
files are identical, some of the steps of generating an editor are
skipped. The new intermediate files are retained for future comparisons.

−s *sysloc*

Use the substitute version of the system from directory
SYNLOC/*sysloc*.

−savessl

Save the input to ssl in file Savessl. This file may be helpful while
debugging a specification.

−S *sysloc*

Use a substitute version of the system from directory *sysloc* instead
of SYNLOC/sys.

−v

> Invoke yacc with the −v flag, so that diagnostic file y.output will
> be produced.

−w *window_type*

> Create an editor for a *window_type* window system. Allowable
> values for *window_type* are VIDEO, SUN, X10, X11 and X. The
> default is installation specific. *Window_type* X denotes the latest
> supported version of the X Window System.

The following options are useful primarily for debugging different parts of the
system.

−interp *interp*

> Use an alternative interpreter from directory *interp* in place of the
> default interpreter, which has the same name as argument *kernel* to
> the −kernel option. (See also the −debug option.)

−lang *lang*

> Use an alternative version of the SSL compiler from directory *lang*.

−misc *misc*

> Use alternative versions of miscellaneous object modules from
> directory *misc*.

−support *support*

> Use alternative versions of supporting object modules from direc-
> tory *support*.

−T *testloc*

> Search the directory structure rooted at *testloc* for parts of the sys-
> tem. Any object module found in *testloc* will be used instead of the
> system copy.

AUTHOR

Thomas Reps and Tim Teitelbaum.

FILES

file.ssl	input file
syn.out	editor created by sgen
sysloc	SYNLOC/sys or location given with −S or −s flag
sysloc/sys/LANG/SSL/ssl	SSL language processor

sysloc/sys/atoms.ssl	standard SSL prefix, including definitions of atomic types
sysloc/sys/KERNEL	editor kernels for the various evaluation schemes
sysloc/sys/MISC	miscellaneous modules needed by an editor
sysloc/sys/SUPPORT	support files needed by an editor
sysloc/sys/include/*	include files needed for compilation
sysloc/sys/eval.c	file into which grammar tables are included and then compiled

SEE ALSO

Reps, T. and Teitelbaum, T., "The Synthesizer Generator," *Proceedings of the ACM SIGSOFT/SIGPLAN Software Engineering Symposium on Practical Software Development Environments*, (Pittsburgh, PA, Apr. 23-25, 1984), *ACM SIGPLAN Notices 19*, 5 (May 1984), pp. 42-48.

Reps, T. and Teitelbaum, T. *The Synthesizer Generator Reference Manual*, Springer-Verlag, New York, NY (Third Edition: 1988).

Reps, T. and Teitelbaum, T. *The Synthesizer Generator: A System for Constructing Language-Based Editors*, Springer-Verlag, New York, NY, 1988.

yacc (1), lex (1), cc (1), dbx (1), gprof (1)

BUGS

Because intermediate-file names are fixed, at most one sgen process can be active in a given directory at a time.

APPENDIX C

Abbreviated List of Editor Commands

This appendix documents the most frequently used editor commands available in generated editors. This summary is intended to serve the needs of new users of the system. Documentation for the rest of the editing commands can be found in *The Synthesizer Generator Reference Manual*.

C.1. Getting Into and Out of an Editor

An editor is created by the sgen command, as described in Appendix B. By default, it is named syn.out. More descriptive names are typically assigned using the −o *output* flag.

An editor can be invoked either with or without parameters. The parameter list specifies a collection of files to be loaded into editor buffers with corresponding names. If the editor is invoked with no arguments, editing begins in a default buffer named main with no associated file.

exit   ^C, ESC-^C, ^X^C

Leave the editor and return to the shell. A warning is issued if any buffers have been modified since their associated files were last written out. Such a warning appears in a form (see *The Synthesizer Generator Reference Manual*). To abort the **exit**, issue a **cancel-command** <ESC-c>. To consummate the **exit**, issue a **start-command** <ESC-s>.

C.2. Changing the Structural Selection by Traversal of the Abstract Syntax Tree

forward-preorder   ^N
    Change the selection to the next resting place in preorder. Do not stop at placeholders for optional constituents.

backward-preorder   ^P
    Change the selection to the previous resting place in preorder. Do not stop at placeholders for optional constituents.

right   ^F
    If there is no text buffer, **right** is the same as **forward-preorder**. Otherwise move the character selection one position to the right.

left   ^B
    If there is no text buffer, **left** is the same as **backward-preorder**. Otherwise move the character selection one position to the left.

forward-with-optionals   ^M
    Change the selection to the next resting place in preorder. Stop at placeholders for optional constituents. Note that the control character ^M is RETURN.

beginning-of-file   ESC-<
    Change the selection to the root of the abstract-syntax tree.

end-of-file   ESC->
    Change the selection to the rightmost resting place in the abstract-syntax tree.

C.3. Executing Commands

execute-command *name*   ^I, ESC-x
    Echo COMMAND: on the command line to signify command mode and redirect subsequent characters to the command line. Entry on the command line is terminated by the first blank, carriage return, or other command key-binding. The entire command name need not be typed; any prefix of a command that uniquely identifies the command is sufficient. Transformations take priority over built-in commands. If the command has no parameters, it is executed immediately. Otherwise, a form for parameters appears; after the parameters have been provided, the command should be initiated by executing **start-command** <ESC-s>. Note that the control character ^I is TAB.

illegal-operation   ^G, ESC-^G, ^X^G
    Cancel any incomplete command key-binding or partial entry on the command line.

start-command   ESC-s

Initiate execution of a command with the parameters contained in the current form. If not currently editing a parameter form, **start-command** does nothing.

cancel-command   ESC-c

Cancel execution of the command awaiting completion of its parameter form. If not currently editing a parameter form, **cancel-command** does nothing.

C.4. Structural Editing

Structural modifications follow the cut-and-paste paradigm. Only whole, well-formed substructures can be removed and inserted.

cut-to-clipped   ^W

Move the selection of the current buffer to the buffer CLIPPED. The new selection becomes a placeholder at the point from which the selection was removed. The previous contents of CLIPPED are lost.

paste-from-clipped   ^Y

Move the contents of the buffer CLIPPED into the buffer at the current selection, which necessarily must be a placeholder. The contents of CLIPPED becomes a placeholder.

delete-selection   ^K

Move the selection of the current buffer to the buffer DELETED. The new selection becomes a placeholder at the point from which the selection was removed. The previous contents of DELETED are lost.

C.5. Moving the Object with Respect to the Window

It is possible to move the object with respect to the window without changing the current selection. In editors generated for video display terminals, this is usually accomplished by issuing scrolling commands. In editors generated for high-resolution, bitmapped workstations, it can also be accomplished by clicking on the appropriate part of a scroll bar. See Appendix D, "Keyboards, Displays, Window Systems, and Mice," for additional details.

next-page   ^V

Move the object up with respect to the window, effectively moving the view of the object down one page.

previous-page   ESC-v

Move the object down with respect to the window, effectively moving the view of the object up one page.

next-line   ^Z

Move the object up with respect to the window by one line, effectively moving the view of the object down one line.

previous-line   ESC-z

Move the object down with respect to the window by one line, effectively moving the view of the object up one line.

C.6. Using the Locator

In editors generated for high-resolution, bitmapped workstations, a mouse is used as a locator or pointer. Using the mouse, it is possible to point anywhere on the object pane, click a button, and change the current selection (see below).

In editors generated for video display terminals, the terminal's cursor is used as a locator or poor man's mouse. It is important to bear in mind that the locator is distinct from the selection. The locator identifies a point on the screen and not a point in the buffer. The following commands are used to move the locator:

pointer-left   ESC-b

Move the locator one character to the left. If already at the left margin of the object pane, scroll the window.

pointer-right   ESC-f

Move the locator one character to the right. If already at the right margin of the object pane, scroll the window.

pointer-up   ESC-p

Move the locator one character up. If already at the top of the object pane, scroll the window.

pointer-down   ESC-d

Move the locator one character down. If already at the bottom of the object pane, scroll the window.

pointer-long-left

Move the locator eight characters to the left. If already at the left margin of the object pane, scroll the window.

pointer-long-right

Move the locator eight characters to the right. If already at the right margin of the object pane, scroll the window.

pointer-long-up

Move the locator eight characters up. If already at the top of the object pane, scroll the window.

pointer-long-down

Move the locator eight characters down. If already at the bottom of the object pane, scroll the window.

select   ESC-@

Change the selection to the production instance whose unparsing scheme caused the printing of the character pointed at by the locator.

C.7. Textual Editing

delete-next-character   ^D

Delete the current character selection.

delete-previous-character   DEL

Delete the character to the left of the character selection.

delete-selection   ^K

Delete all characters in the line containing the character selection.

new-line   ^J

Insert a line feed in the text buffer.

undo   ^X^U

Delete the text buffer, and restore the selection to its state before the text-capture.

C.8. Changing the Character Selection by Textual Traversal of the Text Buffer

forward-preorder   ^N

Move the character selection one position down. If already at the last line of the text buffer, this command causes the text to be parsed. If the parse is successful, **forward-preorder** moves the selection to the first placeholder that exists within the translation of the text, or, if no such placeholder exists, to the first resting place beyond the newly inserted subtree.

backward-preorder   ^P

Move the character selection one position up. If already at the first line of the text buffer, this command is interpreted as **backward-preorder**, provided the text is syntactically correct.

right   ^F

Move the character selection one position to the right.

left   ˆB

Move the character selection one position to the left.

beginning-of-line   ˆA

Move the character selection to the beginning of the line.

end-of-line   ˆE

Move the character selection to the end of the line.

C.9. Buffers, Selections, and Files

list-buffers   ˆXˆB

List all buffers and their associated properties in a textfile buffer and place
that buffer in a window other than the current window, if possible.

switch-to-buffer *buffer-name*   ˆXb

Place the named buffer in the current window. If no such buffer exists,
create a new buffer. The new buffer is associated with the root phylum of
the grammar, and is initialized with the completing term of that phylum.

read-file *file-name*   ˆXˆR

Read a named file into the current buffer, deleting the previous contents of
that buffer. The buffer becomes associated with that file for subsequent
write-current-file commands. If the current buffer is already associated
with a file that has not been written since the buffer was last updated, you
must answer yes to the question Overwrite buffer? before the read will be
executed. If the given file is text, it must be syntactically correct with
respect to the input syntax of the given editor. If syntactically incorrect, the
file is read into a text buffer with the cursor positioned near the error. If the
given file is a structured file, the term contained in the file and the term
currently contained in the buffer must be in the same phylum.

visit-file *file-name*   ˆXˆV

Read a named file into a buffer with the corresponding name, deleting the
previous contents of that buffer if it existed. The buffer becomes associated
with that file for subsequent **write-current-file** commands. If the given file
is text, it must be syntactically correct with respect to the input syntax of the
given editor.

write-current-file   ˆXs

Write the current buffer to its associated file.

write-named-file *file-name format*   ˆXˆW

Write the current buffer to the given file in the given format. The default
value of *format* – structure – can be changed by selecting the *format* field
of the parameter form and invoking the transformation command named
text.

C.10. Creating and Deleting Windows

In editors generated for video display terminals, windows are non-overlapping, are arranged in horizontal stripes across the screen, and are cyclicly ordered from top to bottom for the purpose of the **next-window** and **previous-window** commands.

In editors generated for high-resolution, bitmapped workstations, resizable and overlapping windows with scroll bars are supported. (See Appendix D for further details.)

split-current-window   ˆX2

Split the current window into two windows and display the same buffer in both. Each buffer has only one selection, but each window displaying the given buffer can be independently scrolled.

delete-other-windows   ˆX1

Delete all windows other than the current one.

delete-window   ˆXd

Delete the current window and make the previous window the current window.

next-window   ˆXn

Switch to the next window on the screen.

previous-window   ˆXp

Switch to the previous window on the screen.

redraw-display   ˆL

Refresh the screen image to remove any spurious characters.

Keyboards, Displays, Window Systems, and Mice

Editors may be generated for many different workstations, each with their own sort of keyboard and display screen. This appendix describes information that must be available to a running editor to describe the specific keyboard, display screen, and window system in use.

D.1. Keyboards

Key-bindings for commands are specified in a *keyboard description file*. Each command can have zero or more bindings. Each binding is defined on a separate line in the format

command-name one-or-more-octal-constants **000**

A line in the format

command-name **000**

signifies no key-binding. Each key-binding must be unique and no binding should be the prefix of any other. The lines of a keyboard description file must appear in lexicographic order of key-bindings. File **syn_keyboard** containing the default bindings published in *The Synthesizer Generator Reference Manual* is distributed with the system.

Program **change** is provided to facilitate making a new keyboard description file from an old one, say from **syn_keyboard**. It eliminates the need to know the ASCII sequences generated by a terminal's programmable-function keys, cursor keys, *etc*. The program is located in an installation-specific location and is self-documenting.

A generated editor uses the value of variable SYNKBD of the UNIX environment to know the name of the keyboard description file. If SYNKBD is not defined, the value of variable TERM of the UNIX environment is used. When an editor is executed, a file with this name (optionally preceded by a period) is sought, first in the current working directory, next in the user's home directory, and finally in an installation-specific default directory. If no such file can be found, the same path is searched for a file named syn_keyboard or .syn_keyboard. Typically, the installation-specific default directory contains syn_keyboard.

The exact mechanism used to determine the installation-specific default directory containing keyboard-description files is the following. The directory is named keyboard, and the full path name of its parent directory is contained in file /usr/local/lib/synloc. This file would normally have been created by the system administrator at the time the Synthesizer Generator or the specific language-based editor was installed on the machine. Users wishing to override the default directory with their own can set the environment variable SYNLOC to be the full path name of the directory containing their own version of the keyboard directory. Thus, if the value of SYNLOC is *p* and the value of SYNKBD is *t*, the keyboard-description file sought is *p*/keyboard/*t*.

D.2. Displays and Window Systems

Each editor is generated for a specific window system using flag −w *window_type* of sgen. Allowable values for *window_type* are VIDEO, SUN, X10, X11 and X. X denotes the latest supported version of the X Window System, currently X11. The default window system selected by sgen in the absence of a −w flag is installation specific.

An editor generated with −w VIDEO will run on any video display terminal that is described in the UNIX termcap database. The termcap entry is chosen based on the value of variable TERM of the UNIX environment. An editor generated for video terminals will run in a terminal emulation window of the SunView or X window systems, albeit without supporting mouse-based selection and pop-up menus.

An editor generated for the SunView window system (*i.e.* with −w SUN) can be invoked only from within SunView. The font used by the editor can be selected by setting variable DEFAULT_FONT of the UNIX environment.

An editor generated for the X10 Window System must be invoked after an X10 window manager has been initiated. Editors generated for X10 support the standard X10 geometry and display specifications on the command line. In addition, a number of window properties can be defined in a ˜/.Xdefaults resource file. These window properties are:

Resource Name	Setting
Syn.Foreground	*color*
Syn.Background	*color*
Syn.BodyFont	*fontname*
Syn.PaneFont	*fontname*
Syn.SelectionFont	*fontname*

Syn.Foreground and Syn.Background are the colors of the foreground and background of window elements; the defaults are black and white, respectively. The usage of the various fonts is as follows:

- Syn.BodyFont for text within windows,
- Syn.PaneFont for menu titles, and
- Syn.SelectionFont for menu items.

An editor generated for the X11 Window System must be invoked after an X11 window manager has been initiated. Editors that have been compiled for the X11 window system accept the standard X11 –geometry and –display options on the command line. In addition, a number of window properties can be set on the command line of a running editor, in a ˜/.Xdefaults resource file, and in a XENVIRONMENT resource file. In the event of conflicting settings, the command line has highest precedence and the ˜/.Xdefaults file has lowest precedence. These window properties and their respective command-line flags and resource names are:

Command flag	Resource Name	Setting
–foreground	Syn.Foreground	*color*
–background	Syn.Background	*color*
–lf	Syn.Browser.Label.Font	*fontname*
–mf	Syn.Browser.Menu.Font	*fontname*
–cf	Syn.Browser.Command.Font	*fontname*
–of	Syn.Browser.Object.Font	*fontname*

Syn.Foreground and Syn.Background are the colors of the foreground and background of window elements; the defaults are black and white, respectively. The usage of the various fonts is as follows:

- Syn.Browser.Label.Font for window titles,
- Syn.Browser.Menu.Font for pop-up menus,
- Syn.Browser.Command.Font for the help-pane buttons, and
- Syn.Browser.Object.Font for the object pane.

Editors making use of multiple fonts and font characteristics require a style-definition file, whose location is given by variable SYNSTYLE of the UNIX environment. The form of a style-definition file is described in Section 2.6 of the *Synthesizer Generator Reference Manual*.

D.3. Mice

Editors generated for either the X Window System or SunView can make use of a mouse, while editors generated for video displays cannot. Editors generated for X10 and SunView make use of three buttons. On some workstations, the middle button is simulated by chording both buttons.

The leftmost button has the following uses:

- The selection in the object pane can be changed by clicking or dragging across non-blank characters in the display of an object.
- A transformation can be invoked by clicking on the transformation's name in a help pane.
- The display of an object can be scrolled within the window by clicking on one of the arrows in a scroll bar.

The middle button is used to control a pop-up menu containing language-independent system commands.

The rightmost button is used to control a pop-up menu containing the currently enabled transformations.

In editors generated for X11, system-command and transformation menus are combined under the control of the right button.

Actuators on the vertical scroll bar, from top to bottom, are bound to

scroll-to-top
previous-page
(back-by-half-a-page)
previous-line
next-line
(forward-by-half-a-page)
next-page
scroll-to-bottom

Actuators on the horizontal scroll bar, from left to right, are bound to

page-left
(left-by-half-a-page)
column-left
column-right
(right-by-half-a-page)
page-right

The mouse is used to move, resize, raise, lower, and iconify windows in the fashion of the given window system and its window manager.

Bibliography

Aho86.

    Aho, A.V., Sethi, R., and Ullman, J.D., *Compilers: Principles, Techniques, and Tools,* Addison-Wesley, Reading, MA (1986).

Alberga81.

    Alberga, C.N., Brown, A.L., Leeman, G.B., Mikelsons, M., and Wegman, M.N., "A program development tool," pp. 92-104 in *Conference Record of the Eighth ACM Symposium on Principles of Programming Languages,* (Williamsburg, VA, January 26-28, 1981), ACM, New York, NY (1981).

Bahlke86.

    Bahlke, R. and Snelting, G., "The PSG system: From formal language definitions to interactive programming environments," *ACM Trans. Program. Lang. Syst. 8,* 4 (October 1986), pp. 547-576.

Bates85.

    Bates, J. and Constable, R., "Proofs as programs," *ACM Trans. Program. Lang. Syst. 7,* 1 (January 1985), pp. 113-136.

Burstall69.

    Burstall, R.M., "Proving properties of programs by structural induction," *Computer Journal 12,* 1 (February 1969), pp. 41-48.

Cohen79.

    Cohen, R. and Harry, E., "Automatic generation of near-optimal linear-time translators for non-circular attribute grammars," pp. 121-134 in *Conference Record of the Sixth ACM Symposium on Principles of Programming Languages,* (San Antonio, TX, Jan. 29-31, 1979), ACM, New York, NY (1979).

Delisle84.

    Delisle, N., Menicosy, D., and Schwartz, M., "Viewing a programming environment as a single tool," *Proceedings of the ACM SIGSOFT/SIGPLAN Software Engineering*

Symposium on Practical Software Development Environments, (Pittsburgh, PA, April 23-25, 1984), *ACM SIGPLAN Notices 19,* 5 (May 1984), pp. 49-56.

Demers81.
   Demers, A., Reps, T., and Teitelbaum, T., "Incremental evaluation for attribute grammars with application to syntax-directed editors," pp. 105-116 in *Conference Record of the Eighth ACM Symposium on Principles of Programming Languages,* (Williamsburg, VA, Jan. 26-28, 1981), ACM, New York, NY (1981).

Demers85.
   Demers, A., Rogers, A., and Zadeck, F.K., "Attribute propagation by message passing," *Conference Record of the ACM SIGPLAN 85 Symposium on Language Issues in Programming Environments,* (Seattle, WA, June 25-28, 1985), *ACM SIGPLAN Notices 20,* 7 (July 1985), pp. 43-59.

Deutsch76.
   Deutsch, L.P. and Bobrow, D.G., "An efficient, incremental, automatic garbage collector," *Commun. of the ACM 19,* 7 (July 1976), pp. 522-526.

Dijkstra76.
   Dijkstra, E.W., *A Discipline of Programming,* Prentice-Hall, Englewood Cliffs, NJ (1976).

Donzeau-Gouge75.
   Donzeau-Gouge, V., Huet, G., Kahn, G., Lang, B., and Lévy, J.-J., "A structure-oriented program editor," Tech. Rep. 114, INRIA, Rocquencourt, France (April 1975).

Donzeau-Gouge84.
   Donzeau-Gouge, V., Huet, G., Kahn, G., and Lang, B., "Programming environments based on structured editors: The MENTOR experience," pp. 128-140 in *Interactive Programming Environments,* ed. D. Barstow, E. Sandewall, and H. Shrobe, McGraw-Hill, New York, NY (1984).

Ford85.
   Ford, R. and Sawamiphakdi, D., "A greedy concurrent approach to incremental code generation," pp. 165-178 in *Conference Record of the Twelfth ACM Symposium on Principles of Programming Languages,* (New Orleans, LA, Jan. 14-16, 1985), ACM, New York, NY (1985).

Fritzson84a.
   Fritzson, P., "Preliminary experience from the DICE system, a distributed incremental compiling environment," *Proceedings of the ACM SIGSOFT/SIGPLAN Software Engineering Symposium on Practical Software Development Environments,* (Pittsburgh, PA, Apr. 23-25, 1984), *ACM SIGPLAN Notices 19,* 5 (May 1984), pp. 113-123.

Fritzson84.
   Fritzson, P., "Towards a distributed programming environment based on incremental compilation," Linköping Studies in Science and Technology Dissertation No. 109, Dept. of Comp. and Inf. Sci., Linköping Univ., Linköping, Sweden (1984).

Gentzen69.
   Gentzen, G., "Investigations into logical deductions," pp. 68-131 in *The Collected Papers of Gerhard Gentzen,* ed. M.E. Szabo, North-Holland, Amsterdam (1969).

Gerhart75.

Gerhart, S.L., "Correctness-preserving program transformations," pp. 54-66 in *Confer-ence Record of the Second ACM Symposium on Principles of Programming Languages,* (Palo Alto, CA, Jan. 20-22, 1975), ACM, New York, NY (1975).

Ghezzi79.

Ghezzi, C. and Mandrioli, D., "Incremental parsing," *ACM Trans. on Prog. Lang. and Syst. 1,* 1 (July 1979), pp. 58-70.

Ghezzi80.

Ghezzi, C. and Mandrioli, D., "Augmenting parsers to support incrementality," *Jour-nal of the ACM 27,* 3 (October 1980), pp. 564-579.

Gordon79.

Gordon, M., Milner, R., and Wadsworth, C., *Edinburgh LCF, Lecture Notes in Com-puter Science,* Vol. 78, Springer-Verlag, New York, NY (1979).

Gries81.

Gries, D., *The Science of Programming,* Springer-Verlag, New York, NY (1981).

Hansen71.

Hansen, W., "Creation of hierarchic text with a computer display," Ph.D. dissertation, Dept. of Computer Science, Stanford Univ., Stanford, CA (June 1971).

Henderson84.

Henderson, P., *Proceedings of the ACM SIGSOFT/SIGPLAN Software Engineering Symposium on Practical Software Development Environments,* (Pittsburgh, PA, April 23-25, 1984), *ACM SIGPLAN Notices 19,* 5 (May 1984).

Henderson85.

Henderson, P. and Weiser, M., "Continuous execution: The Visiprog environment," in *Proceedings of the Eighth International Conference on Software Engineering,* (1985).

Henderson87.

Henderson, P., *Proceedings of the ACM SIGSOFT/SIGPLAN Software Engineering Symposium on Practical Software Development Environments,* (Palo Alto, CA, Dec. 9-11, 1986), *ACM SIGPLAN Notices 22,* 1 (January 1987).

Hoare69.

Hoare, C.A.R., "An axiomatic basis for computer programming," *Commun. of the ACM 12,* 10 (October 1969), pp. 576-580, 583.

Hoover87.

Hoover, R., "Incremental graph evaluation," Ph.D. dissertation and Tech. Rep. 87-836, Dept. of Computer Science, Cornell University, Ithaca, NY (May 1987).

Jalili82.

Jalili, F. and Gallier, J., "Building friendly parsers," pp. 196-206 in *Conference Record of the Ninth ACM Symposium on Principles of Programming Languages,* (Albu-querque, NM, Jan. 25-27, 1982), ACM, New York, NY (1982).

Johnson85.

Johnson, G.F. and Fischer, C.N., "A meta-language and system for nonlocal incremen-tal attribute evaluation in language-based editors," pp. 141-151 in *Conference Record of the Twelfth ACM Symposium on Principles of Programming Languages,* (New Orleans, LA, Jan. 14-16, 1985), ACM, New York, NY (1985).

Johnson82.
Johnson, S., *A computer system for checking proofs,* UMI Research Press, Ann Arbor, MI (1982).

Johnson78.
Johnson, S.C., *YACC – Yet another compiler-compiler,* Bell Laboratories, Murray Hill, NJ (July 1978).

Kahn83.
Kahn, G., Lang, B., and Mélèse, B., "Metal: A formalism to specify formalisms," *Science of Computer Programming 3* (1983), pp. 151-188.

Kastens80.
Kastens, U., "Ordered attribute grammars," *Acta Inf. 13,* 3 (1980), pp. 229-256.

Kastens82.
Kastens, U., Hutt, B., and Zimmermann, E., *GAG: A Practical Compiler Generator, Lecture Notes in Computer Science,* Vol. 141, Springer-Verlag, New York, NY (1982).

Kennedy76.
Kennedy, K. and Warren, S.K., "Automatic generation of efficient evaluators for attribute grammars," pp. 32-49 in *Conference Record of the Third ACM Symposium on Principles of Programming Languages,* (Atlanta, GA, Jan. 19-21, 1976), ACM, New York, NY (1976).

Kleene52.
Kleene, S.C., *Introduction to Metamathematics,* North-Holland, Amsterdam (1952).

Knuth68.
Knuth, D.E., "Semantics of context-free languages," *Math. Syst. Theory 2,* 2 (June 1968), pp. 127-145.

Lesk75.
Lesk, M.E., "Lex – A lexical analyzer generator," Comp. Sci. Tech. Rep. 39, Bell Laboratories, Murray Hill, NJ (October 1975).

Medina-Mora81.
Medina-Mora, R. and Feiler, P., "An incremental programming environment," *IEEE Trans. Softw. Eng. SE-7,* 5 (September 1981), pp. 472-482.

Medina-Mora81a.
Medina-Mora, R. and Notkin, D.S., "ALOE users' and implementors' guide," Tech. Rep. CMU-CS-81-145, Dept. of Computer Science, Carnegie-Mellon Univ., Pittsburgh, PA (November 1981).

Milner78.
Milner, R., "A theory of type polymorphism in programming," *Journal of Computer and System Sciences 17* (1978), pp. 348-375.

Milos84.
Milos, D., Pleban, U., and Loegel, G., "Direct implementation of compiler specifications, or the Pascal P-code compiler revisited," pp. 196-207 in *Conference Record of the Eleventh ACM Symposium on Principles of Programming Languages,* (Salt Lake City, UT, Jan. 15-18, 1984), ACM, New York, NY (1984).

Morris81.

Morris, J.M. and Schwartz, M.D., "The design of a language-directed editor for block-structured languages," *Proceedings of the ACM SIGPLAN-SIGOA Symposium on Text Manipulation*, (Portland, OR, June 8-10, 1981), *ACM SIGPLAN Notices 16*, 6 (June 1981), pp. 28-33.

Mughal85.

Mughal, K., "Control-flow aspects of generating runtime facilities for language-based programming environments," pp. 85-91 in *Proceedings of the 1985 IEEE Conference on Software Tools*, (New York, NY, April 15-17, 1985), IEEE Computer Society, Washington, D.C. (1985).

Nelson81.

Nelson, G., "Techniques for program verification," Tech. Rep. CSL-81-10, Computer Science Laboratory, Xerox Palo Alto Research Center, Palo Alto, CA (June 1981).

Notkin85.

Notkin, D., Ellison, R.J., Staudt, B.J., Kaiser, G.E., Kant, E., Habermann, A.N., Ambriola, V., and Montangero, C., Special issue on the GANDALF project, *Journal of Systems and Software 5*, 2 (May 1985).

Reppy84.

Reppy, J. and Kintala, C.M.R., "Generating execution facilities for integrated programming environments," Tech. Mem. 59545-84, A.T.& T. Bell Laboratories, Murray Hill, NJ (March 1984).

Reps82.

Reps, T., "Optimal-time incremental semantic analysis for syntax-directed editors," pp. 169-176 in *Conference Record of the Ninth ACM Symposium on Principles of Programming Languages*, (Albuquerque, NM, January 25-27, 1982), ACM, New York, NY (1982).

Reps83.

Reps, T., Teitelbaum, T., and Demers, A., "Incremental context-dependent analysis for language-based editors," *ACM Trans. Program. Lang. Syst. 5*, 3 (July 1983), pp. 449-477.

Reps84b.

Reps, T. and Alpern, B., "Interactive proof checking," pp. 36-45 in *Conference Record of the Eleventh ACM Symposium on Principles of Programming Languages*, (Salt Lake City, UT, Jan. 15-18, 1984), ACM, New York, NY (1984).

Reps84.

Reps, T., *Generating Language-Based Environments*, The M.I.T. Press, Cambridge, MA (1984).

Reps84a.

Reps, T. and Teitelbaum, T., "The Synthesizer Generator," *Proceedings of the ACM SIGSOFT/SIGPLAN Software Engineering Symposium on Practical Software Development Environments*, (Pittsburgh, PA, Apr. 23-25, 1984), *ACM SIGPLAN Notices 19*, 5 (May 1984), pp. 42-48.

Reps86.

Reps, T., Marceau, C., and Teitelbaum, T., "Remote attribute updating for language-based editors," pp. 1-13 in *Conference Record of the Thirteenth ACM Symposium on Principles of Programming Languages,* (St. Petersburg, FL, Jan 13-15, 1986), ACM, New York, NY (1986).

Reps88.
Reps, T. and Teitelbaum, T., *The Synthesizer Generator Reference Manual,* Springer-Verlag, New York, NY (Third Edition: 1988).

Rovner84.
Rovner, P., "On adding garbage collection and runtime types to a strongly-typed, statically-checked, concurrent language," Rep. CSL-84-7, Xerox Palo Alto Research Center, Palo Alto, CA (July 1984).

Schwartz84.
Schwartz, M., Delisle, N., and Begwani, V., "Incremental compilation in Magpie," *Proceedings of the SIGPLAN 84 Symposium on Compiler Construction,* (Montreal, Can., June 20-22, 1984), *ACM SIGPLAN Notices 19,* 6 (June 1984), pp. 122-131.

Stallman81.
Stallman, R.M., "EMACS: The extensible, customizable self-documenting display editor," *Proceedings of the ACM SIGPLAN-SIGOA Symposium on Text Manipulation,* (Portland, OR, June 8-10, 1981), *ACM SIGPLAN Notices 16,* 6 (June 1981), pp. 147-156.

Teitelbaum81.
Teitelbaum, T. and Reps, T., "The Cornell Program Synthesiszer: A syntax-directed programming environment," *Commun. of the ACM 24,* 9 (September 1981), pp. 563-573.

Teitelman78.
Teitelman, W., *Interlisp Reference Manual,* Xerox Palo Alto Research Center, Palo Alto, CA (December 1978).

Tenenbaum74.
Tenenbaum, A., "Automatic type analysis in a very high level language," Ph.D. dissertation, Computer Science Department, New York University, New York, NY (October 1974).

Turing37.
Turing, A.M., "On computable numbers with an application to the Entscheidungsproblem," *Proc. London Math. Soc., series 2, 42* (1937), pp. 230-265.

Waite83.
Waite, W.M. and Goos, G., *Compiler Construction,* Springer-Verlag, New York, NY (1983).

Warren75.
Warren, S.K., "The efficient evaluation of attribute grammars," M.A. dissertation, Dept. of Mathematical Sciences, Rice University, Houston, TX (April 1975).

Warren76.
Warren, S.K., "The coroutine model of attribute grammar evaluation," Ph.D. dissertation, Dept. of Mathematical Sciences, Rice University, Houston, TX (April 1976).

Wegman80.

Wegman, M., "Parsing for structural editors," pp. 320-327 in *Proceedings of the Twenty-First IEEE Symp. on Foundations of Computer Science* (Syracuse, NY, October 1980), IEEE Computer Society, Washington, D.C. (1980).

Wilcox76.

Wilcox, T.R., Davis, A.M., and Tindall, M.H., "The design and implementation of a table driven, interactive diagnostic programming system," *Commun. of the ACM 19*, 11 (November 1976), pp. 609-616.

Wilner71.

Wilner, W.T., "Declarative semantic definition as illustrated by a definition of Simula 67," Ph.D. dissertation, Dept. of Computer Science, Stanford Univ., Stanford, CA (June 1971).

Wood81.

Wood, S.R., "Z – The 95 percent text editor," *Proceedings of the ACM SIGPLAN-SIGOA Symposium on Text Manipulation,* (Portland, OR, June 8-10, 1981), *ACM SIG-PLAN Notices 16*, 6 (June 1981), pp. 1-7.

Yeh83.

Yeh, D., "On incremental evaluation of ordered attributed grammars," *BIT 23* (1983), pp. 308-320.

Index

Now available from GrammaTech, Inc.:

The Synthesizer Generator System

The Synthesizer Generator System is available on both a research and a commercial basis. For additional information about how to acquire a copy of the system, write:

Synthesizer Generator
GrammaTech, Inc.
One Hopkins Place
Ithaca, NY 14850

Also available from Springer-Verlag:

The Synthesizer Generator Reference Manual: Third Edition
by Thomas W. Reps and Tim Teitelbaum

The Synthesizer Generator Reference Manual is the defining document of the Synthesizer Generator system. Written by the Synthesizer Generator's creators, this volume provides complete documentation on all aspects of specifying, generating, debugging, and running editors.

ISBN 0-387-96910-1

Texts and Monographs in Computer Science